14

The Complete Encyclopedia of Cooking
Supercook

Marshall Cavendish · London Sydney New York

Symbols in Supercook

'Low-Calorie' Recipes

The description 'low-calorie' has been given to recipes in *'Supercook'* which contain fewer calories than other comparable recipes in the book. For instance, the pudding recipes marked 'Low-cal' have the fewest calories when compared to other pudding recipes in *'Supercook'*. Some – but not all – of the recipes labelled

'Low-cal' would be suitable for people who are following strict slimming or low-calorie diets. Each recipe should be examined carefully to ascertain whether the ingredients are permitted for a particular special diet.

The labelling 'Low-cal' will be more helpful for those aiming to lose weight slowly by reducing their calorie intake slightly or those who frequently experiment with new recipes but wish to avoid a very high consumption of calories. These recipes can also guide the person entertaining for weight-conscious friends. However,

thought should also be given to what is to be served *with* the 'low-calorie' recipe. An over-enthusiastic combination of these recipes will not guarantee a low-calorie meal!

In deciding which recipes to consider in the 'low-calorie' category, each ingredient needs to be considered for its calorific contribution. Low-calorie ingredients such as vegetables, fruits, white fish and eggs may be combined with a moderate amount of fat or fat-containing foods and still be relatively 'low-calorie'. A generous combination of fats and fat-containing foods will produce a high-calorie recipe. Similarly, recipes which rely heavily on sugar, alcohol, flour or a combination of these foods with or without fat will be excluded from the 'low-calorie' rating.

In some recipes it may be possible to make further reductions in the amount of fats and sugars used, such as substituting low-fat yogurt for cream, or to grill [broil] food and drain off fat rather than frying, although the end results will differ slightly.

The calorie chart under the alphabetical heading CALORIES (p. 302) may be used to work out the approximate calorific value of individual recipes.

This is the guide to the amount of skill needed for each recipe.

| Easy | Needs special care | Complicated |

This is an estimated guide to the dish's cost, which will, of course, vary with the season.

| Inexpensive | Reasonable | Expensive |

This is an indication of the amount of time needed for preparing and cooking the dish.

| Less than 1 hour | 1 hour to 2½ hours | Over 2½ hours |

Front Cover: Wellington Roast Lamb p. 2759

Published by Marshall Cavendish House
58 Old Compton Street
London W1V 5PA

This Edition Published 1986

©Marshall Cavendish Ltd 1986, 1985, 1979, 1978, 1977, 1976, 1975, 1974, 1973, 1972, 58 Old Compton Street, London W1V 5PA

Printed and bound by
L.E.G.O. Spa Vicenza

Cataloguing in Publication Data

Supercook
1. Cookery
1. Cameron-Smith, Marye
641.5   TX717   79-52319

ISBN (for set) 0 85685 534 0
ISBN (this volume) 0 85685 548 0
Library of Congress catalog card number 78-52319.

Recipes in Volume 14

Piquant Pork Chops

A simple dish to make, Piquant Pork Chops should be served with rice, either fried or plain. No vegetable accompaniment is necessary. If the pork chops are very thick they may need longer initial cooking. Test them with the point of a sharp kitchen knife. If the juices run clear, the chops are cooked.

4 SERVINGS

4 pork chops
2 garlic cloves, crushed
½ teaspoon dried basil
1 teaspoon salt
3 tablespoons vegetable oil
4 fl. oz. [½ cup] dry cider
2 tablespoons wine vinegar
1 tablespoon soft brown sugar
½ teaspoon black pepper
½ teaspoon cayenne pepper
3 large carrots, scraped and sliced on the diagonal
½ cucumber, sliced on the diagonal
1 green pepper, white pith removed, seeded and cut into strips
1 tablespoon cornflour [cornstarch] dissolved in 4 tablespoons dry cider or water

Rub the pork chops all over with the garlic, basil and half of the salt. Set aside.

In a large frying-pan, heat the oil over

These tasty, colourful and easy-to-prepare Piquant Prawns make a delicious lunch or supper dish.

moderate heat. When the oil is hot, add the pork chops and fry them for 5 minutes on each side. Cover the pan, reduce the heat to low and cook the chops for 30 minutes.

Using tongs, transfer the chops to a plate and set aside. Pour off all but 2 tablespoons of the fat from the pan and return it to moderate heat. Stir in the cider, vinegar, sugar, pepper, cayenne and the remaining salt. Bring the sauce to the boil, stirring constantly.

Add the vegetables and stir to mix. Cover the pan and cook the vegetables for 2 minutes. Remove the pan from the heat and stir in the cornflour [cornstarch] mixture. Return the pan to the heat and cook, stirring constantly, for 1 minute or until the sauce is thick and translucent.

Return the pork chops to the pan. Using a large spoon, baste the chops well with the sauce. Cover the pan, reduce the heat to low and simmer the chops for 5 minutes.

Remove the pan from the heat. Transfer the chops to a warmed serving dish. Pour over the sauce and the vegetables.

Serve immediately.

Piquant Prawns

An easy and tasty dish to make, Piquant Prawns should be served in a ring of fried or plain boiled rice. Lager or chilled dry cider makes an excellent accompaniment.

4-6 SERVINGS

3 tablespoons vegetable oil
1 medium-sized onion, finely chopped
2 garlic cloves, crushed
14 oz. canned peeled tomatoes
2 tablespoons tomato purée
2 tablespoons wine vinegar
¼ teaspoon dried basil
¼ teaspoon cayenne pepper
1 teaspoon prepared mustard
½ teaspoon salt
1 teaspoon sugar
1 lb. frozen prawns or shrimps, thawed and drained
2 tablespoons stuffed olives, sliced

In a large frying-pan, heat the oil over moderate heat. When the oil is hot, add the onion and garlic and fry them, stirring occasionally, for 5 to 7 minutes or until the onion is soft and translucent but not brown.

Stir in the tomatoes with the can juice, tomato purée, vinegar, basil, cayenne, mustard, salt and sugar and bring the mixture to the boil. Cover the pan, reduce the heat to low and simmer the sauce for 25 minutes.

Add the prawns or shrimps, and stir them into the sauce. Increase the heat to moderate and bring the mixture to the boil again. Cover the pan, reduce the heat to low and simmer for a further 10 minutes. Taste the sauce and add more salt, pepper or sugar if necessary.

Remove the pan from the heat. Spoon the mixture into a heated serving dish. Scatter over the olives and serve.

Piquant Stew

An unusual combination of sweet and spicy pork and vegetables, Piquant Stew is an adaptation of a Filipino recipe. Serve with an orange salad and boiled rice.

6 SERVINGS

6 tablespoons seasoned flour, made with 6 tablespoons flour, $\frac{1}{2}$ teaspoon salt and $\frac{1}{4}$ teaspoon black pepper
3 lb. pork fillets, cut into $\frac{1}{4}$-inch thick slices
4 oz. [$\frac{1}{2}$ cup] butter
4 tablespoons vegetable oil
12 small onions
2 garlic cloves, crushed
6 medium-sized carrots, scraped and cut into $\frac{1}{2}$-inch slices
3 large potatoes, diced
4 tomatoes, blanched, peeled, seeded and chopped
2 teaspoons sugar
$\frac{1}{2}$ teaspoon salt
1-inch piece fresh root ginger, peeled and finely chopped
1-inch piece cinnamon stick
1 green chilli, seeds removed and finely chopped
2 tablespoons vinegar
6 fl. oz. [$\frac{3}{4}$ cup] red wine
6 fl. oz. [$\frac{3}{4}$ cup] chicken stock

Place the seasoned flour on a plate and dip the pork slices, one by one, in it, shaking off any excess. Set aside.

In a large flameproof casserole, melt half of the butter with half of the oil over moderate heat. When the foam subsides, add the pork pieces, a few at a time, and cook them, turning frequently, for 5 minutes or until they are lightly browned all over. With a slotted spoon, transfer the pork to a large plate. Keep warm while you fry the remaining pork in the same way. Set aside.

Add the remaining butter and oil to the casserole. When the foam subsides, add the onions and garlic and cook, stirring occasionally, for 5 to 7 minutes or

Piroshki are little pies from Poland, made in our recipe with rich pastry and a filling of veal and sour cream. And they're perfect for picnics!

until the onions are soft and translucent but not brown. Stir in the carrots, potatoes and tomatoes and cook for a further 5 minutes.

Stir in the sugar, salt, ginger, cinnamon, chilli and vinegar and cook, stirring occasionally, for 8 minutes. Return the pork to the casserole and pour in the wine and stock. Bring the liquid to the boil over high heat. Cover the casserole, reduce the heat to low and simmer the stew for 1 to 1¼ hours, or until the pork is tender.

Taste the stew and add more salt if necessary.

Remove the casserole from the heat and remove and discard the cinnamon stick. Serve immediately.

Pirogen

POLISH RAVIOLI

Pirogen (peer-row-gen) are little crescent shaped pasta, filled with a variety of sweet and savoury stuffings such as cream cheese, minced [ground] meat and stewed fruit. In Poland, Pirogen are traditionally made with cottage cheese although we have used cream cheese in this recipe. Serve Pirogen with a butter and breadcrumb sauce, as a first course, or with salad as a light meal.

ABOUT 45 PIROGEN

PASTA
12 oz. [3 cups] flour
1 teaspoon salt
3 large eggs, lightly beaten
2 to 3 tablespoons lukewarm water
FILLING
1 oz. [2 tablespoons] butter
1 medium-sized onion, finely grated
1 lb. cream cheese

cloth and leave them to rest for 30 minutes.

Meanwhile, prepare the filling. In a small frying-pan, melt the butter over moderate heat. When the foam subsides, add the grated onion and fry, stirring constantly, for 5 to 7 minutes, or until it is soft and translucent but not brown. Remove the pan from the heat and tip the contents into a medium-sized mixing bowl.

Add the cream cheese to the onion and, using a wooden spoon, mix the ingredients well. Gradually beat in the egg yolks until the mixture is smooth and creamy. Mix in the salt and pepper. Set aside.

Uncover the dough sheets and, with a 3-inch pastry cutter, cut the dough into circles. Place one teaspoon of filling in the centre of each circle.

In a cup, combine the egg and the water for the glaze. Moisten the edges of the dough circles with this mixture. Fold the dough over the fillings to form semi-circles, and seal the edges by pressing them together with a fork. Set aside.

In a large saucepan, bring 4 pints [5 pints] of salted water to the boil over high heat. Drop the pirogen into the boiling water, cover the pan and cook them for 6 to 15 minutes, depending on the thickness of the pasta, or until the pasta is tender.

Remove the pan from the heat and drain the pirogen in a colander. Transfer them to a warmed serving dish and serve immediately.

Piroshki
LITTLE PIES

Piroshki (pee-rosh-kee) are little pies from Eastern Europe made with rich pastry and filled with numerous savoury fillings. They are usually served with soup such as Borscht and also make delicious appetizers.

ABOUT 45 PIES

PASTRY
12 oz. [3 cups] flour
1 teaspoon salt
4 oz. [½ cup] plus 1 teaspoon butter
2 oz. cream cheese
3 tablespoons iced water
2 fl. oz. double cream [¼ cup heavy cream]

FILLING
2 oz. [¼ cup] butter
1 onion, finely chopped
8 oz. minced [ground] veal
4 oz. mushrooms, wiped clean and finely chopped
1 teaspoon salt
½ teaspoon black pepper
½ teaspoon paprika

1 tablespoon finely chopped fresh parsley
3 tablespoons sour cream
1 hard-boiled egg, finely chopped
GLAZE
1 egg
1 teaspoon water

First make the pastry. Sift the flour and salt into a medium-sized mixing bowl. Add the 4 ounces [½ cup] of butter and the cream cheese and cut them into small pieces with a table knife. With your fingertips, rub the butter and cream cheese into the flour until the mixture resembles fine breadcrumbs.

Add 1 tablespoon of iced water and, using the knife, mix it into the flour mixture. Add the cream and repeat the process. With your hands, mix and knead the dough until it is smooth. If the dough is too dry, add the remaining water. Roll the dough into a ball, wrap it in grease-proof or waxed paper and place it in the refrigerator to chill for 30 minutes.

Meanwhile, make the filling. In a medium-sized saucepan, melt the butter over moderate heat. When the foam subsides, add the onion and cook, stirring occasionally, for 5 to 7 minutes or until it is soft and translucent but not brown.

Add the veal, mushrooms, salt, pepper and paprika and cook for 15 minutes, or until the meat is evenly browned and well cooked.

Remove the pan from the heat and stir in the parsley, sour cream and chopped egg. Set aside.

Preheat the oven to fairly hot 400°F (Gas Mark 6, 200°C). With the remaining teaspoon of butter, grease a large baking sheet. Set aside.

Remove the dough from the refrigerator and turn it out on to a lightly floured board. Roll out the dough to about ⅛-inch thick. With a 3-inch pastry cutter, cut the dough into circles.

Place one teaspoon of the filling in the centre of each circle.

In a cup, combine the egg and the water for the glaze. Moisten the edges of the dough circles with this mixture. Fold the dough over the fillings to form semi-circles and seal the edges by pressing them together with a fork. Place the semi-circles on the baking sheet and brush them all over with the remaining egg glaze.

Place the piroshki in the oven and bake them for 20 minutes, or until they are golden brown.

Remove the baking sheet from the oven and serve the piroshki at once if you are serving them hot. Set them aside to cool on a wire rack if they are to be served cold.

2 large egg yolks, beaten
½ teaspoon salt
¼ teaspoon black pepper
GLAZE
1 egg, beaten
1 teaspoon lukewarm water

First make the pasta. Sift the flour and salt into a medium-sized mixing bowl. Make a well in the centre of the flour and pour in the lightly beaten eggs and water.

With your fingertips, draw the flour into the liquid, until all the flour has been incorporated and the mixture forms a stiff dough.

Turn the dough out on to a lightly floured board or working surface and knead it for 10 minutes or until it is smooth but stiff. If necessary add more flour to obtain the necessary stiffness.

Divide the dough in two and roll each piece out into a very thin sheet, pulling it with your hands into a rectangle.

Cover the dough sheets with a damp

Pissaladières

INDIVIDUAL SAVOURY TARTLETS

Pissaladières (pee-sah-lah-dee-yair) are small pastry cases filled with a mixture of onions, garlic, anchovies, olives and tomatoes — and very typical of the cuisine of the South of France. If you prefer, you can make one 9-inch tart instead. Serve with a tossed green salad and a good robust red wine.

9 TARTLETS

PASTRY
8 oz. [2 cups] flour
½ teaspoon salt
2 oz. [¼ cup] plus 2 teaspoons butter
2 oz. [¼ cup] vegetable fat
3 to 4 tablespoons iced water
FILLING
2 fl. oz. [¼ cup] olive oil
6 medium-sized onions, thinly sliced
2 garlic cloves, crushed
3 large tomatoes, blanched, peeled, seeded and finely chopped
1 tablespoon tomato purée
2 oz. canned anchovies, drained and chopped
27 black olives, stoned
½ teaspoon salt
½ teaspoon black pepper

First make the pastry cases. Sift the flour and salt into a medium-sized mixing bowl. Add 2 ounces [¼ cup] of the butter and the vegetable fat and cut them into small pieces with a table knife. With your fingertips, rub the fat into the flour until the mixture resembles coarse breadcrumbs. Add 3 tablespoons of the water and mix it in with the knife. Form the dough into a ball, adding more water if the dough is too dry.

Wrap the dough in greaseproof or waxed paper and place it in the refrigerator to chill for 30 minutes.

Preheat the oven to fairly hot 375°F (Gas Mark 5, 190°C). With the remaining 2 teaspoons of butter, grease 9 fluted tartlet tins. Set aside.

On a lightly floured surface, roll out the dough to an oblong about ¾-inch thick. With a 4-inch pastry cutter, cut out 9 circles of dough. Line the tartlet tins with the dough circles and crimp the edges.

Prick the dough all over with a fork. Line the tins with aluminium foil and place a layer of dried beans on top. Place the tins on a baking sheet and put it in the oven. Bake for 10 minutes.

Remove the baking sheet from the oven and remove the foil and beans. Return the tartlet tins to the oven and bake for a further 5 minutes or until the pastry is golden brown.

Remove the tartlets from the oven. Leave them to cool for 5 minutes. Then carefully remove the pastry cases from the tins. Arrange the pastry cases on a serving platter. Set aside and keep warm while you make the filling.

In a large frying-pan, heat the oil over moderate heat. When the oil is hot, add the onions and garlic. Fry, stirring occasionally, for 5 to 7 minutes or until the onions are soft and translucent but not brown.

Add the tomatoes, purée, anchovies, olives, salt and pepper and stir. Cook for a further 2 to 3 minutes or until the filling is heated through.

Remove the pan from the heat. Spoon the filling into the pastry cases. Serve immediately or allow to cool completely before serving.

Pistachio Nut

The pistachio is the fruit of the deciduous tree, *bistacia vera*, native to the Near East but now grown in many parts of Asia, the Mediterranean and the warmer regions of the Americas.

The nut is about the size of a small olive. It has a small, green kernel with a sweet, distinctive flavour, encased in a thin, yellowish-red wrinkled skin. The kernel separates easily from its shell when the nut is broken open.

Pistachios are sold in their shells or shelled and blanched. They are used in the making of sweets [candies], cakes and frozen desserts. They are also added to meat stuffings and incorporated into many savoury dishes. Sometimes the nuts are crushed and the green colour from the kernel is extracted and used as a food colouring.

Pistachio Ice-Cream

A mouth-watering dessert, Pistachio Ice-Cream may be served sprinkled with toasted almonds or pistachios. For this ice-cream, an ice-cream container equipped with paddles or a hand-propelled ice-cream churn is essential.

1 PINT

8 fl. oz. single cream [1 cup light cream]
4 oz. [1 cup] pistachios, shelled, blanched and chopped
8 fl. oz. double cream [1 cup heavy cream]
½ teaspoon almond essence
3 egg yolks
2 oz. [¼ cup] sugar
3 fl. oz. [⅜ cup] water
3 egg whites, stiffly beaten

Place the single [light] cream and the nuts in an electric blender. Blend, on and off, for 30 seconds or until the nuts are puréed within the cream.

Spoon the cream and nut mixture into a small saucepan and, using a wooden spoon, stir in the double [heavy] cream. Place the pan over low heat and cook gently until the mixture is hot. Remove the pan from the heat. Cover the pan and leave it to cool.

Pour the cream mixture into a small mixing bowl. Beat in the almond essence and set aside.

In a medium-sized mixing bowl, beat the egg yolks with a wire whisk or rotary beater until they are well blended. Set aside.

In a small saucepan, dissolve the sugar in the water over low heat, stirring constantly. When the sugar has dissolved, increase the heat to moderate and boil the syrup until the temperature reaches 220°F on a sugar thermometer or until a little of the syrup spooned out of the pan and cooled, will form a short thread when drawn out between your index finger and thumb. Remove the pan from the heat and let the syrup stand for 1 minute.

Pour the syrup over the egg yolks in a steady stream, whisking constantly with a wire whisk or rotary beater. Continue whisking until the mixture is thick and fluffy. Mix in the cooled cream mixture. With a metal spoon, fold in the egg whites.

Pour the mixture into an ice-cream container equipped with paddles or into a hand-propelled ice-cream churn, and freeze.

Serve as required.

Pistou

ITALIAN VEGETABLE SOUP

A warming soup made with vegetables and spaghetti, Pistou (pee-stoo) is given its distinctive flavour by the addition of garlic and basil, pounded together. Serve with crisp bread.

4 SERVINGS

1½ pints [3¾ cups] water
1 teaspoon salt
1 lb. French beans, trimmed, washed and chopped
4 medium-sized potatoes, peeled and cubed
14 oz. canned peeled tomatoes, drained

Delicious savoury tartlets, Pissaladières are evocative Provençale summertime snacks.

½ teaspoon black pepper
4 oz. spaghetti
2 garlic cloves
3 tablespoons chopped fresh basil
2 tablespoons olive oil
2 oz. [½ cup] **Parmesan cheese,**
  grated

Fill a large saucepan with the water and add the salt. Place the saucepan over high heat and bring the water to the boil. Add the beans, potatoes, tomatoes and pepper. Reduce the heat to moderately low, cover the pan and cook the vegetables for 20 to 25 minutes or until they are tender.

Uncover the pan and add the spaghetti. Continue to cook for a further 10 to 12 minutes, or until the spaghetti is 'al dente' or just tender.

Meanwhile, place the garlic and basil in a mortar. Pound them together with a pestle until they are well mixed. Add the oil and 2 tablespoons of the soup and continue pounding until the mixture is thoroughly combined.

When the spaghetti is cooked, stir the garlic and basil mixture into the soup.

Remove the pan from the heat. Ladle the soup into individual warmed soup bowls and sprinkle with the Parmesan cheese. Serve at once.

Pita

MIDDLE EASTERN BREAD

Pita (pee-tah) is a delicious flat bread which resembles a rather doughy flat pancake in appearance. Pita is made all over the Middle East, Turkey and Greece and is usually cut in half and filled with either Falafel or roast lamb and salad. The secret of making Pita is to heat the baking trays at the same time as the oven is being heated, so that the dough is baked on a very hot tray. This causes the bread to puff up immediately and creates a hollow flat bread. Pita may be stored in a plastic bag in the refrigerator for up to a week or for several months in a home freezer. Before eating Pita, you should heat it in a hot oven for 5 minutes or place it under a moderately hot grill [broiler] for 5 minutes.

12 BREADS

½ oz. fresh yeast
2 tablespoons plus 1 teaspoon sugar
1 pint [2½ cups] plus 1 tablespoon
  lukewarm water
1½ lb. [6 cups] strong white flour
1 tablespoon salt
1 teaspoon olive oil

Crumble the yeast into a small bowl and mash in 1 teaspoon of sugar with a kitchen fork. Add 1 tablespoon of water and cream the water and yeast together to form a smooth paste. Set the bowl aside in a warm, draught-free place for 15 to 20 minutes, or until the yeast has risen and is puffed up and frothy.

Sift the flour, the remaining sugar and the salt into a warmed, large mixing bowl. Make a well in the centre of the flour mixture and pour in the yeast and the remaining lukewarm water. Using your hands or a spatula, gradually draw the flour into the liquid. Continue mixing until all the flour is incorporated and the dough comes away from the sides of the bowl.

Turn the dough out on to a floured board or marble slab and knead for about 10 minutes, reflouring the surface if the dough becomes sticky. The dough should be elastic and smooth.

Rinse, thoroughly dry and lightly grease the large mixing bowl. Shape the dough into a ball and return it to the bowl. With a pastry brush, lightly coat the top of the dough with the oil. Cover the bowl with a clean, damp cloth. Set the bowl in a warm, draught-free place and leave it for 1½ hours, or until the dough has risen and almost doubled in bulk.

Turn the dough out of the bowl on to a floured surface and knead it for 4 minutes. Using a sharp knife, cut the dough into 12 equal pieces and shape each piece into a ball. Place the balls on a large baking sheet, cover with a damp cloth and return to a warm place for 10 minutes.

Place three baking sheets in the oven. Preheat the oven to very hot 450°F (Gas Mark 8, 230°C).

On a floured surface, roll the balls of dough out into circles, approximately 5-inches in diameter.

Remove the hot baking sheets from the oven. Place 2 circles of dough on each sheet. Return the baking sheets to the oven. Bake the dough circles for 8 to 10 minutes or until the bread is puffed up and golden brown.

Remove the baking sheets from the oven. Transfer the bread to a towel spread over your working surface to cool and flatten. Bake the remaining dough in the same way.

Serve the pitas slightly warm.

Pitcaithly Bannock

Pitcaithly Bannock is a delicious Scottish crumbly shortbread, flavoured with almonds and candied peel. Serve it with coffee.

16 SHORTBREADS

8 oz. [1 cup] plus 1 teaspoon butter, softened
2 oz. [¼ cup] plus 1 tablespoon castor sugar
12 oz. [3 cups] flour
2 oz. [⅓ cup] blanched almonds, chopped
2 oz. [⅓ cup] candied peel, chopped

Preheat the oven to moderate 350°F (Gas Mark 4, 180°C).

Lightly grease a 9-inch loose-bottomed flan tin with the teaspoon of butter. Set aside.

In a large mixing bowl, cream the remaining butter and the 2 ounces [¼ cup] of sugar together with a wooden spoon until the mixture is light and creamy.

Add the flour, a little at a time and, using your hands, knead the mixture until it is soft and sticks together. Add the almonds and candied peel and knead lightly until well mixed. Pat the dough into a ball. Place the dough in the flan tin.

Using your hands or the back of a spoon, press the dough out evenly in the bottom of the tin.

Prick the dough all over with a fork

Pita is a flat Middle-Eastern bread, perfect for meat and salad fillings.

and, using a sharp knife, mark the dough circle into 16 equal sections. Place the flan tin in the oven and bake the shortbread for 40 to 45 minutes or until it is a pale golden colour.

Remove the flan tin from the oven and transfer the shortbread to a wire rack. Sprinkle with the remaining tablespoon of sugar and set aside to cool completely. When the shortbread is cold, cut into wedges and serve.

Pithiviers

ALMOND PASTRY

Pithiviers (pee-thee-v'yay) is a classic pastry which is a speciality of Pithiviers near Chartres in France. Serve the pastry, cut into small wedges, with coffee.

ONE 8-INCH PASTRY

PASTRY
8 oz. [2 cups] flour
¼ teaspoon salt
8 oz. [1 cup] unsalted butter
4 fl. oz. [½ cup] iced water
FILLING
6 oz. [1 cup] ground almonds
6 oz. [¾ cup] castor sugar
⅛ teaspoon almond essence
3 tablespoons rum
1 tablespoon unsalted butter, softened
1 large egg, well beaten
GLAZE
1 egg yolk, well beaten with 2 tablespoons milk
1 tablespoon castor sugar

First make the pastry. Sift the flour and salt into a medium-sized mixing bowl. Add 2 ounces [¼ cup] of the butter and cut into small pieces with a table knife. With your fingertips, rub the butter into the flour until the mixture resembles coarse breadcrumbs. Add the water and mix it in with the knife to form a firm dough. Lightly knead the dough for a few minutes until it is smooth and pliable. Shape the dough into a ball and wrap it in greaseproof or waxed paper. Chill the dough in the refrigerator for 15 minutes.

Place the remaining butter between two sheets of greaseproof or waxed paper and beat it with the back of a wooden spoon or a wooden mallet into a flat oblong approximately ½-inch thick. Set aside.

Remove the dough from the refrigerator and remove and discard the paper. Place the dough on a lightly floured board. Using a floured rolling pin, roll the dough out into an oblong approximately ¼-inch thick. Carefully peel off and discard the paper from the butter oblong and

lay the butter in the centre of the dough. Fold the dough in half to enclose the butter and chill it in the refrigerator for 10 minutes.

Remove the dough from the refrigerator and place it, with the folds facing downwards, on the working surface. Roll the dough into an oblong and fold the oblong in three. Turn the dough so that the open ends face you and roll it out again. Fold the dough over in three and chill it in the refrigerator for 15 minutes. Repeat the rolling and folding process twice more, and chill the dough in the refrigerator while you make the filling.

Preheat the oven to fairly hot 400°F (Gas Mark 6, 200°C). Line a large baking sheet with non-stick silicone paper and sprinkle it with a little cold water. Set aside.

To make the filling, place the ground almonds, sugar and almond essence in a medium-sized mixing bowl. Add the rum and the softened butter and beat the mixture with a wooden spoon until it is well blended and the butter is evenly distributed. Add the egg and continue beating until the mixture forms a smooth paste. Set aside.

Remove the dough from the refrigerator and divide it in half. Place one half on a lightly floured working surface and set the other half aside. Using a floured rolling pin, roll the dough out into a circle approximately ¼-inch thick. Trim the circle to make it 8-inches in diameter. Carefully lift the dough circle on the rolling pin and place it on the prepared baking sheet.

Spoon the almond filling on to the dough circle and, using a flat-bladed knife or the back of the spoon, spread it evenly to within ½-inch of the edges of the dough. Moisten the edges of the dough circle with a little cold water and set aside.

Place the second half of the dough on the working surface and roll it out and trim it as before. Using the point of a sharp knife, trace a pattern in the shape of a single rosette in the centre of the circle. Lift the circle on the rolling pin and place it over the almond filling. Crimp the edges of the dough circles together to seal them.

Using a pastry brush, lightly brush the surface of the dough with the egg yolk mixture, and sprinkle with the sugar.

Place the baking sheet in the centre of the oven and bake for 20 minutes, or until the pastry is cooked and golden.

Remove the baking sheet from the oven and set the pastry aside to cool for 30 minutes. Then carefully transfer to a wire rack and set aside to cool completely before cutting into wedges and serving.

Pizzaiola Sauce
ITALIAN TOMATO AND GARLIC SAUCE

A traditional Italian sauce, Pizzaiola (peet-zah-oh-lah) Sauce is a piquant combination of tomatoes, garlic and oregano. It is delicious served with steak or chicken.

4 SERVINGS

2 fl. oz. [¼ cup] olive oil
2 lb. tomatoes, blanched, peeled, seeded and chopped
3 garlic cloves, crushed
1 teaspoon salt
½ teaspoon black pepper
1 tablespoon fresh oregano or 1½ teaspoons dried oregano

In a medium-sized saucepan, heat the oil over moderate heat. When the oil is hot, add the tomatoes, garlic, salt, pepper and oregano and mix well to blend. Reduce the heat to low and simmer the sauce, stirring occasionally, for 15 to 20 minutes, or until it is thick and smooth.

Remove the pan from the heat and serve immediately.

Pizza

Pizza in Italian means pie — a most mundane description of a unique dish. It originated in Naples, Italy and is, basically, a large round cake of bread dough spread with a variety of ingredients — tomatoes, Mozzarella cheese, olives, anchovies, mushrooms, bacon, sausage and shrimps, or a combination of these, being some of the most popular fillings. Pizza is baked in a hot oven for 15 to 20 minutes or until the dough is cooked and the cheese on top has melted.

In some parts of Italy, pizzas are made with pastry instead of bread dough which makes a lighter meal, but for an authentic Neapolitan pizza, the base must be bread dough.

For serving, one small pizza is usually allowed per person, but if preferred, one very large pizza can be made, to serve up to four people.

Pizza alle Asciughe
PIZZA WITH ANCHOVIES AND TUNA

Perfect for those who love the taste of anchovies, Pizza alle Asciughe (peet-zah ah-lay ah-shoo-gay) may be served with crusty rolls and lots of red wine.

2 SERVINGS

½ oz. fresh yeast
¼ teaspoon sugar
4 fl. oz. [½ cup] plus 1 tablespoon lukewarm water

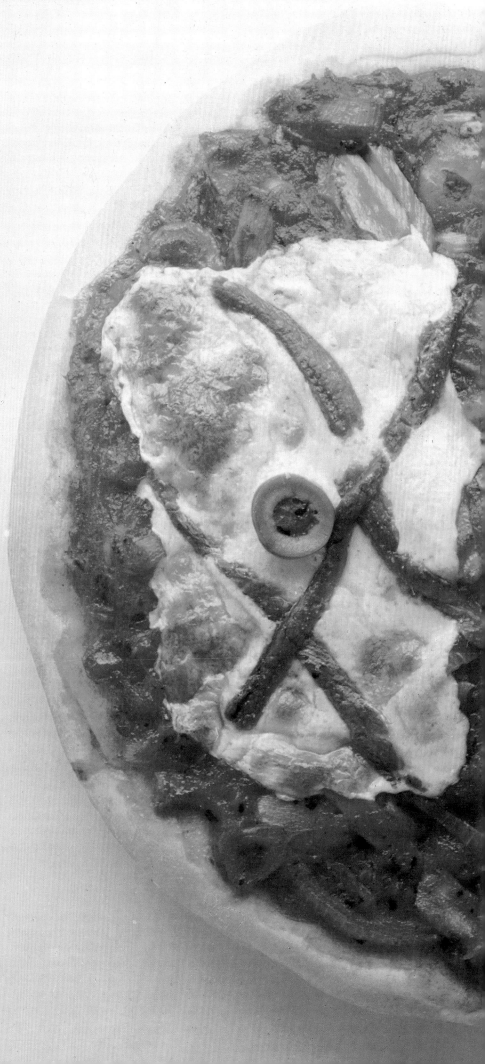

8 oz. [2 cups] flour
1 teaspoon salt
1 teaspoon olive oil
FILLING
1 tablespoon plus 1 teaspoon olive
oil
2 small onions, thinly sliced and
pushed out into rings
14 oz. canned peeled tomatoes,
coarsely chopped
1 tablespoon tomato purée
$\frac{1}{2}$ teaspoon dried basil
$\frac{1}{4}$ teaspoon dried oregano
$\frac{1}{4}$ teaspoon black pepper
1 tablespoon chopped fresh parsley
4 oz. canned tuna, drained and
flaked
6 oz. Mozzarella cheese, thinly
sliced
6 anchovy fillets, halved
4 stuffed olives, halved

Crumble the yeast into a small mixing bowl. Add the sugar and the 1 tablespoon of water and cream the water and yeast together. Set the bowl aside in a warm, draught-free place for 15 to 20 minutes, or until the yeast mixture is puffed up and frothy.

Sift the flour and salt into a warmed, large mixing bowl. Make a well in the centre and pour in the yeast mixture and the remaining water.

Using your fingers or a spatula, gradually draw the flour into the liquids. Continue mixing until all the flour is incorporated and the dough comes away from the sides of the bowl.

Turn the dough out on to a lightly floured board or marble slab and knead it for about 10 minutes, reflouring the surface if the dough becomes sticky. The dough should be elastic and smooth.

Rinse, thoroughly dry and lightly grease the mixing bowl. Shape the dough into a ball and return it to the bowl. Dust the top of the dough with a little flour and cover the bowl with a clean, damp cloth. Set the bowl aside in a warm, draught-free place for 45 minutes to 1 hour, or until the dough has risen and has almost doubled in bulk.

Meanwhile, prepare the filling. In a medium-sized saucepan heat the 1 tablespoon of olive oil over moderate heat. When the oil is hot, add the onions and fry, stirring occasionally, for 5 to 7 minutes or until they are soft and translucent but not brown. Stir in the tomatoes with the can juice, the tomato purée, basil, oregano and pepper. Cook the sauce, stirring occasionally, for 20 to 30 minutes or until it has reduced and thickened. Stir in the parsley and tuna and mix well. Remove the pan from the heat and set aside.

Preheat the oven to very hot 450°F (Gas Mark 8, 230°C). With the 1 teaspoon of olive oil, lightly grease a large baking sheet and set aside.

Turn the risen dough out of the bowl on to a floured surface and knead it for 3 minutes. Cut the dough in half. With a lightly floured rolling pin, roll out each dough half to a circle about ¼-inch thick. Carefully arrange the dough circles, well apart, on the prepared baking sheet.

Spoon half of the tomato sauce on to each dough circle and spread it out with the back of the spoon. Top with the Mozzarella slices and arrange the anchovy fillets and olives over the cheese. Moisten each filling with the remaining teaspoon of oil.

Place the pizzas in the centre of the oven and bake for 15 to 20 minutes, or until the dough is cooked and the cheese has melted.

Remove the pizzas from the oven and transfer them to a warmed serving dish. Serve immediately.

Pizza with Aubergine
[Eggplant]

This pizza has an unusual aubergine [eggplant] filling. Serve it, cut into wedges, with drinks or serve it for supper with a green salad and some red wine, such as Bardolino.

2-4 SERVINGS

½ oz. fresh yeast
¼ teaspoon sugar
4 fl. oz. [½ cup] plus 1 tablespoon lukewarm water
8 oz. [2 cups] flour
1 teaspoon salt
1 teaspoon olive oil
FILLING
4 fl. oz. [½ cup] plus 1 tablespoon olive oil
1 large aubergine [eggplant], cut into ¼-inch slices and dégorged

1 medium-sized onion, finely chopped
1 garlic clove, crushed
14 oz. canned peeled tomatoes, coarsely chopped
1 tablespoon tomato purée
1 teaspoon dried basil
½ teaspoon salt
½ teaspoon pepper
2 oz. [½ cup] Parmesan cheese, grated
6 oz. Mozzarella cheese, sliced

Crumble the yeast into a small mixing bowl. Add the sugar and the 1 tablespoon of water and cream the water and yeast together. Set the bowl aside in a warm, draught-free place for 15 to 20 minutes, or until the yeast mixture is puffed up and frothy.

Sift the flour and salt into a warmed, large mixing bowl. Make a well in the centre and pour in the yeast mixture and the remaining water.

Using your fingers or a spatula, gradually draw the flour into the liquids. Continue mixing until all the flour is incorporated and the dough comes away from the sides of the bowl.

Turn the dough out on to a lightly floured board or marble slab and knead it for about 10 minutes, reflouring the surface if the dough becomes sticky. The dough should be elastic and smooth.

Rinse, thoroughly dry and lightly grease the mixing bowl. Shape the dough into a ball and return it to the bowl. Dust the top of the dough with a little flour and cover the bowl with a clean, damp cloth. Set the bowl aside in a warm, draught-free place for 45 minutes to 1 hour, or until the dough has risen and has almost doubled in bulk.

Meanwhile, prepare the filling. In a medium-sized frying-pan, heat the 4 fluid ounces [½ cup] of oil over moderate heat. When the oil is hot, add the aubergine [eggplant] slices and fry them, turning them frequently, for 6 to 8 minutes or until they are lightly browned on both sides. With a slotted spoon, remove the aubergine [eggplant] slices and set them aside to drain on kitchen paper towels.

In a medium-sized saucepan, heat the remaining tablespoon of oil over moderate heat. When the oil is hot, add the onion and garlic and fry, stirring occasionally, for 5 to 7 minutes or until the onion is soft and translucent but not brown. Stir in the tomatoes with the can juice, the tomato purée, basil, salt and pepper. Cook the sauce, stirring occasionally, for 20 to 30 minutes or until it has reduced and thickened. Remove the pan from the heat and set aside.

Preheat the oven to very hot 450°F

These Pizza Canapés taste every bit as marvellous as they look — serve them as the perfect winter appetizer.

(Gas Mark 8, 230°C). Using the 1 teaspoon of olive oil, lightly grease a large baking sheet and set aside.

Turn the risen dough out of the bowl on to a floured surface and knead it for 3 minutes. Cut the dough in half. With a lightly floured rolling pin, roll out each dough half to a circle about ¼-inch thick. Carefully arrange the dough circles, well apart, on the prepared baking sheet.

Spoon half of the tomato sauce on to each dough circle and spread it out with the back of the spoon. Place the aubergine [eggplant] slices over the tomato sauce. Sprinkle with the grated cheese and arrange the Mozzarella slices on top.

Place the pizzas in the centre of the oven and bake for 15 to 20 minutes, or

together. Set the bowl aside in a warm, draught-free place for 15 to 20 minutes, or until the yeast mixture is puffed up and frothy.

Sift the flour and salt into a warmed, large mixing bowl. Make a well in the centre and pour in the yeast mixture and the remaining water.

Using your fingers or a spatula, gradually draw the flour into the liquids. Continue mixing until all the flour is incorporated and the dough comes away from the sides of the bowl.

Turn the dough out on to a lightly floured board or marble slab and knead it for about 10 minutes, reflouring the surface if the dough becomes sticky. The dough should be elastic and smooth.

Rinse, thoroughly dry and lightly grease the large mixing bowl. Shape the dough into a ball and return it to the bowl. Dust the top of the dough with a little flour and cover the bowl with a clean, damp cloth. Set the bowl aside in a warm, draught-free place for 45 minutes to 1 hour or until the dough has risen and has almost doubled in bulk.

Meanwhile, prepare the filling. In a medium-sized saucepan, heat the 1 table-spoon of oil over moderate heat. When the oil is hot, add the onion and garlic and fry, stirring occasionally, for 5 to 7 minutes or until the onion is soft and translucent but not brown. Add the tomatoes with the can juice, the tomato purée, thyme, oregano, salt and pepper. Cook the sauce, stirring occasionally, for 20 to 30 minutes or until it has reduced and thickened. Remove the pan from the heat and set aside.

Preheat the oven to very hot 450°F (Gas Mark 8, 230°C). With the 1 teaspoon of olive oil, lightly grease a large baking sheet and set aside.

Turn the risen dough out of the bowl on to a floured surface and knead it for 3 minutes. With a lightly floured rolling pin, roll out the dough to a rectangle about $\frac{1}{8}$-inch thick. Carefully place the dough on the prepared baking sheet.

Spoon the tomato sauce on to the dough and spread it out with the back of the spoon. Place the Mozzarella slices on top and arrange the anchovy fillets and olives over the cheese. Moisten the filling with the remaining teaspoon of olive oil.

Place the pizza in the centre of the oven and bake for 10 to 15 minutes, or until the dough is cooked and the cheese has melted.

Remove the baking sheet from the oven. With a sharp knife, cut the pizza into $1\frac{1}{2}$-inch squares. Transfer the can-apés to a serving dish and either serve them immediately or set them aside to cool completely before serving.

until the dough is cooked and the cheese has melted.

Remove the pizzas from the oven and transfer them to a warmed serving dish. Serve immediately.

Pizza Canapés

These small pizzas make interesting appetizers. The dough is rolled out very thinly and cut into small squares but apart from this, Pizza Canapés are made in the same way as ordinary pizzas. This recipe is for a basic filling, but you can vary it in any way you like as long as you do not overload the dough with filling.

40 CANAPES

$\frac{1}{2}$ oz. fresh yeast
$\frac{1}{4}$ teaspoon sugar
4 fl. oz. [$\frac{1}{2}$ cup] plus 1 tablespoon lukewarm water

8 oz. [2 cups] flour
1 teaspoon salt
1 teaspoon olive oil
FILLING
1 tablespoon plus 1 teaspoon olive oil
1 small onion, finely chopped
1 garlic clove, crushed
14 oz. canned peeled tomatoes, finely chopped
1 tablespoon tomato purée
$\frac{1}{2}$ teaspoon dried thyme
$\frac{1}{4}$ teaspoon dried oregano
$\frac{1}{4}$ teaspoon salt
$\frac{1}{4}$ teaspoon black pepper
6 oz. Mozzarella cheese, thinly sliced
8 anchovy fillets, halved
8 black olives, halved and stoned

Crumble the yeast into a small mixing bowl. Add the sugar and the 1 tablespoon of water and cream the water and yeast

Pizza Capri
PIZZA WITH TOMATOES, CHEESE AND CAPERS

Pizza Capri (peet-zah cap-ree) *is a delicious tomato, cheese, caper and olive pizza from the Naples region of Italy. Serve with a tossed green salad and a glass of Italian white wine.*

2 SERVINGS

$\frac{1}{2}$ oz. fresh yeast
$\frac{1}{4}$ teaspoon sugar
4 fl. oz. [$\frac{1}{2}$ cup] plus 1 tablespoon lukewarm water
8 oz. [2 cups] flour
1 teaspoon salt
1 teaspoon olive oil
FILLING
1 tablespoon plus 1 teaspoon olive oil
1 small onion, finely chopped
1 garlic clove, crushed
14 oz. canned peeled tomatoes, coarsely chopped
$\frac{1}{2}$ teaspoon dried marjoram
$\frac{1}{4}$ teaspoon dried oregano
$\frac{1}{2}$ teaspoon salt
$\frac{1}{4}$ teaspoon black pepper
6 oz. Mozzarella cheese, thinly sliced
2 tablespoons capers
6 black olives, halved and stoned

Crumble the yeast into a small mixing bowl. Add the sugar and the 1 tablespoon of water and cream the water and yeast together. Set the bowl aside in a warm, draught-free place for 15 to 20 minutes, or until the yeast mixture is puffed up and frothy.

Sift the flour and salt into a warmed, large mixing bowl. Make a well in the centre and pour in the yeast mixture and the remaining water.

Using your fingers or a spatula, gradually draw the flour into the liquids. Continue mixing until all the flour is incorporated and the dough comes away from the sides of the bowl.

Turn the dough out on to a lightly floured board or marble slab and knead it for about 10 minutes, reflouring the surface if the dough becomes sticky. The dough should be elastic and smooth.

Rinse, thoroughly dry and lightly grease the mixing bowl. Shape the dough into a ball and return it to the bowl. Dust the top of the dough with a little flour and cover the bowl with a clean, damp cloth.

Set the bowl aside in a warm, draught-free place for 45 minutes to 1 hour, or until the dough has risen and has almost doubled in bulk.

Meanwhile, prepare the filling. In a medium-sized saucepan, heat the 1 table-spoon of oil over moderate heat. When the oil is hot, add the onion and garlic and fry, stirring occasionally, for 5 to 7 minutes or until the onion is soft and translucent but not brown. Stir in the tomatoes with the can juice, the marjoram, oregano, salt and pepper. Cook the sauce, stirring occasionally, for 20 to 30 minutes or until it has reduced and thickened. Remove the pan from the heat and set aside.

Preheat the oven to very hot 450°F (Gas Mark 8, 230°C). Using the 1 teaspoon of olive oil, lightly grease a large baking sheet and set aside.

Turn the risen dough out of the bowl on to a floured surface and knead it for 3 minutes. Cut the dough in half. With a lightly floured rolling pin, roll out each dough half to a circle about $\frac{1}{4}$-inch thick. Carefully arrange the dough circles, well apart, on the prepared baking sheet.

Spoon half of the tomato sauce on to each dough circle and spread it out with the back of the spoon. Place the Mozzarella slices over the tomato sauce and arrange the capers and olives over them.

Mozzarella, tomatoes, capers and olives make up the filling for Pizza Capri. Serve with lots of white wine.

Moisten each filling with the remaining teaspoon of oil.

Place the pizzas in the centre of the oven and bake for 15 to 20 minutes, or until the dough is cooked and the cheese has melted.

Remove the pizzas from the oven and transfer them to a warmed serving dish. Serve immediately.

Pizza ai Funghi
PIZZA WITH MUSHROOMS

Pizza ai Funghi (peet-zah eye foon-gee) is made from tomatoes, cheese, pimiento and mushrooms. Serve with a mixed salad and some Italian red wine, such as Valpolicella.

2 SERVINGS

$\frac{1}{2}$ oz. fresh yeast
$\frac{1}{4}$ teaspoon sugar
4 fl. oz. [$\frac{1}{2}$ cup] plus 1 tablespoon lukewarm water
8 oz. [2 cups] flour
1 teaspoon salt
1 teaspoon olive oil
FILLING
1 tablespoon plus 1 teaspoon olive oil
1 small onion, finely chopped
4 oz. mushrooms, wiped clean and sliced

14 oz. canned peeled tomatoes, drained and coarsely chopped
$\frac{1}{2}$ teaspoon dried basil
$\frac{1}{2}$ teaspoon dried oregano
$\frac{1}{4}$ teaspoon salt
$\frac{1}{4}$ teaspoon black pepper
4 tablespoons chopped pimiento
6 oz. Mozzarella cheese, thinly sliced

Crumble the yeast into a small mixing bowl. Add the sugar and the 1 tablespoon of water and cream the water and yeast together. Set the bowl aside in a warm, draught-free place for 15 to 20 minutes, or until the yeast mixture is puffed up and frothy.

Sift the flour and salt into a warmed, large mixing bowl. Make a well in the centre and pour in the yeast mixture and the remaining water.

Using your fingers or a spatula, gradually draw the flour into the liquids. Continue mixing until all the flour is incorporated and the dough comes away from the sides of the bowl.

Turn the dough out on to a lightly floured board or marble slab and knead it for about 10 minutes, reflouring the surface if the dough becomes sticky. The dough should be elastic and smooth.

Rinse, thoroughly dry and lightly grease the mixing bowl. Shape the dough into a ball and return it to the bowl. Dust

Mushrooms are what make this colourful Pizza ai Funghi really delicious. Serve as a filling supper dish.

the top of the dough with a little flour and cover the bowl with a clean, damp cloth. Set the bowl aside in a warm, draught-free place for 45 minutes to 1 hour, or until the dough has risen and has almost doubled in bulk.

Meanwhile, prepare the filling. In a small frying-pan, heat the 1 tablespoon of oil over moderate heat. When the oil is hot, add the onion and fry, stirring occasionally, for 5 to 7 minutes or until it is soft and translucent but not brown. Add the mushrooms and fry, stirring occasionally, for 3 minutes or until they are tender. Remove the pan from the heat and set aside.

Preheat the oven to very hot 450°F (Gas Mark 8, 230°C). Using the 1 teaspoon of olive oil, lightly grease a large baking sheet and set aside.

Turn the risen dough out of the bowl on to a floured surface and knead it for 3 minutes. Cut the dough in half. With a lightly floured rolling pin, roll out each dough half to a circle about $\frac{1}{4}$-inch thick. Carefully arrange the dough circles, well apart, on the prepared sheet.

Arrange the chopped tomatoes over the dough circles to cover them completely.

Sprinkle over the basil, oregano, salt, pepper and chopped pimiento. Cover with the Mozzarella slices. Using a slotted spoon, remove the onion and mushroom mixture from the frying-pan and arrange it over the cheese. Moisten each filling with the remaining teaspoon of oil.

Place the pizzas in the centre of the oven and bake for 15 to 20 minutes or until the dough is cooked and the cheese has melted.

Remove the pizzas from the oven and transfer them to a warmed serving dish. Serve immediately.

Pizza al Prosciutto
PIZZA WITH HAM

Pizza al Prosciutto (peet-zah al proh-shoo-toh) is one of the most delicious and simplest of pizza recipes. If you cannot obtain prosciutto, substitute any cooked ham, although the flavour will not be so authentically Italian.

2 SERVINGS

½ oz. fresh yeast
¼ teaspoon sugar
4 fl. oz. [½ cup] plus 1 tablespoon lukewarm water
8 oz. [2 cups] flour
1 teaspoon salt
1 teaspoon olive oil
FILLING
14 oz. canned peeled tomatoes, drained and coarsely chopped
½ teaspoon dried basil
¼ teaspoon dried oregano
¼ teaspoon salt
¼ teaspoon black pepper
6 oz. Mozzarella cheese, thinly sliced
4 oz. prosciutto, cut into strips
6 black olives, halved and stoned
1 teaspoon olive oil

Crumble the yeast into a small mixing bowl. Add the sugar and the 1 tablespoon of water and cream the water and yeast together. Set the bowl aside in a warm, draught-free place for 15 to 20 minutes, or until the yeast mixture is puffed up and frothy.

Sift the flour and salt into a warmed, large mixing bowl. Make a well in the centre and pour in the yeast mixture and the remaining water.

Using your fingers or a spatula, gradually draw the flour into the liquids. Continue mixing until all the flour is incorporated and the dough comes away from the sides of the bowl.

Turn the dough out on to a lightly floured board or marble slab and knead it

for about 10 minutes, reflouring the surface if the dough becomes sticky. The dough should be elastic and smooth.

Rinse, thoroughly dry and lightly grease the mixing bowl. Shape the dough into a ball and return it to the bowl. Dust the top of the dough with a little flour and cover the bowl with a clean, damp cloth. Set the bowl aside in a warm, draught-free place for 45 minutes to 1 hour, or until the dough has risen and has almost doubled in bulk.

Preheat the oven to very hot 450°F (Gas Mark 8, 230°C). With the 1 teaspoon of olive oil, lightly grease a large baking sheet and set aside.

Turn the risen dough out of the bowl on to a floured surface and knead it for 3 minutes. Cut the dough in half. With a lightly floured rolling pin, roll out each dough half to a circle about ¼-inch thick. Carefully arrange the dough circles, well apart, on the prepared baking sheet.

Arrange the chopped tomatoes over the dough circles to cover them completely. Sprinkle over the basil, oregano, salt and pepper. Place the Mozzarella slices on top and arrange the prosciutto and olives over the cheese.

Moisten each filling with the remaining teaspoon of olive oil.

Place the pizzas in the centre of the oven and bake for 15 to 20 minutes or until the dough is cooked and the cheese has melted.

Remove the pizzas from the oven and transfer them to a warmed serving dish. Serve immediately.

Plaice
Plaice, sometimes known as FLOUNDER, is a flat, saltwater fish. It is oval in shape, has both eyes on the same side of the head and a brown skin with bright orange-red spots on one side and completely white on the other. Plaice grows to a maximum weight of 8 pounds, but the average weight is usually just a little over 1 pound.

The flesh of plaice is soft and the flavour rather bland. It therefore requires accompaniments and sauces to give it extra flavour and texture. Plaice is often filleted before cooking but may be cooked whole, on the bone.

When buying plaice, allow a 1-pound fish or 8 ounces of fillet per person.

To shallow-fry plaice fillets, first dip them in beaten egg and then in breadcrumbs, coating both sides thoroughly. Fry them in butter over moderate heat for 5 to 7 minutes on each side depending on the thickness of the fillets. The fish may be fried omitting the egg and breadcrumbs, in which case reduce the cooking time slightly.

To deep-fry plaice fillets, coat each piece of fish with a little flour, and then dip them in batter. Fill a large saucepan one-third full of vegetable oil. Heat the oil over moderate heat until it reaches 375°F on a deep-fat thermometer, or until a cube of stale bread dropped into the oil browns in 40 seconds. Place the fish in a deep-frying basket. Lower the basket into the oil and fry for 4 to 5 minutes, again depending on the thickness of the fillets.

To grill [broil] plaice fillets, preheat the grill [broiler] to high. Brush each fillet with a little melted butter and place under the heat. Cook for 8 to 10 minutes, turning occasionally, depending on the thickness of the fillets.

Poaching is an ideal way to cook whole plaice, although fillets may also be poached. Poaching can be done in the oven or on top of the stove. To prepare a whole plaice for poaching, clean and gut the fish, trim the fins and gills and remove the eyes if the head is left on.

To poach plaice in the oven, preheat the oven to moderate 350°F (Gas Mark 4, 180°C). Lay the fish in a shallow baking dish. Heat the poaching liquid (milk, COURT BOUILLON, FISH STOCK, wine or water), until it is boiling, and pour it over the fish. Cover the dish with aluminium foil and place it in the oven. Cook for 15 to 20 minutes or until the flesh flakes easily when tested with a fork.

To poach plaice on top of the stove, place the fish in a large flameproof casserole and cover with the chosen poaching liquid. Place the casserole over moderate heat and bring to the boil. Reduce the heat to low and simmer the fish until it is cooked. Allow 12 to 15 minutes per pound for whole fish and 8 to 12 minutes for fillets.

To steam plaice, fill a large double-boiler with hot COURT BOUILLON, FISH STOCK or water and lay the fish on the steaming shelf. Place the pan over moderately low heat, cover and steam until cooked. Cooking times are the same as for poaching.

To bake plaice fillets, preheat the oven to moderate 350°F (Gas Mark 4, 180°C). Brush the fillets with melted butter and bake, uncovered, for 25 to 30 minutes or until tender. Baked plaice is generally served with parsley, herb or lemon sauce.

Plaice [Flounder] Anatole

A delicious soufflé-like dish, Plaice [Flounder] Anatole is quick and easy to make. The creamy cheese topping is very rich and the dish requires no accompaniment, except perhaps a green salad.

*Rich Plaice [Flounder] Anatole is a
superb dinner dish.*

4-6 SERVINGS

2 oz. [¼ cup] plus 1 teaspoon butter
2 lb. plaice [flounder] fillets
1 large green pepper, white pith
    removed, seeded and thinly
    sliced
1 pint [2½ cups] mayonnaise
8 oz. [2 cups] Cheddar cheese,
    grated
½ teaspoon salt
¼ teaspoon white pepper

2 fl. oz. double cream [¼ cup heavy
    cream]
4 egg whites, stiffly beaten

Preheat the oven to moderate 350°F (Gas
Mark 4, 180°C). With the teaspoon of
butter, grease a large ovenproof dish.
Set aside.

In a large frying-pan, melt the remaining butter over moderate heat. When the
foam subsides, add the plaice [flounder]
fillets, a few at a time, and fry for 2
minutes on each side. Remove the pan
from the heat and carefully remove the
skin from the fish fillets. Transfer the

fillets to the prepared dish. Arrange the
green pepper slices over the fish and set
aside.

Place the mayonnaise in a medium-
sized mixing bowl. Using a wooden spoon,
stir in the cheese, salt and pepper and then
the cream. With a metal spoon, carefully
fold in the beaten egg whites until the
mixture is thoroughly combined.

Pour the mayonnaise mixture evenly
over the fish. Place the dish in the oven
and bake for 20 minutes or until the top
has risen and turned a golden brown.

Remove the dish from the oven and
serve immediately.

Plaice [Flounder] with Artichoke Sauce is quick and easy to prepare — and tastes delicious too!

Plaice [Flounder] with Artichoke Sauce

Plaice [flounder] fillets, simmered in Court Bouillon and served with a creamy artichoke sauce, is quick and easy to prepare and tastes delicious. Serve with steamed broccoli or peas.

6 SERVINGS

2 lb. plaice [flounder] fillets
$\frac{1}{2}$ teaspoon salt
$\frac{1}{4}$ teaspoon black pepper
1 small onion, sliced and pushed out into rings
1 celery stalk, trimmed and chopped
1 mace blade
   bouquet garni, consisting of 4 parsley sprigs, 1 thyme spray and 1 bay leaf tied together
6 white peppercorns, crushed
10 fl. oz. [1$\frac{1}{4}$ cups] fish stock
6 fl. oz. [$\frac{3}{4}$ cup] dry white wine
1 tablespoon lemon juice
1 tablespoon chopped fresh parsley
SAUCE
1 oz. [2 tablespoons] butter
1 oz. [$\frac{1}{4}$ cup] flour
$\frac{1}{4}$ teaspoon salt

$\frac{1}{8}$ teaspoon white pepper
$\frac{1}{8}$ teaspoon cayenne pepper
2 fl. oz. double cream [$\frac{1}{4}$ cup heavy cream]
3 artichoke hearts, cooked, drained and chopped

Put the plaice [flounder] fillets on a working surface and rub them all over with the salt and pepper. Lay the fillets, in one layer if possible, on the bottom of a large flameproof casserole. Add the onion, celery, mace blade, bouquet garni and peppercorns. Pour over the stock and wine and add the lemon juice.

Place the casserole over moderately high heat and bring the liquid to the boil. Reduce the heat to moderately low, cover the casserole and cook for 8 to 12 minutes, or until the fish flakes easily when tested with a fork.

Remove the casserole from the heat. Using a slotted spoon, transfer the fish to a warmed serving dish. Keep hot while you make the sauce.

Pour 10 fluid ounces [1$\frac{1}{4}$ cups] of the cooking liquid through a fine wire strainer set over a medium-sized bowl. Discard the contents of the strainer.

In a large frying-pan, melt the butter over moderate heat. Remove the pan from the heat and, with a wooden spoon, stir in the flour to make a smooth paste. Gradually add the strained cooking liquid, stirring constantly. Return the pan to the

heat and cook, stirring constantly, for 2 to 3 minutes, or until the sauce is thick and smooth.

Remove the pan from the heat. Stir in the salt, pepper and cayenne. Stir in the cream, and then the artichoke heart pieces. Taste the sauce and add more salt and pepper if necessary. Pour the sauce over the fish fillets, sprinkle with the parsley and serve at once.

Plaice [Flounder] Baked with Garlic and Tomatoes

An unusual and tasty way of cooking plaice [flounder], Plaice [Flounder] Baked with Garlic and Tomatoes is easy to make. It requires no accompaniments except some good French bread and a chilled white Provençal wine.

4 SERVINGS

1 tablespoon butter
4 oz. [1$\frac{1}{3}$ cups] dry breadcrumbs
2 tablespoons finely chopped fresh parsley
2 large garlic cloves, crushed
   finely grated rind of 1 lemon
2$\frac{1}{2}$ teaspoons salt
$\frac{1}{2}$ teaspoon black pepper
1 egg, lightly beaten with 4 tablespoons milk
4 large plaice [flounder], filleted
3 tablespoons olive oil

2 medium-sized onions, sliced and
   pushed out into rings
2 large green peppers, white pith
   removed, seeded and sliced
4 large tomatoes, blanched, peeled
   and cut into thick slices
12 large black olives, stoned and
   halved
2 fl. oz. [¼ cup] melted butter

Preheat the oven to very hot 450°F (Gas
Mark 8, 230°C). Generously grease a
large baking dish with the butter. Set
aside.

On a large plate, combine the breadcrumbs, parsley, garlic, lemon rind, 2
teaspoons of the salt and half of the
pepper together. Put the egg and milk
mixture on another plate.

Dip the fish fillets, first in the egg and
milk mixture and then in the breadcrumb
mixture, coating the fillets well. Place the
fillets in the baking dish, in one layer.
(Use two baking dishes if necessary.) Set
aside.

In a large frying-pan, heat the oil over
moderate heat. When the oil is hot, add
the onions and peppers and fry, stirring
occasionally, for 5 to 7 minutes or until
they are soft and translucent but not
brown. Add the tomatoes, the remaining
salt and pepper and the olives. Reduce the
heat to low and cook, stirring occasionally, for 15 minutes or until the mixture
has thickened.

*Serve Plaice [Flounder] Baked with
Mushrooms with vegetables and some
well-chilled white wine for supper.*

Meanwhile, sprinkle a little of the
melted butter over the fish. Put the baking
dish in the upper part of the oven and
bake the fish, basting occasionally with the
remaining melted butter, for 12 to 15
minutes or until the fish flakes easily when
tested with a fork.

Remove the baking dish from the oven.
Using a fish slice or spatula, carefully
transfer the fillets to a warmed serving
dish. Arrange the fillets in a circle.

Remove the frying-pan from the heat
and pile the tomato mixture in the middle
of the fillets. Serve immediately.

Plaice [Flounder] Baked with Mushrooms

*A tasty main meal dish, Plaice [Flounder]
Baked with Mushrooms may be served with
croquette or creamed potatoes. A well
chilled white wine, such as Chablis or
Niersteiner makes a good accompaniment.*

4 SERVINGS
10 fl. oz. [1¼ cups] dry white wine
 4 fl. oz. [½ cup] water
1 tablespoon lemon juice
1 bay leaf

6 black peppercorns
1 small onion, thinly sliced
½ teaspoon salt
8 plaice [flounder] fillets
2 oz. [¼ cup] butter
1 lb. small button mushrooms,
   wiped clean and thickly sliced
2 tablespoons flour
2 fl. oz. double cream [¼ cup heavy
   cream]
1 tablespoon finely chopped fresh
   chervil or 1½ teaspoons dried
   chervil
⅛ teaspoon cayenne pepper
2 oz. [½ cup] Cheddar cheese, grated

Preheat the oven to moderate 350°F (Gas
Mark 4, 180°C).

In a large baking dish, combine the
wine, water, lemon juice, bay leaf, peppercorns, onion and salt. Place the fish fillets
in the dish and baste them thoroughly
with the mixture. Cover the dish and
place it in the centre of the oven. Bake the
fish for 25 to 30 minutes or until the flesh
flakes easily when tested with a fork.

Remove the dish from the oven and
allow it to cool for a few minutes. With a
fish slice or spatula, remove the fish fillets
from the dish and transfer them to a large,
flameproof casserole. Set aside and keep
warm. Strain and reserve 10 fluid ounces
[1¼ cups] of the cooking liquid. Set aside.

In a medium-sized frying-pan, melt 1½
ounces [3 tablespoons] of the butter over

1837

moderate heat. When the foam subsides, add the mushrooms and cook, stirring frequently, for 3 minutes. Remove the pan from the heat and, with a slotted spoon, transfer the mushrooms to a plate. Set aside and keep warm.

Preheat the grill [broiler] to high.

In a medium-sized saucepan, melt the remaining butter over moderate heat. Remove the pan from the heat and, with a wooden spoon, stir in the flour to make a smooth paste. Gradually add the reserved cooking liquid, stirring constantly. Return the pan to the heat and cook, stirring constantly, for 2 to 3 minutes or until the sauce is thick and smooth. Remove the pan from the heat and stir in the cream, chervil and cayenne. Add the mushrooms to the sauce, stirring constantly until they are well blended.

Pour the mushroom sauce over the fish. Sprinkle on the grated cheese and place

the casserole under the grill [broiler]. Grill [broil] for 5 minutes or until the cheese has melted.

Remove the casserole from the grill [broiler] and serve at once.

Plaice [Flounder] Baked with Sour Cream and Peppers

 ① ①

A delicious main meal, Plaice [Flounder] Baked with Sour Cream and Peppers may be served with cauliflower and boiled new potatoes for an informal lunch or dinner.

6 SERVINGS

4 oz. [½ cup] plus 1 teaspoon butter
2 oz. [½ cup] seasoned flour, made with 2 oz. [½ cup] flour, ½ teaspoon salt, ¼ teaspoon black pepper, ⅛ teaspoon cayenne pepper and 1 teaspoon dried chervil
2 lb. plaice [flounder] fillets
2 tablespoons lemon juice
1 small green pepper, white pith removed, seeded and chopped
1 small red pepper, white pith removed, seeded and chopped
3 shallots, finely chopped
10 fl. oz. [1¼ cups] sour cream
2 teaspoons paprika
1 oz. [⅓ cup] dry white breadcrumbs mixed with 1 oz. [¼ cup] Cheddar cheese, finely grated

Preheat the oven to moderate 350°F (Gas Mark 4, 180°C). Grease a medium-sized, oblong baking dish with the teaspoon of butter and set it aside.

Place the seasoned flour on a large plate. Dip the fish fillets in it, one by one, coating them thoroughly and shaking off any excess flour.

In a large, heavy frying-pan, melt half

of the remaining butter over moderate heat. When the foam subsides, add the fish fillets and cook them for 2 minutes on each side. With a fish slice or spatula remove the fish fillets from the pan and arrange them in the prepared baking dish. Sprinkle over the lemon juice. Add the remaining butter to the pan. When the foam subsides, add the peppers and shallots and cook them, stirring occasionally, for 3 to 4 minutes, or until the shallots are soft and translucent but not brown. Remove the pan from the heat. With a slotted spoon, transfer the vegetables to the baking dish and spread them over the fish.

In a small mixing bowl, combine the

Plaice [Flounder] Indonesian-Style may be served with rice, shrimp crisps and a Sambal for an exotic meal.

sour cream with the paprika. Spread the mixture over the fish fillets. Sprinkle over the cheese and breadcrumb mixture. Place the dish in the centre of the oven and bake for 25 to 30 minutes or until the fish flesh flakes easily when tested with a fork, and the top is lightly browned.

Remove the dish from the oven and serve immediately, straight from the dish.

Plaice [Flounder] Indonesian-Style

This is a highly spiced but delicious way of cooking plaice [flounder]. Serve with boiled rice, prawn or shrimp crisps and a Sambal.

4 SERVINGS

4 fl. oz. [½ cup] dark soy sauce
2 tablespoons soft brown sugar
1 teaspoon hot chilli powder
2 garlic cloves, crushed
4 whole plaice [flounder], cleaned and prepared for cooking
1 oz. [2 tablespoons] butter
juice of 1 lemon

Low Cal

In a small mixing bowl, combine the soy sauce, sugar, chilli powder and garlic together, mixing well to blend.

Put the fish in a shallow dish and pour over the soy sauce mixture. Cover the dish and set it aside at room temperature to marinate, basting occasionally, for 1 hour.

Preheat the grill [broiler] to high. Line the grill [broiler] rack with aluminium foil and place it in the grill [broiler] pan.

Arrange the fish on the lined rack and place the pan under the heat. Grill [broil] the fish, turning them once, for 8 to 10 minutes or until the flesh flakes easily when tested with a fork. Baste the fish occasionally during the cooking time with the marinade.

In a small saucepan, melt the butter over low heat. When the foam subsides stir in the lemon juice.

Remove the grill [broiler] pan from under the heat. Carefully transfer the fish to individual plates. Discard the remaining marinade.

Pour the melted butter and lemon juice over the fish and serve immediately.

Planking

Planking is a method of cooking and serving meat or fish on a hardwood board. Usually oval in shape, the board, or plank, is specially carved with a hollow at one end to catch the meat or fish juices. The board is heated in the oven, then oil or butter is rubbed in. The meat or fish, usually half cooked, is placed on the board and then baked or grilled [broiled]. Care

should be taken to keep the board as far away from the source of heat as possible.

Plantain

Plantain is a tropical fruit which greatly resembles the BANANA in appearance. (It is, in fact, sometimes known as the cooking banana.) Plantain is slightly larger, has coarser flesh and a higher starch content than the banana.

Plantain is grown in many tropical regions of the world, including the West Indies, South America, Africa and India.

Plantain may be boiled, fried or baked and may be served as a vegetable or, depending on how ripe it is, as a dessert.

Plantain Chips

A delicious change from potato crisps [chips], Plantain Chips are perfect served with drinks, or with Avocado Dip.

4-6 SERVINGS

4 ripe plantain, peeled and cut into very thin slices
12 fl. oz. [1½ cups] salt water
sufficient vegetable oil for deep-frying
2 teaspoons salt

In a large mixing bowl, soak the plantain in the salt water for 15 minutes. Drain the plantain slices and dry them thoroughly on kitchen paper towels.

Fill a medium-sized deep-frying pan one-third full with the oil. Place the pan over moderate heat and heat the oil until it reaches 375°F on a deep-fat thermometer, or until a small cube of stale bread dropped into the oil turns golden brown in 40 seconds.

Place half of the plantain slices in a deep-frying basket and gently lower the basket into the oil. Fry the slices for 1 minute or until they are crisp and golden.

Remove the chips from the pan and transfer them to kitchen paper towels to drain. Set aside to cool while you fry the remaining plantain in the same way.

Serve cold, sprinkled with the salt.

Plantain Coated with Sesame Seeds

Plantain Coated with Sesame Seeds is a most versatile dish, which may be served either as a vegetable or as a dessert. It may also be served as an appetizer.

4 SERVINGS

6 oz. [1 cup] sesame seeds, roasted
3 oz. [⅜ cup] butter
4 ripe plantains, peeled, quartered lengthways and then cut into 1-inch pieces
1 teaspoon salt or 1 tablespoon sugar

Place the sesame seeds in a large, shallow dish and set aside.

In a large frying-pan, melt half of the butter over moderate heat. When the foam subsides, add half of the plantain pieces and fry, turning them once, for 10 to 12 minutes, or until they are golden brown. With a slotted spoon, remove the plantain from the pan and roll each piece in the sesame seeds.

Keep warm while you fry the remaining plantain in the same way.

Transfer the plantain to a warmed serving dish. Sprinkle with the salt or sugar, depending on whether you are serving it as a vegetable dish or as a dessert. Serve immediately.

Planters' Beef

A tasty and quickly made dish, Planters' Beef can also be economical if you use rump ends rather than the more expensive rump steak.

4 SERVINGS

4 tablespoons olive oil
1½ lb. rump steak or rump ends, trimmed of all fat and cut into strips
1 medium-sized onion, thinly sliced
1 large garlic clove, crushed
1 large green pepper, white pith removed, seeded and sliced
1 teaspoon cumin seed
14 oz. canned peeled tomatoes
1 teaspoon salt
1 teaspoon sugar
ACCOMPANIMENTS
2 lb. sweet potatoes, washed
1 teaspoon salt
1 oz. [2 tablespoons] butter
2 tablespoons olive oil
4 bananas, halved lengthways

In a large frying-pan, heat the oil over moderately high heat. When the oil is hot, add the beef strips, a few at a time, and fry them, turning them constantly, for 2 to 3 minutes or until they are lightly browned. Using a slotted spoon, transfer the beef strips as they brown to a plate. Set aside.

Reduce the heat to moderate and add the onion, garlic and green pepper and cook, stirring occasionally, for 8 to 10 minutes or until the onion is golden brown.

Add the cumin seed, tomatoes with the can juice, the salt and sugar. Stir to mix. When the mixture comes to the boil, reduce the heat to low and simmer the sauce, uncovered, for 25 minutes or until it is beginning to thicken.

Return the beef strips to the pan, cover it and continue cooking, stirring occasionally, for 15 minutes.

Meanwhile prepare the accompaniments. Place the sweet potatoes in a large saucepan and pour over enough water just to cover. Place the pan over high heat and bring the water to the boil. Add half of the salt, cover the pan and reduce the heat to low. Cook the sweet potatoes for 20 to 30 minutes or until they are tender when pierced with the point of a sharp knife. Using tongs, remove the sweet potatoes from the pan and set them aside to cool. When they are cool enough to handle, remove and discard the skin. Place the potatoes on a board and cut them into thick slices. Set aside.

In a medium-sized frying-pan, melt the butter with the oil over moderate heat. When the foam subsides, add the bananas and fry them, turning them frequently, for 2 minutes. Using a slotted spoon, transfer the bananas to a plate and keep them warm while you fry the potatoes.

Add the potato slices to the pan and fry them for 3 to 4 minutes on each side or until they are slightly crisp. Remove the pan from the heat.

Spoon the beef mixture on to a warmed serving dish. Arrange the sweet potato slices all around and sprinkle them with the remaining salt. Garnish with the bananas and serve immediately.

Planters' Pork Chops

These sweet and tasty pork chops with fruit sauce may be accompanied by mashed potatoes and peas.

4 SERVINGS

1 oz. [2 tablespoons] butter
1 tablespoon vegetable oil
1 garlic clove, crushed
4 pork chops
4 tablespoons lemon juice
2 teaspoons soft brown sugar
½ teaspoon salt

Low Cal

½ teaspoon black pepper
5 fl. oz. [⅝ cup] dry white wine
1 banana
4 pineapple rings
4 orange slices
4 watercress sprigs

Preheat the oven to moderate 350°F (Gas Mark 4, 180°C).

In a large frying-pan, melt the butter with the oil over moderate heat. When the foam subsides, add the garlic and fry, stirring constantly, for 1 minute. Add the pork chops and fry them for 4 minutes on each side. Using tongs, transfer the chops to an ovenproof dish large enough to hold them in one layer.

Pour off the cooking liquid from the pan.

Return the pan to the heat and add 3 tablespoons of lemon juice, the sugar, salt, pepper and wine and bring to the boil, stirring frequently. Remove the pan from the heat and pour the mixture over the pork chops.

Place the dish in the oven and bake the chops for 25 minutes.

Meanwhile, with a stainless steel or silver knife, cut the banana lengthways, then cut it crosswise to make four pieces. Place the banana pieces on a small plate and sprinkle over the remaining 1 tablespoon of lemon juice. Set aside.

Remove the dish from the oven and place a pineapple ring, an orange slice and a piece of banana on top of each pork chop.

Return the dish to the oven. Continue baking the chops for 5 minutes or until they are tender and the juices which run out are clear when they are pierced with the point of a sharp knife.

Remove the dish from the oven. Garnish the pork chops with the watercress sprigs and serve immediately.

Planters' Punch

This is a popular rum-based drink, made in almost as many different ways as there are bar tenders. This version is a basic one and the fruit and juices may be increased or decreased according to taste.

1 SERVING

1 tablespoon sugar
2 tablespoons water
1 tablespoon fresh orange juice juice of 1 lime
5 fl. oz. [⅝ cup] rum
4 ice cubes, crushed
1 orange slice
1 pineapple slice

Planters' Beef makes a colourful and tasty dinner party dish.

Combine the sugar, water and orange juice together in a tall glass and stir with a long-handled spoon until the sugar has dissolved. Stir in the lime juice and rum.

Add the crushed ice and, when the outside of the glass has frosted, garnish with the orange and pineapple slices.

Serve immediately.

Plastic Icing

This icing, which is pliable and easily rolled, resembles Fondant in texture. Plastic Icing does not need cooking and any excess may be stored in a plastic bag. Stored Plastic Icing may be prepared for use by kneading it until it is soft and pliable again.

Use Plastic Icing for covering Petits Fours, gâteaux and birthday and Christmas cakes. If you wish to colour the icing, add 2 to 4 drops of food colouring — depending on the strength of the colouring and the depth of colour required — to the liquid ingredients.

Liquid glucose may be obtained from many pharmacies or chemists.

This quantity of icing makes enough to cover the top and sides of an 8- to 9-inch cake.

ABOUT 2½ POUNDS [10 CUPS]
2½ lb. icing sugar [10 cups confectioners' sugar]
4 tablespoons liquid glucose
2 egg whites
2 tablespoons lemon juice
½ teaspoon rose water (optional)

Sift the icing [confectioners'] sugar into a large mixing bowl. Add the glucose, egg whites, lemon juice and rose water, if you are using it. Stir the ingredients with a wooden spoon until they are well mixed. Using your hands, knead the mixture into a ball, which should be firm and pliable.

If the mixture is too sticky, work in some more sifted icing [confectioners'] sugar.

Turn the mixture out on to a working surface and knead it lightly until it is smooth.

On a working surface lightly sprinkled with cornflour [cornstarch], roll out the icing to a ¼-inch thick and use as required.

Plastic Icing for Moulding

This is an ideal icing for moulding into shapes for cake decorations. It must be firm but pliable and, if handled carefully, can be formed into fine, life-like floral sprays. The flowers and leaves may be delicately colour-ed and shaded with a clean water-colour

Flatten a piece of Plastic Icing for Moulding into an oval shape, and roll it up to form the centre of a flower.

Flatten a slightly larger piece of the icing, and roll it around the flower centre to make a rose shape.

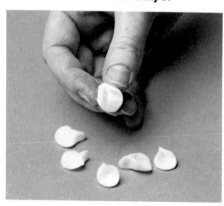

Flatten a small piece of the icing into a round shape and pinch it together to form the base of a petal.

Arrange several petals together to form a flower shape and place a tiny flower centre in the middle.

paint brush and diluted food colouring.

This quantity of icing makes enough for 3 or 4 medium-sized flowers to form a spray. If you have any icing left over, store it in a plastic bag to prevent it from drying out.

10 OUNCES [2½ CUPS]
1 teaspoon gelatine
1 tablespoon lemon juice
1 teaspoon rose water (optional)
10 oz. icing sugar [2½ cups confectioners' sugar]
1 tablespoon liquid glucose

In a heatproof jug or cup, placed in a pan of boiling water, dissolve the gelatine in the lemon juice, stirring occasionally with a teaspoon. Remove the pan from the heat and lift out the jug or cup. Stir in the rose water, if you are using it.

Sift the icing [confectioners'] sugar into a medium-sized mixing bowl. Add the glucose and the gelatine mixture and stir the ingredients with a wooden spoon until they are well mixed.

Using your hands, knead the mixture into a ball, which should be very firm but still pliable.

If the mixture is too sticky, work in some more sifted icing [confectioners'] sugar.

The icing is now ready to use.

Plate Pie

A plate pie is, as its name suggests, a pie baked in a deep plate instead of a pie dish. You will need an ovenproof plate, and any meat or fruit filling may be used. We have filled our Plate Pie with an unusual mixture of lamb and currants.

ONE 9-INCH PIE
1½ oz. [3 tablespoons] plus 1 teaspoon butter
1 tablespoon vegetable oil
2 lb. boned leg of lamb, cut into fine dice
1 teaspoon salt
½ teaspoon black pepper
2 oz. [⅓ cup] currants
4 fl. oz. [½ cup] dry sherry
1 large egg, lightly beaten
¼ teaspoon ground mace
1 tablespoon chopped fresh parsley
PASTRY
8 oz. [2 cups] flour
¼ teaspoon salt
4 oz. [½ cup] butter
3 to 4 tablespoons iced water
1 egg, lightly beaten

In a large flameproof casserole, melt 1½ ounces [3 tablespoons] of the butter with the oil over moderate heat. When the foam subsides, add the lamb dice to the

casserole and fry, turning frequently, for 5 minutes or until the meat is lightly and evenly browned.

Add the salt, pepper and currants, and pour over the sherry. Increase the heat to high and bring the liquid to the boil. Reduce the heat to moderately low, cover the casserole and simmer for 30 minutes. Uncover the casserole and continue cooking for a further 30 minutes.

Meanwhile, make the pastry. Sift the flour and salt into a medium-sized mixing bowl. Add the butter and cut it into small pieces with a table knife. Using your fingertips, rub the butter into the flour until the mixture resembles coarse breadcrumbs.

Add 2 tablespoons of the iced water and, with the knife, mix it into the flour mixture. With your hands, mix and knead the dough until it is smooth. Add more water if the dough is too dry. Form the

dough into a ball and wrap it in greaseproof or waxed paper. Place the ball in the refrigerator and chill for 20 minutes.

Preheat the oven to fairly hot 400°F (Gas Mark 6, 200°C). With the remaining teaspoon of butter, grease a 9-inch ovenproof pie plate.

Remove the casserole from the heat. Pour off and discard any liquid left in the casserole. Mix in the egg and set aside.

Remove the dough from the refrigerator. Divide the dough into two equal pieces. On a lightly floured surface, using a rolling pin, roll out one piece of dough into a circle slightly larger than the plate. Carefully lift the dough on the rolling-pin and place it on the plate. Press it down with your fingertips to line the plate, trimming off any excess dough. Reserve the trimmings. Moisten the edge of the dough with water. Spoon the meat filling into the centre of the plate, leaving the

Crisp, melt-in-the-mouth pastry envelops an unusual filling of lamb, sherry and currants in our version of traditional Plate Pie.

rim clear. Sprinkle the mace and parsley over the filling.

Roll the remaining dough out into another circle, large enough to fit the plate. Lift the dough circle on to the plate. Trim off any excess dough and crimp the edges together to seal them. Roll out the trimmings and use to decorate the pie. Using a pastry brush, brush the dough with the beaten egg.

Place the plate on a baking sheet and put the baking sheet in the oven. Bake for 20 to 25 minutes or until the pastry is golden brown and crisp.

Remove the baking sheet from the oven and serve the pie at once.

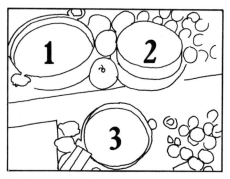

1 Plum and Apple Marmalade, 2 Plum Cake and 3 Plum and Cherry Soup are only three of, literally, scores of delicious recipes for plums.

Plön Strudel

GERMAN LIVER STRUDEL

A delicious savoury strudel with a liver pâté filling, Plön Strudel (pl-ehn shtrood-'l) makes an excellent hors d'oeuvre.

8-10 SERVINGS

PASTRY
5 oz. [1¼ cups] flour
¼ teaspoon salt
½ egg, lightly beaten
3 fl. oz. [⅜ cup] plus 1 tablespoon warm water
2 oz. [¼ cup] plus 2 tablespoons butter, melted

FILLING
1 lb. soft liver pâté
2 tablespoons finely chopped fresh parsley

First make the pastry. Sift the flour and salt into a large mixing bowl. In a small mixing bowl, combine the egg, water and 1 tablespoon of the melted butter. With a wooden spoon, stir the egg and water mixture into the flour and mix well. Using your hands, knead the dough until it is firm.

Place the dough on a floured board and continue kneading for 10 minutes, or until it is smooth and elastic. Place the dough in a warmed, large mixing bowl. Cover the bowl with a cloth and set it aside in a warm draught-free place for 30 minutes.

Spread out a large, clean cloth (a sheet is ideal) on a table. Sprinkle the cloth with flour. Place the dough on the cloth and, with a floured rolling pin, roll the dough out as thinly as possible.

With the back of your hands, lift and stretch the dough, pulling the dough until it is paper thin. This should be done as carefully as possible. Do not worry if a few small holes appear in the dough. With scissors, trim the outer edges of the dough so that the sides are straight.

Preheat the oven to very hot 450°F (Gas Mark 8, 230°C). Using the remaining tablespoon of melted butter, grease two large baking sheets.

Using a pastry brush, carefully brush the dough with half of the remaining melted butter. Using a palette knife or spatula, spread the pâté on to the dough, 3-inches away from the edges of the dough nearest to you, and within 2-inches of each end. Sprinkle with the parsley.

Using the cloth, lift the dough over the filling and roll up Swiss [jelly] roll style. Tuck in the ends. Brush the top of the dough with the remaining butter.

With a sharp knife, divide the strudel into two pieces, small enough to fit the baking sheets. Carefully lift the pieces on to the prepared baking sheets, with the seams underneath.

Bake the strudels in the centre of the oven for 10 minutes. Reduce the oven temperature to fairly hot 400°F (Gas Mark 6, 200°C) and continue to bake for a further 20 minutes or until the strudels are crisp and golden brown.

Remove the baking sheets from the oven. Leave the strudels to cool on the baking sheets before transferring to a wire rack to cool completely.

Cut the strudels into thin slices and serve immediately.

Plover

The plover is a small game bird related to the sandpiper. There are many species, the most common being green plover, or lapwing as it is often called, golden plover, stone curlew and grey plover.

Plovers are often cooked undrawn. They should therefore be eaten while they are fresh and should not be hung. The gizzard is removed but the liver should be left, whether the bird is to be cooked, drawn or undrawn.

To roast plover, the head should be skinned but left on the bird — the beak is used as a skewer to hold the legs and wings together. Lard and truss the bird and place it on a buttered baking dish. Roast in an oven preheated to fairly hot 400°F (Gas Mark 6, 200°C), basting occasionally, for 15 to 20 minutes. Plovers are sometimes baked on a piece of toast so that all their juices are absorbed.

The traditional way to serve roast plover is to place it on a slice of toast and garnish it with watercress.

Pluck

Pluck is the collective term for the LIGHTS (lungs), HEART, LIVER and entrails of any animal slaughtered for consumption.

Plucking

Plucking poultry or game requires a considerable amount of time and patience, and is rarely necessary these days when most poultry is sold oven-ready.

If you have to pluck a bird, it should be done in a small room or enclosed space where there are no draughts — otherwise the feathers will fly all over the place! Have a large cardboard box near you to put the feathers in, and also cover the floor with newspaper to catch any small pieces of down and feathers.

Lay the bird on a table in front of you, feet towards you. Sharply pull the feathers in the opposite direction to the way they lie. Any hard pieces of quill can be pulled out with a pair of tweezers. To remove any small feathers, singe the bird over an open flame. Alternatively, the bird can be plunged in boiling water, which will soften the pores of the skin and make these small feathers easier to remove. However, this is not recommended unless the bird is to be cooked immediately after plucking.

The bird is now ready to be cut into serving pieces, or stuffed and trussed.

Plum

The plum is a stone fruit belonging to the same genus, *prunus* and family, *rosaceae*, as the PEACH and the CHERRY.

There are numerous varieties of plum, which grow all over the world. Most of those grown in Europe have common ancestors which were native to West Asia; those grown on the Pacific coast of the United States and in other warmer parts of the world most probably derive from a Japanese species.

For culinary purposes plums are classed as either dessert or cooking varieties. Cooking varieties, such as damsons, have very dry flesh with little flavour and a high acid and pectin content. These fruit make excellent jams, compôtes and fillings for tarts and flans, since cooking with sugar brings out their flavour.

Dessert plums, such as greengages, are sweet, juicy and finely flavoured, and are best eaten uncooked. Many dessert plums may also be cooked, such as Victorias and those delicious purple-blue plums from Yugoslavia, called Switzers.

Plum and Apple Marmalade

This is a delicious, and unusual marmalade made from plums and apples. Serve it for breakfast, or tea, on hot buttered toast. Or eat it the way the French do — with hot Croissants.

ABOUT 5 POUNDS

1½ lb. plums, halved and stoned
1½ lb. cooking apples, peeled, cored and sliced
1 tablespoon lemon juice
10 fl. oz. [1¼ cups] water
3 lb. [6 cups] sugar

In a preserving pan or large saucepan, bring the plums, apples, lemon juice and water to the boil over high heat.

Reduce the heat to moderate and cook for 20 minutes or until the fruit is soft. Add the sugar and stir until it has dissolved.

Bring the jam to the boil and boil for 15 minutes or until setting point is reached.

To test for setting point, remove the pan from the heat and spoon a small amount of the jam on to a saucer. Allow it to cool. If it sets and wrinkles when you push it with your finger, the jam is ready. If not, return the pan to the heat and continue boiling, testing frequently. If you use a sugar thermometer, the jam should register 220°F to 222°F.

When setting point has been reached, remove the pan from the heat. With a slotted spoon, skim off the scum from the surface of the jam.

Pour the jam into clean, dry, warmed jam jars. Seal each jar with a jam cover, label and store in a cool, dry place.

Plum Cake

A rich, old-fashioned fruit cake, Plum Cake keeps for at least three months if stored in an airtight tin. A little rum poured gradually over the cake each week will add to the flavour and keep the cake moist.

ONE 9-INCH CAKE

8 oz. [1 cup] plus 2 teaspoons butter
8 oz. [1⅓ cups] raisins
6 oz. [1 cup] currants
8 oz. [1⅓ cups] sultanas or seedless raisins
3 oz. [½ cup] glacé cherries, chopped
2 strips candied orange peel, chopped
2 tablespoons chopped candied angelica
4 fl. oz. [½ cup] dark rum
10 oz. [2½ cups] self-raising flour
½ teaspoon ground cinnamon
1 teaspoon ground allspice
¼ teaspoon salt
8 oz. [1⅓ cups] soft brown sugar
3 eggs
3 oz. [½ cup] walnuts, chopped

Preheat the oven to cool 300°F (Gas Mark 2, 150°C). With 1 teaspoon of the

butter, lightly grease a 9-inch cake tin. Line the bottom and sides of the tin with a double layer of greaseproof or waxed paper and grease this with the remaining teaspoon of butter. Set aside.

In a medium-sized mixing bowl, combine the raisins, currants, sultanas or seedless raisins, glacé cherries, orange peel, angelica and rum. Set aside.

Sift the flour, cinnamon, allspice and salt into another medium-sized mixing bowl. Set aside.

In a large mixing bowl, cream the remaining butter with a wooden spoon until it is light and fluffy. Gradually add the sugar and beat until the mixture is creamy and smooth. Beat in the eggs, one at a time, adding a tablespoon of the flour mixture with each one. Fold in the remaining flour mixture.

Stir in the fruit and rum mixture and the walnuts. Combine the ingredients thoroughly.

Pour the batter into the prepared cake tin and place the tin in the centre of the oven. Bake the cake for 2¼ to 2½ hours or until a skewer inserted into the centre comes out clean.

Remove the cake from the oven and let it stand in the tin for 2 hours. Turn the cake out on to a rack and peel off the paper. Leave the cake to cool for at least 12 hours before wrapping it in aluminium foil and storing it in an airtight tin.

Plum and Cherry Soup

An Israeli recipe, Plum and Cherry Soup makes a light and delicious first course for a summer meal. It is traditionally served chilled with sour cream and garnished with fresh mint sprigs.

4 SERVINGS

1 lb. plums, halved and stoned
8 oz. pears, halved and cored
10 oz. cherries, halved and stoned
2 oz. [¼ cup] sugar
¼ teaspoon salt
1 teaspoon cinnamon
juice and finely grated rind of 1 lemon
2 pints [5 cups] water
1 teaspoon cornflour [cornstarch]

Place the fruit in a large saucepan. Add the sugar, salt, cinnamon and lemon juice and rind. Pour in the water and bring the mixture to the boil over high heat, stirring occasionally. Reduce the heat to low, cover the pan and cook the fruit for 10 to 15 minutes or until it is tender.

Remove the pan from the heat. Strain the contents of the pan into a large bowl, rubbing the fruit through the strainer

with the back of a wooden spoon. Discard any pulp remaining in the strainer.

Return the soup to the pan. In a small mixing bowl, mix the cornflour [cornstarch] with 2 tablespoons of the soup. Add it, a little at a time, to the soup, stirring constantly. Place the pan over high heat and bring to the boil, stirring constantly.

Reduce the heat to moderate and cook for a further 5 to 8 minutes or until the soup is smooth and has thickened slightly. Taste the soup and add more sugar if necessary.

Remove the pan from the heat. Pour the soup into a large serving bowl and set it aside at room temperature to cool. When it is cool, cover the bowl and place it in the refrigerator to chill for 1 hour before serving.

Plum Compôte

Plum Compôte (kawm-pot) is a simple but delicious dessert which may be served cold or chilled, with whipped cream.

4 SERVINGS

10 fl. oz. [1¼ cups] water
6 oz. [¾ cup] sugar
grated rind of ½ lemon
1½ lb. plums, stoned

In a medium-sized saucepan, combine the water, sugar and lemon rind together. Set the pan over low heat and cook the mixture, stirring occasionally, until the sugar has dissolved. Increase the heat to moderate and boil the syrup for 5 minutes, without stirring, or until it has reduced and thickened slightly.

Add the plums to the pan, reduce the heat to low and simmer, stirring occasionally, for 3 to 5 minutes or until the plums are cooked but still retain their shape.

Remove the pan from the heat and set the compôte aside for 30 minutes. Turn the compôte into a serving dish and set aside to cool completely or chill in the refrigerator before serving.

Plum Jam

Plum Jam is one of the most popular of home-made jams. Plums have a high pectin content so the jam sets easily. Choose firm, ripe plums, discarding any that are bruised.

ABOUT 5 POUNDS

3 lb. plums, halved and stoned
10 fl. oz. [1¼ cups] water
3 lb. [6 cups] sugar

In a preserving pan or large saucepan,

bring the plums and water to the boil over high heat.

Reduce the heat to moderate and cook for 20 minutes, or until the plums are soft. Add the sugar and stir until it has dissolved.

Bring the jam to the boil and boil for 15 minutes or until setting point is reached.

To test for setting point, remove the pan from the heat and spoon a small amount of the jam on to a saucer. Allow it to cool. If it sets and wrinkles when you push it with your finger, the jam is ready. If not, return the pan to the heat and continue boiling, testing frequently. If you use a sugar thermometer, the jam should register 220°F to 222°F.

When setting point has been reached, remove the pan from the heat. With a slotted spoon, skim off the scum from the surface of the jam.

Pour the jam into clean, dry, warmed jam jars. Seal each jar with a jam cover, label and store in a cool, dry place.

Plum Sauce

Plum Sauce is a dark red, thick sauce which is used as a condiment in Chinese cookery. It has a sweet and sour flavour and is made from plums, apricots, chillis, vinegar and sugar. It is used as an accompaniment to roasted meat. Sold bottled and canned in oriental stores, plum sauce will keep, opened, in the refrigerator for several months.

Plum-Stuffed Crêpes

Serve these delicious Plum-Stuffed Crêpes hot with whipped cream or Crème à la Vanille for a warming dessert.

4-6 SERVINGS
5 oz. [1¼ cups] sweet Crêpe Batter
1½ lb. sweet dark plums, stoned and chopped
1 oz. [2 tablespoons] butter
2 tablespoons castor sugar
¼ teaspoon ground allspice
2 teaspoons arrowroot dissolved in 1 tablespoon water
5 tablespoons soft brown sugar

Fry the crêpes according to the instructions in the basic recipe and keep them warm.

In a medium-sized saucepan, combine the plums, butter, sugar and allspice together. Cover the pan and set it over moderately low heat. Cook the plums, stirring occasionally, for 8 to 10 minutes, or until they are beginning to pulp. Stir in the dissolved arrowroot and increase the heat to moderate. Cook the mixture, stirring constantly, for 3 minutes or until it is thick. Remove the pan from the heat.

Preheat the grill [broiler] to moderate.

Lay the crêpes out flat. Spoon equal amounts of the plum mixture on to the centre of each crêpe. Roll up the crêpes and place them, in one layer if possible, in a large, oblong flameproof dish. Sprinkle over the brown sugar.

Place the dish under the grill [broiler] and grill [broil] the crêpes for 4 to 5 minutes or until the sugar has melted and caramelized.

Remove the dish from the grill [broiler] and serve immediately.

Sweet and tasty Plum-Stuffed Crêpes may be served on their own or with cream or Crème à la Vanille for an ideal dessert.

Poaching

Poaching is a method of simmering various food, in particular eggs, fish and fruit, in liquid.

Poco Albondiga
LITTLE MEATBALLS

An ideal supper for the family, Poco Albondiga (poh-koh al-bon-dee-gah), beef mixed with rice to make meatballs, is cooked in a creamy tomato sauce. Serve with creamed potatoes and glazed carrots.

4-6 SERVINGS

1½ lb. lean beef, minced [ground]
1 large onion, finely chopped
1 red pepper, white pith removed, seeded and chopped
3 oz. [½ cup] long-grain rice, washed, soaked in cold water for 30 minutes and drained
1 teaspoon salt
½ teaspoon black pepper
1 tablespoon paprika
1 large egg, lightly beaten

Low Cal

SAUCE
14 oz. canned peeled tomatoes
1 onion, coarsely chopped
1 celery stalk, trimmed and chopped
4 tablespoons tomato purée
1 tablespoon soft brown sugar
1 teaspoon salt
½ teaspoon black pepper
½ teaspoon dried thyme
1 bay leaf
8 fl. oz. [1 cup] milk
⅛ teaspoon cayenne pepper

First, make the sauce. Place the tomatoes with the can juice, the onion, celery, tomato purée, sugar, salt, pepper, thyme and bay leaf in a large flameproof casserole. Pour in the milk. Place the casserole over moderate heat and bring the mixture to the boil, stirring frequently.

Reduce the heat to low, cover the casserole and simmer the sauce for 30 minutes.

Meanwhile, prepare the meatballs. In a large mixing bowl, using a fork or your hands, combine all the ingredients together until they are thoroughly mixed. With lightly floured hands form the mixture into about 16 balls approximately 2-inches in diameter. Set aside.

Remove the casserole from the heat. Pour the sauce through a fine wire strainer set over a medium-sized bowl. Remove and discard the bay leaf. Using the back of a wooden spoon, rub the cooked vegetables through the strainer until only a dry pulp is left. Discard the pulp. Return the sauce to the casserole and return the casserole to the heat. Stir in the cayenne and add the meatballs. Increase the heat to high and bring the mixture to the boil. Reduce the heat to low, cover the casserole and simmer for 40 to 45 minutes or until the meat balls are cooked.

Remove the casserole from the heat and serve at once, straight from the casserole.

Poireaux à l'Hongroise, leeks cooked with sour cream and nuts, tastes delicious with cheese dishes.

Poireaux à l'Hongroise
LEEKS HUNGARIAN-STYLE

Poireaux à l'Hongroise (pwar-oh ah l'ang-wahz) is an excellent vegetable accompaniment for cheese dishes. If the quantity of nuts is increased, it may also be served as a light and nourishing vegetarian dish.

4 SERVINGS

8 fl. oz. [1 cup] water
2 lb. leeks, trimmed, washed and cut into ½-inch lengths
½ teaspoon salt
8 fl. oz. [1 cup] sour cream
½ teaspoon dried marjoram
½ teaspoon black pepper
2 tablespoons toasted and chopped hazelnuts
2 tablespoons toasted and chopped almonds
3 tablespoons flaked almonds

In a medium-sized saucepan, bring the water to the boil over high heat. Add the leeks and the salt. When the water comes to the boil again, cover the pan, reduce the heat to low and simmer the leeks for 8 to 12 minutes, or until they are just tender. Remove the pan from the heat and drain the leeks in a colander.

In a small saucepan, combine the sour cream, marjoram, pepper, hazelnuts and chopped almonds together. Place the pan over low heat and cook the sauce for 5 minutes or until it has heated through. Remove the pan from the heat and set aside.

Preheat the grill [broiler] to high.

Arrange the leeks on the bottom of a flameproof dish. Pour over the sauce and sprinkle the flaked almonds on top.

Place the dish under the grill [broiler] and grill [broil] for 3 minutes or until the almonds are brown and the sauce is bubbling.

Remove the dish from under the grill [broiler] and serve immediately.

Poireaux au Miel

LEEKS WITH HONEY DRESSING

A delicately flavoured salad, Poireaux au Miel (pwar-oh oh mee-ell) is a delightful way of using young leeks or 'thinnings'. Serve the salad with grilled [broiled] steak, cold roast chicken or turkey.

4 SERVINGS

1½ lb. young leeks, trimmed and washed
½ large onion, thinly sliced
2 shallots, finely chopped
4 canned artichoke hearts, drained and chopped
1 small green pepper, white pith removed, seeded and thinly sliced
½ bunch watercress, trimmed and chopped
1 small cos [romaine] lettuce, coarse outer leaves removed, washed and torn into pieces
DRESSING
4 tablespoons olive oil
3 tablespoons white wine vinegar
2 tablespoons clear honey
½ teaspoon salt
¼ teaspoon black pepper
1 teaspoon prepared French mustard

Half-fill a large saucepan with water. Place the pan over high heat and bring the water to the boil. Add the leeks and blanch them for 3 minutes. Remove the pan from the heat and drain the leeks in a colander. Set them aside to cool.

In a large salad bowl, combine the onion, shallots, artichoke hearts, green pepper, watercress and lettuce. Set aside.

To make the dressing, place all the dressing ingredients in a small mixing bowl and beat them with a fork until they are well combined. Set aside.

When the leeks are completely cold, cut them into 2-inch pieces and add them to the salad bowl. Pour the dressing over the vegetables and toss with two forks until they are well coated with the dressing.

Serve immediately.

Poires Belle Hélène

PEARS WITH ICE-CREAM AND CHOCOLATE SAUCE

A classic French dessert, Poires Belle Hélène (pwar bel ay-lehn) is a delicious mixture of poached pears, ice-cream and hot chocolate sauce. The chocolate sauce may be either poured over the pears or served separately in a sauceboat.

Pears cooked with caramel, Poires au Caramel may be served with cream.

4-8 SERVINGS

6 oz. [¾ cup] sugar
10 fl. oz. [1¼ cups] water
1 vanilla pod, split in half
4 large ripe pears, peeled, halved and cored
1½ pints [3¾ cups] vanilla ice-cream
10 fl. oz. [1¼ cups] Chocolate Sauce, hot

In a large, heavy saucepan, dissolve the sugar in the water with the vanilla pod over low heat, stirring constantly. When the sugar has dissolved, increase the heat to moderate and boil the syrup for 2 minutes, without stirring. Remove and discard the vanilla pod.

Reduce the heat to low, add the pear halves and poach them for 12 to 15 minutes or until they are tender but still firm.

Remove the pan from the heat and set the pears aside to cool in the syrup. Transfer the pears and the syrup to a large bowl and place the bowl in the refrigerator. Chill the pears for 30 minutes.

Scoop the vanilla ice-cream into a chilled serving dish.

Remove the bowl from the refrigerator and, using a slotted spoon, remove the pear halves from the syrup and arrange them around the ice-cream. Discard the syrup. Pour the chocolate sauce into a warmed sauceboat or over the pears and serve immediately.

Poires au Caramel
PEARS WITH CARAMEL SAUCE

A simple and attractive dessert, Poires au Caramel (pwar oh kah-rah-mehl) takes only a short time to make. It is an ideal dessert when you're entertaining, as it may be prepared well in advance.

6 SERVINGS

6 oz. [¾ cup] sugar
15 fl. oz. [1⅞ cups] dry white wine
10 pears, peeled and with the stalks left on
10 sponge finger biscuits [cookies]

In a large saucepan, dissolve the sugar in the wine over low heat, stirring con-

stantly. When the sugar has dissolved, place the pears in the pan. Poach, basting the pears frequently, for 15 to 20 minutes or until they are tender but hold their shape.

Meanwhile, arrange the biscuits [cookies] on a serving dish.

With a slotted spoon, remove the pears from the pan and arrange them on top of the biscuits [cookies]. Set aside.

Increase the heat to moderate and boil the syrup for 8 to 10 minutes or until it turns a light golden brown. Do not let the syrup darken too much or it will become too stiff.

Remove the pan from the heat. Spoon enough of the syrup over the pears to glaze them. Allow to cool completely before serving.

Poissons à la Niçoise
SMALL RED MULLET IN TOMATO SAUCE

Serve Poissons à la Niçoise (pwah-sohn ah lah nee-swahz) with peppery buttered rice and, to follow, a green salad. The red mullet should be quite small as two are allowed per person. If you cannot find very

---

Serve colourful Poissons à la Niçoise with peppery, buttered rice.

small fish, use six medium-sized fish.

6 SERVINGS

4 tablespoons olive oil
2½ lb. tomatoes, blanched, peeled, seeded and coarsely chopped
4 garlic cloves, crushed
1 teaspoon dried thyme
1 bay leaf
1 teaspoon salt
1 teaspoon black pepper
8 oz. [2 cups] black olives, stoned
2 lemons, cut into 12 slices
12 small red mullet, cleaned and scaled but with the heads and tails left on

In a very large frying-pan, heat the oil over moderate heat. When the oil is hot, add the tomatoes, garlic, thyme, bay leaf, salt and pepper. Reduce the heat to low and cook, stirring occasionally, for 15 to 20 minutes or until the sauce is very thick.

Add the olives and lemon slices and stir well. Transfer half of the mixture to another large frying-pan. Place six fish in each pan and turn them over in the sauce until they are well coated.

Cover the pans and cook, turning the fish occasionally, for 15 to 20 minutes or until the flesh flakes easily when it is tested with a fork.

Remove the pans from the heat. Remove and discard the bay leaf and serve.

Poissons aux Poivrons

FISH STEW WITH PEPPERS

A slightly spicy fish stew, Poissons aux Poivrons (pwah-sohn oh pwah-vrohn) is made with sole fillets, green peppers, new potatoes and a tomato sauce. It is a delicious meal in itself.

4 SERVINGS

2 tablespoons olive oil
1 lb. canned peeled tomatoes
1 red chilli, seeded and finely chopped
2 green peppers, white pith removed, seeded and sliced
2 medium-sized onions, finely chopped
3 garlic cloves, crushed
2 fl. oz. [¼ cup] dry white wine
1 teaspoon dried thyme
1 bay leaf
2 lb. sole fillets, cut into 1-inch cubes
1 lb. small new potatoes, scrubbed, cooked until just tender and kept warm

In a large, flameproof casserole, heat the oil over moderate heat. When the oil is hot, add the tomatoes with the can juice, and the chopped chilli. Cook, stirring occasionally, for 15 minutes or until the mixture is thick.

Stir in the green peppers, onions, garlic, wine, thyme, bay leaf and fish cubes. Cover the casserole, reduce the heat to low and cook, stirring occasionally, for 10 minutes.

Add the potatoes and turn them over in the fish mixture. Cover again and cook for a further 5 minutes or until the fish flakes easily when tested with a fork.

Remove the casserole from the heat. Remove and discard the bay leaf and serve at once.

Polenta

Polenta (pohl-ehn-tah) is a type of porridge usually made from corn meal. It is popular in Italy and in Corsica, where it is made with chestnut flour.

Water, butter and sometimes grated Parmesan cheese are mixed into and cooked with the corn meal. When the mixture is cooked, it is left to cool, then cut into various shapes, fried and served as a garnish. The same mixture, omitting

the cheese and adding sugar, can be used to make a pudding.

Polenta is also used as a bed for serving small roasted birds.

Polish Beetroot [Beets]

Freshly cooked beetroot [beets], served with a sour cream sauce, makes an excellent accompaniment for roast meat and poultry.

4 SERVINGS

1 tablespoon butter
2 teaspoons flour
8 fl. oz. [1 cup] sour cream
2 tablespoons vinegar
½ teaspoon dill seed
½ teaspoon salt
¼ teaspoon black pepper
1 tablespoon sugar
1 lb. beetroot [beets], cooked, peeled, sliced and kept hot

In a medium-sized saucepan, melt the butter over moderate heat. Remove the pan from the heat and, with a wooden

---

Poissons aux Poivrons is a succulent fish stew made with sole, tomatoes, chilli, green peppers, onions and wine, and it makes a meal in itself.

spoon, stir in the flour to make a smooth paste. Gradually add the sour cream, vinegar, dill seed, salt, pepper and sugar. Return the pan to low heat and cook, stirring constantly, for 5 minutes or until the sauce is very hot and smooth.

Place the beetroot [beet] slices in a warmed serving dish. Pour over the sauce and serve immediately.

Polish Bigos

An adaptation of a well-known Polish dish, Polish Bigos (bee-goss) is a deliciously warming dish. There are many types of Bigos in Poland, all using different meats, cooked and uncooked — this particular version uses veal and sausage. Serve Polish Bigos with rye bread and beer.

6 SERVINGS

6 tablespoons seasoned flour, made with 6 tablespoons flour, 1 teaspoon salt and ½ teaspoon black pepper
2 lb. stewing veal, cut into 1-inch cubes
8 oz. streaky bacon, diced
2 tablespoons olive oil
2 medium-sized onions, thinly sliced and pushed out into rings
2 garlic cloves, crushed

Polish Beetroot [Beets], with a dill and sour cream sauce, is a refreshing vegetable accompaniment.

---

1 lb. smoked Polish sausage, cut into 1-inch slices
8 oz. garlic sausage, cut into ½-inch cubes
1 tablespoon sugar
2 lb. canned sauerkraut, drained
1 large cooking apple, peeled, cored and coarsely chopped
1 large pear, peeled, cored and coarsely chopped
2 teaspoons dried marjoram
6 fl. oz. [¾ cup] red wine
8 fl. oz. [1 cup] beef stock

Place the seasoned flour on a plate and coat the veal cubes in it, shaking off any excess. Set aside.

In a large flameproof casserole, fry the bacon over moderate heat for 5 minutes or until it is golden brown and has rendered most of its fat. With a slotted spoon, transfer the bacon to a plate. Set aside.

Add the olive oil to the casserole and heat it over moderate heat. When the oil is hot, add the veal cubes, a few at a time, and fry, turning occasionally, for 6 to 8 minutes or until they are lightly and evenly browned. With a slotted spoon, transfer them to a plate and keep warm while you fry the remaining cubes in the same way.

Add the onions and garlic to the casserole and cook, stirring occasionally, for 5 to 7 minutes or until the onions are soft and translucent but not brown.

Stir in the bacon, veal, Polish sausage, garlic sausage, sugar, sauerkraut, apple, pear and marjoram and cook for 5 minutes. Pour over the wine and stock.

Increase the heat to high and bring the contents of the casserole to the boil. Cover the casserole, reduce the heat to low and simmer the stew for 45 minutes to 1 hour or until the veal is tender when pierced with the point of a sharp knife.

Remove the casserole from the heat and serve immediately, from the casserole.

Polish Carp

Polish Carp is a succulent fish dish which may be served either hot or cold, with an oil and vinegar dressing. Accompany it with some well chilled Hungarian Riesling.

6 SERVINGS

1 oz. [2 tablespoons] butter
2 tablespoons olive oil
2 medium-sized onions, thinly sliced and pushed out into rings
2 tablespoons chopped spring onions [scallions]
6 carrots, scraped and thinly sliced
1 tablespoon sugar
1 tablespoon wine vinegar
1 teaspoon salt
½ teaspoon black pepper
1 x 3 lb. carp, cleaned and prepared for cooking
6 fl. oz. [¾ cup] white wine
6 fl. oz. [¾ cup] fish stock
bouquet garni, consisting of 4 parsley sprigs, 1 thyme spray and 1 bay leaf tied together
1 tablespoon beurre manié (if serving hot)

In a fish kettle, melt the butter with the oil over moderate heat. When the foam subsides, add the onions, spring onions [scallions] and carrots and cook, stirring occasionally, for 5 to 7 minutes or until the onions are soft and translucent but not brown. Add the sugar, vinegar, salt and pepper and cook, stirring occasionally, for a further 5 minutes. Place the carp on top of the vegetables, pour over the wine and stock and add the bouquet garni. Increase the heat to high and bring the liquid to the boil.

Cover the kettle, reduce the heat to low and simmer the fish for 40 to 45 minutes

or until it flakes easily when tested with a fork.

Remove the fish kettle from the heat. Carefully transfer the fish to a warmed serving dish and keep warm while you finish making the sauce.

Remove and discard the bouquet garni. Return the kettle to moderate heat and bring the liquid to the boil. Reduce the heat to low and stir in the beurre manié, a little at a time. Cook, stirring constantly, for 2 minutes or until the sauce is smooth and has thickened slightly. Pour the sauce and vegetables over the carp and serve immediately.

If the carp is to be served cold, allow it to cool in the cooking juices. Carefully transfer the fish to a serving dish. Pour the juices and vegetables over the carp, cover the dish and place it in the refrigerator to chill and set.

Polish Meat Loaf

This delicious adaptation of a Polish recipe is both economical and delicious. Serve it with a green vegetable for a sustaining lunch or supper.

4-6 SERVINGS

2 oz. [¼ cup] butter
2 medium-sized onions, thinly sliced
2 garlic cloves, crushed
2 lb. lean minced [ground] beef
3 oz. [1½ cups] fresh breadcrumbs
1 teaspoon horseradish sauce
½ teaspoon salt
¼ teaspoon black pepper
¼ teaspoon dried dill
1 egg
2 fl. oz. [¼ cup] sour cream
SAUCE
1 oz. [2 tablespoons] butter
4 oz. button mushrooms, wiped clean and thinly sliced
12 fl. oz. [1½ cups] sour cream
⅛ teaspoon white pepper

Preheat the oven to moderate 350°F (Gas Mark 4, 180°C).

In a medium-sized frying-pan, melt the butter over moderate heat. When the foam subsides, add the onions and garlic and cook, stirring occasionally, for 5 to 7 minutes or until the onions are soft and translucent but not brown. Remove the pan from the heat and transfer the mixture to a large mixing bowl. Set aside to cool.

When the mixture is cool, add all the remaining ingredients to the bowl. With your hands, mix and knead the ingredients together. Spoon the mixture into a 2-pound loaf tin and smooth the top

with a flat-bladed knife. Cover tightly with aluminium foil.

Place the loaf tin in a baking tin and pour enough boiling water into the tin to come 1½-inches up the sides of the loaf tin.

Place the baking tin in the oven and bake the meat loaf for 1¼ to 1½ hours or until a skewer inserted into the centre of the meat comes out clean.

Meanwhile, prepare the sauce. In a medium-sized saucepan, melt the butter over moderate heat. When the foam subsides, add the mushrooms and cook for 3 minutes or until they are tender. Stir in the sour cream and pepper and cook for a further 5 to 8 minutes or until the sauce is

Two delectable dishes from Poland to make a complete meal — Polish Carp and Polish Orange and Almond Flan.

smooth. Remove the pan from the heat and pour the sauce into a warmed sauce-boat. Set aside and keep warm.

Remove the baking tin from the oven. Lift out the loaf tin and set aside to cool slightly. Remove the aluminium foil. Run a knife around the edge of the meat loaf and turn it out on to a warmed serving dish. Serve immediately, with the sauce.

Polish Orange and Almond Flan

Moist and crunchy, Polish Orange and Almond Flan may be served either as a dessert with whipped cream or by itself with coffee.

ONE 8-INCH FLAN

1 teaspoon vegetable oil
6 oz. [1 cup] ground almonds
3 oz. [$\frac{3}{8}$ cup] sugar
juice of $\frac{1}{2}$ orange
TOPPING
4 oranges, peeled, white pith removed and segmented
2 tablespoons orange-flavoured liqueur

juice of 3 oranges
4 oz. [$\frac{1}{2}$ cup] sugar
2 tablespoons water
grated rind of 2 oranges

Preheat the oven to very cool 250°F (Gas Mark $\frac{1}{2}$, 130°C).

With the teaspoon of vegetable oil, grease a shallow 8-inch round flan tin. Set aside.

In a medium-sized mixing bowl, combine the almonds and sugar together. Pour in the orange juice and stir until the ingredients are thoroughly combined. (The mixture should be just moist enough to spread.) With a palette knife or spatula, spread the almond mixture over the bottom of the flan tin. Place the tin in the centre of the oven and bake for 20 to 25 minutes, or until the mixture is firm. Remove the tin from the oven and set aside to cool. Gently remove the flan base and place it on a wire rack. Set aside.

Meanwhile, make the topping. Place the orange segments in a shallow bowl and pour over the orange-flavoured liqueur. Set aside.

In a medium-sized saucepan, combine the orange juice, sugar and water. Place the pan over low heat and cook the mixture, stirring constantly, until all the sugar has dissolved. Increase the heat to moderate and bring the mixture to the boil. Boil the mixture for 10 minutes or until it is thick and will coat the back of the spoon. Remove the pan from the heat and stir in the orange rind. Set the syrup aside.

Arrange the orange segments decoratively on top of the flan base and pour over the juices. Pour the orange syrup over the oranges, smoothing it over evenly with a flat-bladed knife. Set aside until the topping is cool. Place the flan in the refrigerator to chill for 1 hour before serving.

To serve, remove the flan from the refrigerator. Transfer it to a serving plate and cut with a warm knife.

Pollo alla Bolognese

CHICKEN BREASTS WITH HAM AND CHEESE

A delicious Italian dish, Pollo alla Bolognese (poh-loh ahl-lah boh-lohn-yay-zay) is chicken breasts with smoked ham and cheese. Serve it with sautéed potatoes and creamed spinach and, to drink, a light Italian white wine, such as Soave.

4 SERVINGS

4 chicken breasts, skinned and boned
2 tablespoons seasoned flour, made with 2 tablespoons flour, $\frac{1}{2}$ teaspoon salt and $\frac{1}{4}$ teaspoon black pepper
2 oz. [$\frac{1}{4}$ cup] butter
8 slices smoked ham, thinly sliced and cut a little smaller than the chicken breasts
2 oz. [$\frac{1}{2}$ cup] Parmesan cheese, grated

Using a sharp knife, cut each chicken breast in half, crosswise. Place each piece between two sheets of greaseproof or waxed paper and, using a mallet, pound it to flatten.

Place the seasoned flour on a shallow plate. Remove the chicken pieces from the paper and dip them in the flour, one

by one, to coat them thoroughly. Shake off any excess flour and set aside.

In a large frying-pan, melt 1 ounce [2 tablespoons] of the butter over moderate heat. When the foam subsides, add the chicken pieces and cook, turning frequently, for 10 to 15 minutes or until they are cooked and lightly and evenly browned. Remove the pan from the heat.

Meanwhile, in a small saucepan, melt the remaining butter over moderate heat. Remove the pan from the heat and set aside.

Place a slice of ham on each chicken piece and sprinkle over about one-quarter of the grated cheese. Pour over the melted butter. Return the frying-pan to moderate heat, cover and cook the mixture for 3 to 4 minutes or until the ham is hot and the cheese has melted.

Remove the pan from the heat. Using a slotted spoon, transfer the chicken breast mixture to warmed serving plates and serve at once.

Pollo alla Cacciatora

CHICKEN WITH WINE, TOMATOES AND MUSHROOMS

A traditional Italian dish, Pollo alla Cacciatora (poh-loh ahl-lah kah-chi-at-tor-rah) may be served with mashed potatoes and green beans or steamed broccoli.

4-6 SERVINGS

1 tablespoon butter
2 tablespoons olive oil
2 garlic cloves, crushed
2 spring onions [scallions], finely chopped
6 oz. mushrooms, wiped clean and sliced
1 x 4 lb. chicken, cut into 8 serving pieces
1 teaspoon salt
$\frac{1}{2}$ teaspoon black pepper
6 fl. oz. [$\frac{3}{4}$ cup] dry white wine
2 fl. oz. [$\frac{1}{4}$ cup] chicken stock
6 medium-sized tomatoes, blanched, peeled, seeded and coarsely chopped
1 large bay leaf
2 teaspoons beurre manié
1 tablespoon chopped fresh parsley

In a medium-sized flameproof casserole, melt the butter with the oil over moderate heat. When the foam subsides, add the garlic and spring onions [scallions] and cook, stirring occasionally, for 3 to 4

Two super Italian chicken dishes ideal for dinner parties — Pollo alla Bolognese and Pollo alla Cacciatora.

minutes or until the onions are soft and translucent but not brown. Add the mushrooms and cook for a further 3 minutes, stirring frequently. Using a slotted spoon, remove the vegetables from the casserole and set them aside on a plate.

Add the chicken pieces to the casserole and cook, turning them frequently with tongs, for 8 to 10 minutes or until they are lightly and evenly browned. Add the salt, pepper, wine, stock, tomatoes, bay leaf and the mushroom and onion mixture. Bring the liquid to the boil, stirring constantly. Reduce the heat to low, cover the casserole and simmer for 40 minutes or until the chicken pieces are tender.

Remove the casserole from the heat and, using a slotted spoon, transfer the chicken pieces to a warmed serving dish. Set aside and keep warm.

Place the casserole over moderate heat and boil the sauce, stirring frequently, for 3 to 5 minutes or until it has reduced slightly. Stir in the beurre manié, a little at a time, and cook for a further 3 minutes or until the sauce is smooth and fairly thick.

Remove the casserole from the heat and remove and discard the bay leaf. Pour the sauce over the chicken pieces, sprinkle over the parsley and serve immediately.

Pollo alla Diavola

GRILLED [BROILED] CHICKEN WITH HERBS

Pollo alla Diavola (poh-loh ahl-lah dee-ah-voh-lah) *is a well-known Italian dish of grilled* [broiled] *chicken basted with a herb and butter sauce. It is very quick to prepare, and so is an ideal dish to make when you are in a hurry. Serve with boiled new potatoes and a crisp green salad. A well-chilled Soave or Verdiccho Bianco would be the ideal wines to accompany it.*

4 SERVINGS

- **2 x 2 lb. chickens, cut in half lengthways**
- **1 large garlic clove, halved**
- **1 teaspoon salt**
- **$\frac{1}{2}$ teaspoon black pepper**
- **4 oz. [$\frac{1}{2}$ cup] butter**
- **2 tablespoons olive oil**
- **juice of $\frac{1}{2}$ lemon**
- **1 tablespoon chopped fresh parsley**
- **1 tablespoon chopped fresh basil or $1\frac{1}{2}$ teaspoons dried basil**

Preheat the grill [broiler] to moderate.

Rub the chicken halves all over with the garlic clove halves, then with the salt and pepper. Discard the garlic and set the chicken aside.

In a small saucepan, melt the butter with the oil over moderate heat. Remove the pan from the heat and stir in the lemon juice, parsley and basil.

Using a pastry brush, brush the chicken halves all over with the butter and herb mixture. Place the chicken halves, skin side down, on the grill [broiler] rack.

Place the chicken under the grill [broiler] and grill [broil] for 7 to 10 minutes on each side, basting frequently with the butter and herb mixture.

After 15 minutes, test the chicken by inserting a skewer into one of the thighs. If the juices run clear, they are cooked.

Remove the chicken halves from the grill [broiler]. Using tongs, transfer the halves to a warmed serving dish and spoon over any remaining butter and herb mixture. Serve immediately.

Pollo en Pepitoria

CHICKEN WITH GARLIC AND ALMONDS

Pollo en Pepitoria (poh-loh on pehpee-tor-ee-ah) *is a Spanish dish of chicken in white wine with garlic and almonds. It is delicious served with boiled rice and green beans. A light Spanish white wine, such as Spanish Chablis, would make an ideal accompaniment.*

4-6 SERVINGS

- **2 oz. [$\frac{1}{2}$ cup] seasoned flour, made with 2 oz. [$\frac{1}{2}$ cup] flour, $\frac{1}{2}$ teaspoon salt and $\frac{1}{2}$ teaspoon black pepper**
- **1 x 5 lb. chicken, cut into 8 serving pieces**
- **4 tablespoons vegetable oil**
- **1 large onion, finely chopped**
- **2 garlic cloves, crushed**
- **1 large green pepper, white pith removed, seeded and chopped**
- **5 fl. oz. [$\frac{5}{8}$ cup] dry white wine**
- **10 fl. oz. [$1\frac{1}{4}$ cups] chicken stock**
- **$\frac{1}{8}$ teaspoon cayenne pepper**
- **bouquet garni, consisting of 4 parsley sprigs, 1 thyme spray and 1 bay leaf tied together**
- **2 hard-boiled egg yolks**
- **2 oz. [$\frac{1}{3}$ cup] ground almonds**

Place the seasoned flour on a plate. Dip the chicken pieces, one by one, in the flour, coating them thoroughly and shaking off any excess. Set the chicken aside.

In a large, flameproof casserole, heat the oil over moderate heat. When the oil is hot, add the onion, garlic and green pepper and cook, stirring occasionally, for 5 to 7 minutes or until the onion is soft and translucent but not brown. Using a slotted spoon, remove the vegetables from the pan and set them aside on a plate.

Add the chicken pieces to the casserole and fry them, stirring and turning frequently, for 10 to 12 minutes or until they are well browned all over.

Return the vegetables to the casserole and add the wine, stock, cayenne and bouquet garni. Bring the liquid to the boil. Reduce the heat to low, cover the casserole and simmer for 40 minutes or until the chicken pieces are tender.

In a small mixing bowl, mash the egg yolks and 3 tablespoons of the cooking liquid together with a fork until the mixture forms a smooth paste. Add the ground almonds and combine the mixture thoroughly. Stir this paste, a little at a time, into the casserole. Increase the heat to moderate and cook for a further 10 minutes.

Remove the casserole from the heat. Using tongs or a slotted spoon, remove the chicken pieces from the casserole and transfer them to a warmed serving dish. Keep warm while you finish the sauce.

Remove and discard the bouquet garni and return the casserole to the heat. Boil the sauce, stirring occasionally, for 3 to 5 minutes or until it has reduced and thickened slightly.

Remove the casserole from the heat. Pour the sauce over the chicken pieces and serve immediately.

Poloni

STEAMED MEAT LOAF

Poloni, or Polony, is the name given to an Italian sausage made with partly cooked or smoked meat and spices. A meat loaf, popular in Scotland, is also called Poloni and this recipe is made with minced [ground] *beef and ham then glazed with a tomato-flavoured aspic. Serve it cold with a potato salad and a lightly dressed green salad.*

4 SERVINGS

- **1 lb. lean beef, minced [ground]**
- **1 lb. ham, minced [ground] or very finely chopped**
- **2 oz. [1 cup] fresh breadcrumbs**
- **1 small onion, finely chopped**
- **1 tablespoon chopped fresh parsley**
- **1 tablespoon tomato ketchup**
- **1 teaspoon salt**
- **$\frac{1}{2}$ teaspoon black pepper**
- **$\frac{1}{2}$ teaspoon dried thyme**
- **2 eggs, lightly beaten**
- **2 teaspoons vegetable oil**

GLAZE

- **$\frac{1}{2}$ oz. gelatine, softened in 3 tablespoons warm water**

Chicken grilled [broiled] with herbs and garlic, Pollo alla Diavola should be served with a mixed green salad.

10 fl. oz. [1¼ cups] beef stock
1 tablespoon tomato purée
¼ teaspoon salt
¼ teaspoon black pepper

In a large mixing bowl, combine the beef, ham, breadcrumbs, onion, parsley, ketchup, salt, pepper and thyme and mix well.

Add the eggs and beat the mixture with a wooden spoon until all the ingredients are well blended.

Using a pastry brush, lightly grease the inside of a 2½-pint [1½-quart] pudding basin with 1 teaspoon of the oil. Place the mould upside-down on kitchen paper towels to drain off the excess oil.

Spoon the meat mixture into the pudding basin. Cut out a circle of greaseproof or waxed paper about 4-inches wider in diameter than the rim of the basin. Brush the paper with the remaining oil. Cut out a circle of aluminium foil the same size as the paper circle.

Put the greaseproof or waxed paper circle and foil circle together and, holding them firmly together, make a 1-inch pleat across the centre. Place the pleated paper and foil circles, foil uppermost, over the pudding basin. With a piece of string, securely tie the paper and foil circle around the rim of the basin, leaving a loop

with which to lift the pudding out of the saucepan when it is cooked.

Place the basin in a large saucepan and pour in enough boiling water to come about two-thirds of the way up the sides of the basin. Cover the pan and place it over low heat.

Steam the pudding for 3 hours, adding more boiling water as necessary.

When the pudding has finished steaming, remove the pan from the heat and lift the basin out of the water. Remove the foil and paper circles. Tip the pudding basin carefully over the sink and pour away any surplus fat. Place a large serving plate, inverted, on top of the basin. Holding them firmly together, reverse them. The meat loaf should slide out easily. Set it aside at room temperature until it cools slightly. Then place it in the refrigerator for 30 minutes to cool completely.

Meanwhile, make the glaze. In a medium-sized saucepan, heat the softened gelatine mixture over low heat, stirring constantly until the gelatine has dissolved. Add the stock, tomato purée, salt and pepper and stir until the ingredients are well mixed.

Remove the pan from the heat and set aside. When the glaze has cooled but just

before it has started to set, using a pastry brush, brush it over the meat loaf in a thin layer.

Set the meat loaf aside until the glaze has set completely before serving.

Pomarez Pineapple

This very simple dessert is ideal as a light and refreshing end to a rich meal.

4 SERVINGS
1 medium-sized fresh pineapple, peeled, cored and sliced into rings
1 tablespoon castor sugar
2 fl. oz. [¼ cup] kirsch

Low Cal

Lay the pineapple rings in a medium-sized, shallow serving dish. Sprinkle on the sugar and pour over the kirsch.

Place the dish in the refrigerator and marinate the pineapple for 3 hours, basting and turning the slices frequently.

Remove the dish from the refrigerator and serve immediately.

Pomarez Pineapple is a very simple pineapple and kirsch dessert

Pomegranate

The pomegranate is the fruit of a small, hardy tree, *punica granatum,* and is the only member of the family, *punicaceae.* It is said to be native to Iran but now grows all over the world. The best fruit grow in a hot dry climate, where the fresh juicy flesh is most appreciated.

An ancient fruit, the pomegranate was known in biblical times and regarded as a symbol of fruitfulness.

The pomegranate is a hard, round fruit with a leathery skin. It ranges in colour from pale whitish pink to deep red. In size too, it varies from that of a small orange to as large as a grapefruit. Inside it is divided into numerous cells containing translucent pale to deep red pulpy oval beads, each enclosing a seed. The taste of pomegranate is refreshing and slightly astringent.

The fruit is most usually crushed for its juice, but the pulp can be chewed and the seeds either crushed and eaten or discarded.

In India, pomegranate seeds are dried and used as a souring agent in cooking. In Mexico, the juice is made into a liqueur. GRENADINE syrup, which is used in many cocktails, is also made from pomegranate juice.

Pomelo

A citrus fruit from which the GRAPEFRUIT is descended, Pomelo, sometimes called shaddock, is larger than the grapefruit but resembles it in shape. The skin is thick, the flesh pink in colour, acid and coarse in texture.

Pomelo are not produced commercially for export but are grown for domestic consumption in South-East Asia and other tropical regions.

Pomerol

Pomerol is the smallest of the five major wine-producing areas of Bordeaux. It makes only red wine.

Pomerol wines tend to be softer, slightly less full than those produced in the other regions of Bordeaux. For that reason they do not need to be 'laid down' to mature for such a long period before they reach their peak of perfection.

Although the wines of Pomerol were not included in the great 1855 classification of Bordeaux wines, an 'unofficial' local division does exist. The quality rating used, however, seems to be rather more flexible than that governing the original 'official' classification since over 20 Pomerol châteaux can claim to produce *premier cru* wines as opposed to three Médocs and one Sauternes granted this distinction in 1855. Of these 20-odd *premiers crus,* Château Petrus and Château Certan are usually considered to be the leading wines of the district.

Pomerol wines go particularly well with chicken, veal and game dishes.

Pomeroy Rolls

Delightful little yeast rolls in the shape of clover leaves, Pomeroy Rolls have dried apricots, marinated in sweet wine, added to the dough before cooking. Serve warm, with plenty of butter and honey or home-made apricot jam.

24 ROLLS

6 oz. [1 cup] dried apricots, finely chopped
2 fl. oz. [¼ cup] lukewarm sweet white wine
½ oz. fresh yeast
2 oz. [¼ cup] plus ½ teaspoon sugar
10 fl. oz. [1¼ cups] lukewarm milk
1 lb. [4 cups] flour
1 teaspoon salt
3 oz. [⅜ cup] plus 2 teaspoons butter, melted

Place the apricots in a small bowl and pour over the wine. Set aside to marinate for 30 minutes. Drain the apricots and reserve the wine.

Meanwhile, crumble the yeast into a small bowl and mash in the ½ teaspoon of sugar with a fork. Add 2 fluid ounces [¼ cup] of the milk and cream the milk and yeast together. Set the bowl aside in a warm, draught-free place for 15 to 20 minutes or until the yeast mixture is puffed up and frothy.

Sift the flour, the remaining sugar and the salt into a warmed, large mixing bowl. Make a well in the centre and pour in the

Little clover leaf-shaped rolls filled with dried apricots marinated in wine, Pomeroy Rolls should be served warm with lots of butter.

reserved wine, yeast mixture, the remaining milk and 2 ounces [¼ cup] of the butter. Using your fingers or a spatula, gradually draw the flour mixture into the liquids. Continue mixing until all the flour is incorporated and the dough comes away from the sides of the bowl.

Turn the dough out on to a lightly floured board or marble slab and knead it for 10 minutes, reflouring the surface if the dough becomes sticky. The dough should be elastic and smooth.

Rinse, thoroughly dry and lightly grease the large mixing bowl. Shape the dough into a ball and return it to the bowl. Cover the bowl with a clean, damp cloth and set it in a warm, draught-free place for 1 to 1½ hours, or until the dough has risen and has almost doubled in bulk.

Using the 2 teaspoons of butter, grease 24 patty tins. Set aside.

Turn the risen dough out of the bowl on to a floured surface. Roll the dough out slightly and sprinkle with the apricots. Press the apricots into the dough and knead it for 8 minutes. Make 72 very small balls by rolling pieces of the dough between the palms of your hands. Place 3 balls into each patty tin and return the tins to a warm, draught-free place for 45 minutes to 1 hour or until the dough has almost doubled in bulk and risen to the tops of the tins.

Preheat the oven to hot 425°F (Gas Mark 7, 220°C).

Using a pastry brush, brush the dough with the remaining melted butter. Place the tins in the oven and bake for 15 to 20 minutes or until the rolls are golden brown.

Remove the tins from the oven. Turn the rolls out on to a wire rack to cool before serving.

Pommes et Abricots à l'Ancienne

APPLE AND APRICOT DESSERT

A delicious pudding to end that special meal, Pommes et Abricots à l'Ancienne (pohm ay ab-bree-coh ah l'on-see-en) may be served on its own or, if you prefer, with whipped cream or ice-cream.

4-6 SERVINGS

4 oz. [1½ cups] stale cake crumbs
3 tablespoons rum
5 oz. [⅝ cup] plus 1 tablespoon sugar
12 fl. oz. [1½ cups] water
1 vanilla pod
2 eating apples, peeled, cored and thickly sliced
4 apricots, stoned and thickly sliced
1 oz. [2 tablespoons] plus 1 teaspoon butter, melted

6 fl. oz. [¾ cup] Apple Sauce
3 tablespoons slivered almonds
SAUCE
6 tablespoons apricot jam
3 tablespoons rum

Arrange the cake crumbs in a shallow dish and pour over the rum. Set the dish aside for 30 minutes or until the crumbs have absorbed most of the rum.

Meanwhile, in a large saucepan, dissolve the 5 ounces [⅝ cup] of sugar in the water with the vanilla pod over moderate heat, stirring constantly until the sugar has dissolved. Reduce the heat to low and cook the syrup for 6 minutes, without stirring. Add the apples and apricots to the pan and spoon over the syrup to coat them thoroughly. Cover the pan and poach the fruit gently, basting and turning them in the syrup from time to time, for 10 minutes or until they are tender but still firm.

Preheat the oven to moderate 350°F (Gas Mark 4, 180°C). With the 1 teaspoon of butter, lightly grease a 2-pint [1½-quart] soufflé or baking dish and set aside.

When the fruit is done, remove the pan from the heat and remove and discard the vanilla pod. Using a slotted spoon, remove the fruit from the pan and arrange them in the prepared baking dish. Pour over 4 fluid ounces [½ cup] of the poaching liquid and discard the rest.

Spoon over the cake crumb mixture, to cover the fruit completely. Then spread over the apple sauce. Sprinkle the almonds on top, then the remaining sugar and the remaining melted butter.

Place the dish in the oven and bake for 20 to 25 minutes or until the topping is lightly browned. Remove the dish from the oven and set aside.

Meanwhile, make the sauce. In a small saucepan, heat the jam over moderate heat, stirring constantly until it is hot and has thinned slightly. Pour in the rum and continue mixing until the sauce is hot but not boiling and the ingredients are well blended.

Remove the pan from the heat and pour the sauce over the fruit mixture in the dish. Serve at once.

Pommes à la Bourguignonne

APPLES IN BURGUNDY WINE

A delicious dessert, Pommes à la Bourguignonne (pohm ah lah boor-gheen-yon) may be served plain or with whipped cream. Use a good quality red Burgundy wine for this dish.

6 SERVINGS

8 oz. [1 cup] sugar

1 pint [2½ cups] red Burgundy wine
6 cooking apples

In a large saucepan, dissolve the sugar in the wine over moderate heat, stirring constantly until the sugar has dissolved. Boil the mixture for 2 minutes, without stirring.

Core and peel the apples. Place them in

the sweetened wine as you peel them, and baste them to prevent them from discolouring. When all the apples have been added to the pan, cover the pan. Reduce the heat to low and poach the apples, basting frequently, for 10 to 15 minutes or until they are tender but still retain their shape. Test the apples frequently with a skewer so that you do not over-cook them.

Remove the pan from the heat and set the apples aside to cool in the syrup.

When the apples are cold, with a slotted spoon, transfer them to a serving dish. Cover the dish and set aside. Place the saucepan over high heat and boil the wine syrup, uncovered, for 8 to 10 minutes or until it has reduced by about half.

Remove the pan from the heat. Leave

the syrup to cool slightly, then pour it over the apples. Place the apples in the refrigerator to chill before serving.

Pommes à la Bourguignonne, apples cooked with Burgundy, and Pommes et Abricots à l'Ancienne, apple and apricot pudding, are two French classics.

Pommes au Cognac

APPLES BAKED IN BRANDY AND VERMOUTH

A sophisticated version of baked apples, Pommes au Cognac (pohm oh cawn-yac) is apples baked in brandy and vermouth. Although we have served Pommes au Cognac hot, they may also be served cold, with chilled whipped cream or even vanilla ice-cream.

4 SERVINGS

4 cooking apples
1 oz. [2 tablespoons] plus 4 teaspoons butter
2 tablespoons castor sugar
4 fl. oz. [½ cup] dry white vermouth
4 fl. oz. [½ cup] water
3 fl. oz. [⅜ cup] Cognac
4 slices white bread, crusts removed, and cut into circles about ½-inch thick and 3-inches in diameter
2 tablespoons redcurrant jelly

Preheat the oven to moderate 350°F (Gas Mark 4, 180°C).

Wash the apples and, with an apple corer, remove the cores. Using a sharp knife, make shallow slits all round the apples, starting from the centre and extending halfway down the sides. This will prevent the skins from bursting.

Put 1 teaspoon of the butter in the centre of each apple and place them, upright, in a medium-sized flameproof baking dish. Sprinkle over the sugar and pour in the vermouth, water and 2 tablespoons of the Cognac.

Place the baking dish in the oven and bake the apples for 30 to 35 minutes or until they are tender when pierced with a skewer.

Meanwhile, in a medium-sized frying-pan, melt the 1 ounce [2 tablespoons] of butter over moderate heat. When the foam subsides, add the bread slices and fry for 1 to 2 minutes on each side or until they are crisp and golden brown. Using a fish slice or spatula, remove the fried bread from the pan and set them aside to drain on kitchen paper towels. Arrange them on a serving dish.

When the apples have cooked, remove the baking dish from the oven and, with a slotted spoon, carefully place one apple on each slice of fried bread. Set aside and keep warm.

Place the baking dish over high heat, add the remaining Cognac and the red-currant jelly and cook, stirring frequently, for 5 to 7 minutes or until the sauce has reduced by about half.

Remove the pan from the heat and spoon the sauce over the apples. Serve at once.

Pommes Gratinées

APPLES WITH MERINGUE TOPPING

A lovely dessert, Pommes Gratinées (pohm gra-tee-nay) is apple purée topped with a light meringue mixture. It is best served cold, with vanilla ice-cream.

4-6 SERVINGS

1 oz. [2 tablespoons] plus 1 teaspoon butter
3 lb. cooking apples, peeled, cored and sliced
finely grated rind of 1 lemon
½ teaspoon ground allspice
3 tablespoons apricot jam
TOPPING
2 oz. [¼ cup] butter
2 oz. [¼ cup] sugar
2 eggs, separated
juice and finely grated rind of 1 small lemon
1 tablespoon flour
2 oz. [1 cup] fresh breadcrumbs
2 oz. [¼ cup] plus 1 teaspoon castor sugar

In a large saucepan, melt the 1 ounce [2 tablespoons] of butter over low heat. When the foam subsides, add the apples, lemon rind and allspice. Cover the pan and cook the mixture for 15 to 20 minutes or until the apples are very soft.

Remove the pan from the heat and beat in the jam with a wooden spoon, beating until the mixture becomes pulpy. Return the pan to the heat and cook, uncovered, for a further 3 to 5 minutes or until the mixture has thickened.

Remove the pan from the heat. Preheat the oven to warm 325°F (Gas Mark 3, 170°C).

Using the remaining teaspoon of butter, lightly grease a 2½-pint [1½-quart] baking dish.

Spoon the apple mixture into the baking dish and set aside.

To make the topping, in a medium-sized mixing bowl, cream the butter and sugar together with a wooden spoon until the mixture is light and fluffy. Add the egg yolks, lemon juice and rind, flour and breadcrumbs and mix well.

In another medium-sized mixing bowl, beat the egg whites with a wire whisk or rotary beater until they form soft peaks. Gradually beat in the 2 ounces [¼ cup] of castor sugar and continue beating until the egg whites form stiff peaks.

With a metal spoon, fold the egg white mixture into the breadcrumb mixture, then spoon it over the apples in the baking dish. Sprinkle with the remaining castor sugar and place the baking dish in the oven. Bake for 35 to 40 minutes or until the top is golden brown.

Remove the dish from the oven and set aside at room temperature to cool. Place it in the refrigerator to chill for at least 2 hours before serving.

Pommes Grimaldi

APPLE AND RICE FLAN

Pommes Grimaldi (pohm gree-mahl-dey) is an unusual dessert of apples and rice baked in a flan case.

4-6 SERVINGS

12 fl. oz. [1½ cups] milk
1 vanilla pod
3 oz. [½ cup] round-grain rice, washed, soaked in cold water for 30 minutes and drained
2 tablespoons castor sugar
1 tablespoon chopped candied peel
1½ oz. [3 tablespoons] butter
1 tablespoon orange-flavoured liqueur
1 x 9-inch Flan Case made with rich shortcrust pastry, baked blind and cooled
2 lb. cooking apples, peeled, cored and sliced

In a medium-sized saucepan, scald the milk with the vanilla pod (bring to just below boiling point) over moderate heat.

Remove the pan from the heat, cover it and leave the milk to infuse for 20 minutes. Remove the vanilla pod.

Return the pan to the heat and bring the milk to the boil over moderate heat. Add the rice, reduce the heat to low and simmer for 15 to 20 minutes or until all the liquid has been absorbed.

Remove the pan from the heat. Stir in 1 tablespoon of the sugar, the candied peel, 1 tablespoon of the butter and the liqueur. Spread the rice mixture evenly over the bottom of the flan case.

Preheat the oven to fairly hot 375°F (Gas Mark 5, 190°C).

In a large frying-pan, melt the remaining butter over moderate heat. When the foam subsides, add the apple slices and cook, turning them occasionally, for 8 to 12 minutes or until they are tender. Remove the pan from the heat.

Using a slotted spoon, arrange the apple slices in an overlapping layer in the flan case, on top of the rice. Sprinkle over the remaining sugar and place the flan in the oven. Bake the flan for 10 to 15 minutes or until it is hot and the sugar has melted.

Remove the flan from the oven and serve immediately.

Pommes Gratinées and Pommes au Cognac are really worth trying!

Pommes Normandes
APPLE AND CARAMEL MOULD

A stunning and quite delicious dinner party dessert, Pommes Normandes (pohm nor-mahnd) is an apple custard flavoured with Calvados and set in a caramel-lined mould. Serve it with whipped cream.

4-6 SERVINGS

2 fl. oz. [¼ cup] Caramel, hot
3 lb. cooking apples, peeled, cored and sliced
½ teaspoon ground allspice
¼ teaspoon ground cloves
2 oz. [¼ cup] castor sugar
2 fl. oz. [¼ cup] Calvados
2 oz. [¼ cup] butter
3 eggs
1 egg white, lightly beaten

Warm a 1½ pint [1 quart] mould in hot water. Dry the mould thoroughly then pour in the caramel, tilting and rotating the mould so that the insides are evenly coated. Set the mould aside while you prepare the apples.

In a large, heavy saucepan, combine the apples, allspice and cloves together. Cover the pan, place it over low heat and cook for 20 to 25 minutes, or until the apples are very soft. Remove the pan from the heat and set aside.

Preheat the oven to fairly hot 375°F (Gas Mark 5, 190°C).

Purée the apples with a fork, then return the pan, uncovered, to the heat and cook for 10 to 15 minutes longer or until the purée is dry and stiff.

Remove the pan from the heat and beat in the sugar, Calvados, butter and eggs. Fold in the egg white and pour the mixture into the caramel-lined mould. Cover the mould with aluminium foil and put it in a bain-marie, or baking tin, three-quarters filled with boiling water.

Place the bain-marie, or baking tin, in the oven and cook the mixture for 1¼ to 1½ hours or until it is set and firm.

Remove the mould from the oven and set aside for 15 minutes to allow the mixture to cool slightly.

If you are serving it warm, turn it out on to a serving dish. It should slide out easily.

If you are serving it cold, chill the mould in the refrigerator until just before serving. Remove the mould from the refrigerator and quickly dip the bottom in hot water. Run a sharp knife around the edge of the mould. Place a serving dish, inverted, over the top of the mould and, holding them firmly together, reverse the two. The pudding should slide easily out of the mould.

Serve the pudding immediately.

Pommes de Terre Anna
POTATO SLICES BAKED WITH BUTTER

This delicious potato dish requires some care in its preparation but the result is well worth the effort. Serve Pommes de Terre Anna (pohm d'tair anna) with roast or grilled [broiled] meat.

2-4 SERVINGS

1 lb. potatoes, weighed after peeling
2 oz. [¼ cup] butter
1 teaspoon salt
½ teaspoon black pepper

Preheat the oven to fairly hot 375°F (Gas Mark 5, 190°C).

Using a very sharp knife, a mandolin or a vegetable cutter, cut the potatoes into ⅟₁₆-inch thick slices.

Using 1 tablespoon of the butter generously grease a 6-inch soufflé or straight-sided ovenproof dish. Arrange about one-sixth of the potato slices on the bottom of the dish, in circles. Sprinkle the slices with one-sixth of the salt and pepper. Cut one-sixth of the remaining butter into pieces and dot these over the potato slices. Continue making layers in this way until all the ingredients are used up, ending with a layer of potato slices dotted with butter.

Cover the dish and place it in the oven. Bake the potatoes for 1¼ hours or until they are tender when pierced with the point of a sharp knife.

Remove the dish from the oven, and pour off and discard any excess butter.

Serve immediately, from the dish, or unmould the potatoes on to a warmed serving plate and serve.

Pommes de Terre Campagnardes
POTATOES COUNTRY-STYLE

Pommes de Terre Campagnardes (pohm d'tair cam-pan-yard), a sustaining mixture of fried potato cubes, onion, bread croûtons and eggs, makes a filling accompaniment to lamb chops or ham. Or, served with lots of cold beer and crusty bread, it may be served as a snack lunch.

4-6 SERVINGS

1½ lb. potatoes, weighed after peeling
2 teaspoons salt
2 oz. [¼ cup] butter
2 medium-sized onions, finely chopped
1 garlic clove, crushed
2 thick slices day-old white bread, crusts removed and cut into cubes
3 eggs
3 fl. oz. [⅜ cup] milk

½ teaspoon black pepper
¼ teaspoon dried thyme
1 tablespoon chopped fresh parsley

Place the potatoes in a large saucepan and pour over enough water just to cover. Add 1 teaspoon of the salt and place the pan over high heat. Bring the water to the boil, reduce the heat to moderate and cook the potatoes for 8 minutes. Remove the pan from the heat and drain the potatoes.

Set aside to cool slightly.

When the potatoes are cool enough to handle, transfer them to a chopping board. With a sharp knife, cut them into cubes and set aside.

Meanwhile, in a large, deep frying-pan, melt the butter over moderate heat. When the foam subsides, add the onions, garlic and bread cubes and cook, stirring occasionally, for 8 to 10 minutes or until the onions are golden brown.

Add the potato cubes to the pan and cook them, turning occasionally, for 5 to 8 minutes or until the potatoes are tender when pierced with the point of a sharp knife.

Meanwhile, in a small mixing bowl, beat the eggs, milk, the remaining salt, the pepper and thyme together until they are well blended.

Pour the egg mixture over the potato mixture and cook, stirring and turning constantly, for 3 minutes or until the eggs are cooked and the mixture is still moist.

Remove the pan from the heat and transfer the mixture to a warmed serving dish. Sprinkle over the parsley and serve at once.

A hearty potato and egg mixture, Pommes de Terre Campagnardes may be served with meat or fish.

Pommes de Terre Dauphine
DEEP-FRIED POTATO SHAPES

Pommes de Terre Dauphine (pohm d'tair doh-feen) is a classic French way of cooking potatoes. The potato mixture must be stiff enough to hold its shape if a good appearance is to be achieved. The use of a large forcing bag and a $\frac{3}{4}$-inch nozzle gives the best result. The potato mixture can also be moulded into balls or other shapes.

4 SERVINGS

5 oz. [1$\frac{1}{4}$ cups] Choux Pastry
8 oz. Duchess Potato purée
    sufficient vegetable oil for
    deep-frying

In a medium-sized mixing bowl, combine the choux pastry and the duchess potato purée together, beating with a wooden spoon until they are thoroughly mixed.

Spoon the potato mixture into a large forcing bag fitted with a $\frac{3}{4}$-inch nozzle.

Fill a deep-frying pan one-third full with the vegetable oil. Place the pan over moderate heat and heat the oil until it reaches 375°F on a deep-fat thermometer, or until a cube of stale bread dropped into the oil turns golden brown in 40 seconds.

Pipe 2-inch pieces of the potato mixture into the hot oil, cutting off the ends with a knife. Do not crowd the pan. Fry the potato pieces for 4 to 5 minutes or until they are golden brown. Using a

slotted spoon, transfer the potato pieces to kitchen paper towels to drain. Keep warm while you fry the remaining mixture in the same way.

Serve immediately.

Pommes de Terre Fondantes
OLIVE-SHAPED POTATOES

A classic way of preparing and cooking potatoes, Pommes de Terre Fondantes (pohm d'tair fawn-dohn) is simply olive-shaped potatoes cooked in butter. Serve them with grilled [broiled] or roasted meat or chicken.

Three super dishes—Pommes de Terre à la Provençale, Pommes de Terre Dauphine and Pommes de Terre Fondantes.

4 SERVINGS

3 oz. [⅜ cup] butter
2 lb. potatoes, peeled, quartered and cut into olive shapes about 2-inches long
1 teaspoon salt

In a deep frying-pan, melt the butter over moderate heat. When the foam subsides, add the potatoes and cook them, shaking the pan frequently, for 2 to 3 minutes or until they are well coated in the butter. Reduce the heat to low, cover the pan and cook the potatoes, shaking the pan and turning the potatoes occasionally, for 20 to 30 minutes or until they are golden brown and tender when pierced with the point of a sharp knife.

Remove the pan from the heat and drain the potatoes on kitchen paper towels.

Sprinkle with the salt and serve immediately.

Pommes de Terre Galette
POTATO CAKE

A golden, crisp potato cake, Pommes de Terre Galette (pohm d'tair ga-leht) is excellent served with grilled [broiled] fish or meat.

4 SERVINGS

2 lb. potatoes, peeled and cooked
1 small onion, finely chopped
2 teaspoons salt
¼ teaspoon black pepper
1 tablespoon chopped fresh parsley
2 oz. [¼ cup] butter, softened
2 eggs, lightly beaten
½ teaspoon paprika

Preheat the oven to fairly hot 375°F (Gas Mark 5, 190°C).

With a potato masher or fork, mash the potatoes and place them in a medium-sized mixing bowl. Add the onion, salt, pepper and parsley and mix well.

Beat in 1½ ounces [3 tablespoons] of the butter and the eggs and stir until the ingredients are well blended.

Using the remaining butter, generously grease a medium-sized baking dish. Spoon the mixture into the dish, flattening the top with a palette knife. Sprinkle over the paprika.

Place the dish in the oven and bake the mixture for 20 to 30 minutes or until it is golden brown and crisp.

Remove the dish from the oven and

cut the galette into wedges. Serve immediately.

Pommes de Terre à la Lyonnaise
POTATOES WITH ONIONS

A classic French way of cooking potatoes, Pommes de Terre à la Lyonnaise (pohm d'tair ah la lee-yon-eze) makes a delicious accompaniment to grilled [broiled] steak or roast beef or pork.

4-6 SERVINGS

2 lb. potatoes, weighed after peeling
1½ teaspoons salt
2 oz. [¼ cup] butter
2 medium-sized onions, thinly sliced
1 teaspoon black pepper

Place the potatoes in a large saucepan and pour in enough water just to cover. Add 1 teaspoon of salt and place the pan over high heat. Bring the water to the boil, reduce the heat to moderate and cook the potatoes for 10 minutes.

Remove the pan from the heat and drain the potatoes. Set them aside to cool a little.

When the potatoes are cool enough to handle, place them on a chopping board and cut them into thick slices. Set them aside.

In a large frying-pan, melt the butter over moderate heat. When the foam subsides, add the potato slices and cook, turning them occasionally, for 5 minutes or until they are lightly and evenly browned.

Add the onions, the remaining salt and the pepper and cook, stirring occasionally, for 5 to 7 minutes or until the onions are soft and translucent but not brown and the potatoes are tender when pierced with the point of a sharp knife.

Remove the pan from the heat and transfer the mixture to a warmed serving dish. Serve at once.

Pommes de Terre Ménagère
MASHED POTATOES WITH HAM

A classic French method of preparing mashed potatoes, Pommes de Terre Ménagère (pohm d'tair main-ah-jer) may be served with grilled [broiled] steak or roast beef or pork.

4 SERVINGS

1 oz. [2 tablespoons] butter
2 lb. potatoes, peeled, cooked, mashed and kept hot

1 small onion, finely chopped
4 oz. cooked ham, finely chopped
1 oz. Emmenthal cheese, chopped
2 tablespoons grated Emmenthal cheese

Beat half of the butter into the mashed potatoes with a kitchen fork. Set aside and keep warm.

In a small frying-pan melt the remaining butter over moderate heat. When the foam subsides, add the onion and fry, stirring occasionally, for 5 to 7 minutes or until it is soft and translucent but not brown. Remove the frying-pan from the heat and pour the onion and cooking juices on to the potatoes. Add the ham and beat the mixture well.

Preheat the grill [broiler] to high.

Spoon the potato mixture into a medium-sized flameproof dish. Smooth down the top with the back of the spoon.

Sprinkle the top of the potato with the chopped and grated cheese and place the dish under the grill [broiler]. Grill [broil] the mixture for 2 to 3 minutes or until the cheese has melted and is lightly browned.

Remove the dish from under the grill [broiler] and serve immediately.

Pommes de Terre à la Provençale
POTATOES WITH GARLIC

A rustic, hearty dish of potatoes cooked in oil, garlic and anchovies, Pommes de Terre à la Provençale (pohm d'tair ah lah prohvan-sahl) is an excellent accompaniment to stews and casseroles.

4 SERVINGS

2 fl. oz. [¼ cup] olive oil
2 garlic cloves, crushed
2 lb. potatoes, parboiled in their skins for 10 minutes
½ teaspoon salt
¼ teaspoon black pepper
6 anchovy fillets, halved
1 tablespoon chopped fresh parsley

In a large frying-pan, heat the oil over moderate heat. When the oil is hot, add the garlic and cook, stirring constantly, for 5 minutes.

Peel the potatoes and cut them into ½-inch slices. Add the potatoes to the pan, sprinkle over the salt and pepper and cook them, turning once, for 10 to 15 minutes or until they are well cooked and golden brown.

Just before serving, add the anchovy fillets and cook for a further 2 minutes.

Using a slotted spoon, transfer the potatoes to a warmed serving dish. Sprinkle with the parsley and serve.

Pommes de Terre au Roquefort

BAKED POTATOES WITH BLUE CHEESE

Baked potatoes stuffed with Roquefort cheese and sour cream, Pommes de Terre au Roquefort (pohm d'tair oh rock-fawr) makes an ideal snack lunch, served with a mixed salad. Or serve them as an extra-special accompaniment to grilled [broiled] steak.

4 SERVINGS

4 large potatoes, scrubbed
5 fl. oz. [⅝ cup] sour cream
4 oz. Roquefort cheese, crumbled
2 tablespoons chopped fresh chives
⅛ teaspoon cayenne pepper
½ teaspoon salt
¼ teaspoon black pepper

Preheat the oven to fairly hot 375°F (Gas Mark 5, 190°C).

Put the potatoes in the centre of the oven and bake them for 1½ hours.

Remove the potatoes from the oven and set aside to cool a little. When they are cool enough to handle, lay them on their sides. Cut off a thin slice, lengthways, from the top of each one. Using a tea-spoon, scoop out the inside of each potato to within ¼-inch of the shell, taking care not to break the skin.

In a medium-sized mixing bowl, mash together the scooped-out potato, sour cream, cheese, chives, cayenne, salt and pepper.

Stuff equal amounts of the potato and cheese filling into each potato. Place the potatoes in a baking dish and return them to the oven. Bake for 10 to 15 minutes or until the top of the filling is lightly browned. Remove the dish from the oven and serve the potatoes immediately.

Pommes de Terre Sautées au Citron

SAUTEED POTATOES FLAVOURED WITH LEMON

Garlic-flavoured sautéed potatoes with a touch of lemon, Pommes de Terre Sautées au Citron (pohm d'tair soh-tay oh see-trawn) makes a delightful accompaniment to grilled [broiled] steak or roast lamb.

4-6 SERVINGS

2 lb. small even-sized potatoes, scraped
1 oz. [2 tablespoons] butter
1 tablespoon vegetable oil
grated rind of ½ lemon
½ teaspoon salt
½ teaspoon black pepper
1 garlic clove, crushed
SAUCE
1 oz. [2 tablespoons] butter

Two appetizing potato recipes from France — Pommes de Terre au Roque-fort and Pommes de Terre Soufflées.

2 garlic cloves, crushed
1 tablespoon lemon juice

Check the potatoes and cut away any lumps or oddly shaped parts, so that the potatoes are uniform in shape.

In a large frying-pan, melt the butter with the oil over moderate heat. When the foam subsides, add enough potatoes to cover the bottom of the pan and fry them, turning frequently and shaking the pan, for 6 to 8 minutes or until they are evenly browned on all sides. As the potatoes brown, push them to one side and add more potatoes. Add more oil and butter if necessary.

When all the potatoes have browned, add the lemon rind, salt, pepper and garlic and stir to coat the potatoes with the flavourings. Reduce the heat to low, cover the pan and continue cooking for a further 10 to 15 minutes, shaking the pan frequently, or until the potatoes are tender and deeply and evenly browned.

Remove the pan from the heat. Drain off and discard the cooking juices. Keep the potatoes warm.

To make the sauce, in a small sauce-pan, melt the butter over moderate heat.

When the foam subsides, stir in the garlic and fry for 3 to 5 minutes or until it is golden brown. Do not let the butter brown.

Remove the pan from the heat, stir in the lemon juice and strain the sauce over the potatoes. Discard the contents of the strainer. Return the pan containing the potatoes to moderate heat and, stirring constantly, heat the potatoes for 4 minutes or until they are very hot and are coated with the sauce.

Remove the pan from the heat. Transfer the potatoes into a heated serving dish and serve immediately.

Pommes de Terre Soufflées
POTATO PUFFS

Pommes de Terre Soufflées (pohm d'tair sou-flay) are thinly sliced potatoes fried in two lots of oil — the first at a low temperature, the second at a high temperature. This method of frying makes the potatoes puff up. Serve Pommes de Terre Soufflées with grilled [broiled] meat or fish. If any of the potato slices do not puff up when fried the second time, remove them and serve them as fried potatoes.

2-4 SERVINGS

1 lb. potatoes, peeled and cut into ⅛-inch thick slices
sufficient vegetable oil for deep-frying
1 teaspoon salt

Place the potato slices in a large bowl of cold water for 30 minutes. Drain them and dry thoroughly with a clean cloth.

Fill two large saucepans one-third full with oil. Heat the oil in one pan over moderate heat until it reaches 325°F on a deep-fat thermometer or until a piece of stale bread dropped into the oil turns golden brown in 65 seconds.

Heat the oil in the other pan over moderate heat until it reaches 375°F on a deep-fat thermometer or until a piece of stale bread dropped into the oil turns golden brown in 40 seconds.

Drop the potato slices into the first pan and fry them for 4 minutes.

Using a slotted spoon, transfer the slices to the second pan and fry them for 2 to 3 minutes or until they puff up. Immediately the slices puff up, remove them from the oil and drain them on kitchen paper towels.

Sprinkle with the salt and serve immediately.

Pomodori alla Siciliana
SICILIAN STUFFED TOMATOES

A tasty dish to serve as a first course, Pomodori alla Siciliana (pom-oh-dor-ee ahl-lah si-chi-li-ah-na) may be served either hot or cold.

4 SERVINGS

8 large firm tomatoes
6 tablespoons olive oil
2 medium-sized onions, finely chopped
1 garlic clove, crushed
4 oz. [2 cups] fresh breadcrumbs
8 anchovy fillets, chopped
3 tablespoons black olives, stoned and chopped
2 tablespoons chopped fresh parsley
2 teaspoons chopped fresh oregano or 1 teaspoon dried oregano
3 tablespoons grated Parmesan cheese
1 tablespoon butter, cut into 8 pieces

Pomodori alla Siciliana, tomatoes stuffed with anchovies, herbs and cheese, may be served hot or cold as a tempting first course.

Tasty rice and chicken Poona Pilaff is easy and inexpensive to make.

Preheat the oven to moderate 350°F (Gas Mark 4, 180°C).

Place the tomatoes on a board and cut off the tops with a sharp knife. Discard the tops. With a teaspoon, scoop out and discard the seeds, taking care not to pierce the skin. Set the tomatoes aside.

In a medium-sized frying-pan, heat the oil over moderate heat. When the oil is hot, add the onions and garlic and fry, stirring occasionally, for 5 to 7 minutes or until the onions are soft and translucent but not brown. Remove the pan from the heat and stir in the breadcrumbs, anchovies, olives, parsley and oregano.

Using a teaspoon, fill the tomatoes with the breadcrumb mixture. Place the tomatoes in an ovenproof dish large enough to take them in one layer.

Sprinkle the Parmesan cheese over the stuffed tomatoes and top each one with a piece of butter.

Place the dish in the oven and bake the tomatoes for 20 to 25 minutes or until the tops are lightly browned and the tomatoes are tender but still firm.

Remove the dish from the oven and serve immediately. If you wish to serve the tomatoes cold, allow them to cool in the dish, then chill them in the refrigerator for at least 1 hour before serving.

Ponche de Crème
MILK PUNCH

A potent drink from the West Indies, Ponche de Crème (pawnsh-d'krem) *may be served chilled, with crushed ice. It may be stored for up to 4 weeks in the refrigerator.*

ABOUT 4 PINTS

2 tablespoons cornflour [cornstarch]
2 pints [5 cups] milk
6 oz. [¾ cup] sugar
5 eggs, lightly beaten
26 fl. oz. [3¼ cups] (1 bottle) rum
½ teaspoon vanilla essence

In a large mixing bowl, mix the cornflour [cornstarch] with 2 tablespoons of the milk. Set aside.

In a large saucepan, scald the remaining milk over moderate heat (bring to just below boiling). Remove the pan from the heat and pour the milk, stirring well, on to the cornflour [cornstarch] mixture. Return the mixture to the pan and return the pan to moderate heat. Bring the mixture to the boil, stirring constantly. Reduce the heat to low and cook the mixture for 2 minutes, stirring constantly. Remove the pan from the heat. Beat in the sugar and the eggs.

Strain the milk and egg mixture into a large mixing bowl. Stir in the rum and vanilla essence. Cover the bowl and set aside to cool completely. Place the bowl in the refrigerator and chill for 1 hour before serving.

If you wish to keep the punch, pour it into clean, dry bottles. Cover and store it in the refrigerator for up to 4 weeks.

Poona Pilaff

The tastiest way to make this dish is to use a whole chicken so that you can make the stock from the carcass and giblets. If you do not have the time to do this, chicken pieces and a stock cube will do, though the flavour of the pilaff will not be as good.

4 SERVINGS

2 oz. [¼ cup] butter
1 x 4 lb. chicken, cut into serving pieces, or 8 chicken pieces
1 teaspoon salt
½ teaspoon black pepper
½ teaspoon dried tarragon
8 oz. button mushrooms, wiped clean
12 oz. [2 cups] long-grain rice, washed, soaked in cold water for 30 minutes and drained
1 pint [2½ cups] chicken stock
5 fl. oz. single cream [⅝ cup light cream]

In a large saucepan, melt the butter over moderate heat. When the foam subsides, add the chicken pieces and cook them, turning them frequently, for 6 to 8 minutes or until they are lightly browned. Sprinkle the chicken pieces with half of the salt, the pepper and tarragon. Reduce the heat to low, cover the pan and cook the chicken pieces for 25 minutes.

Uncover the pan, increase the heat to moderate and add the mushrooms. Continue cooking for 10 minutes, stirring occasionally.

Add the rice and the remaining salt and cook, stirring constantly, for 5 minutes.

Pour in the stock and bring the mixture to the boil. Cover the pan, reduce the heat to low and cook the pilaff for 20 to 25 minutes or until the rice is tender and all the liquid has been absorbed. Remove the pan from the heat and stir in the cream.

Spoon the pilaff on to a warmed serving platter and serve immediately.

Popcorn

Popcorn is MAIZE or Indian corn kernels which are roasted until the heat causes the moisture in the kernels to expand and explode. (They explode with a popping sound, hence the name.)

To make popcorn, buy the special packaged corn selected for popping. Use a large saucepan with a tight-fitting lid. Heat 2 tablespoons of vegetable oil in the pan over moderate heat. When the oil is hot, add 2 ounces [½ cup] of popcorn and cover the pan. Shaking the pan frequently, cook the corn until the popping stops. Do not uncover the pan while the corn is popping.

Remove the pan from the heat and, using a slotted spoon, lift out the popcorn, discarding any imperfect kernels, and drain them on kitchen paper towels. Place on a serving dish, sprinkle with salt and melted butter or cheese and serve while hot.

This quantity will make about 1 quart of popcorn.

Pope

Pope is a fish belonging to the same family as PERCH, which it closely resembles. It is a freshwater fish, delicate in flavour, which is often used in fish stews.

Pope may be cooked in the same way as perch.

Pope's Eye or Ear

Pope's eye or ear is the name given to a small circle of fat found in the middle of a leg of lamb or pork.

Pope's Nose

Pope's Nose or Parson's Nose as it is sometimes called, is the name for the bottom or tail end of poultry. It is edible although it is a matter of individual preference whether it is eaten or discarded.

Popovers

Popovers are individual batter puddings which may be made plain for serving with roast meat, or they may have a sweet or savoury filling.

To make popovers, heat a patty tin in a hot oven 425°F (Gas Mark 7, 220°C) for 3 minutes. Remove the tin from the oven, coat the inside of each cup with 1 teaspoon of oil and return the tin to the oven for 5 minutes. Remove the tin from the oven and fill each cup two-thirds full with CREPE batter. Place the patty tin in the oven and bake the popovers for 10 to 15 minutes or until they have puffed up and are deep golden brown.

Remove the tin from the oven and serve immediately, if you are serving the popovers plain.

Poppadum

Poppadums are thin, round, crisp, puffed savoury pastries. They originated in India and are usually served with Indian food and curries, or with other savoury food, although they are also sometimes served as appetizers.

Poppadums are made from lentil flour and may be plain or spiced. They are sold, prepacked in Indian and Pakistani food stores and, increasingly, in the larger supermarkets. They are cooked by grilling [broiling] or frying.

To grill [broil] poppadums, preheat the grill [broiler] to hot. Place two poppadums on the grill [broiler] rack and place the rack under the grill [broiler]. Grill [broil] the poppadums for 1 minute on each side or until they have puffed up and are very crisp.

To fry poppadums, heat about a tablespoon of vegetable oil over moderate heat. When the oil is hot, place a poppadum in the oil and fry it for 2 minutes, turning once, or until it has puffed up and is very crisp. Remove the poppadum from the pan and drain it on kitchen paper towels.

Poppy Seed

Poppy seed, as the name indicates, is the seed of a poppy. The most common type of poppy seed is blue-grey in colour, with a mild flavour which is released when the seed is cooked. Poppy seeds are used extensively in Central European and Jewish cookery, in cakes, puddings, strudels and noodle dishes. They are also

often sprinkled on bread, rolls and biscuits [cookies].

There is another type of poppy seed, white in colour, which is used mainly in Indian cookery. It has a sweet, nutty flavour.

Poppy seeds are very hard and therefore difficult to grind. Special poppy seed grinders are available in some European countries and in the United States but are not often seen in the United Kingdom.

Poppy Seed Bread

Poppy Seed Bread is a delicious white milky bread. Traditionally the dough is braided before cooking, but it may be shaped into rounds or baked in a loaf tin.

ONE 2-POUND LOAF

¾ oz. yeast
½ teaspoon sugar
16 fl. oz. [2 cups] lukewarm milk
2 lb. [8 cups] flour
2 teaspoons salt
4 oz. [½ cup] plus 1 teaspoon butter
1 egg, lightly beaten with 1 tablespoon milk
2 tablespoons poppy seeds

Crumble the yeast into a small bowl and mash in the sugar with a kitchen fork. Add 2 fluid ounces [¼ cup] of milk and cream the milk and yeast together. Set the bowl aside in a warm, draught-free place for 15 to 20 minutes or until the yeast mixture is puffed up and frothy.

Sift the flour and salt into a warmed, large mixing bowl. Add the 4 ounces [½ cup] of butter, and, using your fingertips, rub the fat into the flour until the mixture resembles fine breadcrumbs. Make a well in the centre and pour in the yeast mixture and remaining milk. Using your fingers or a spatula, gradually draw the flour mixture into the liquids. Continue mixing until all the flour is incorporated and the dough comes away from the sides of the bowl.

Poppy Seed Cake and Poppy Seed Bread are both delicious sliced, spread with butter and served with coffee.

Turn the dough out on to a lightly floured board or marble slab and knead it for 10 minutes, reflouring the surface if the dough becomes sticky. The dough should be elastic and smooth.

Rinse, thoroughly dry and lightly grease the large mixing bowl. Shape the dough into a ball and return it to the bowl. Cover the bowl with a clean damp cloth and set it in a warm, draught-free place. Leave it for 1 to 1½ hours or until the dough has risen and has almost doubled in bulk.

Turn the risen dough out of the bowl on to a floured surface and knead it for about 8 minutes.

Using the remaining teaspoon of butter, grease a large baking sheet. Roll the dough out into a large oblong. Using a sharp knife, cut the dough, lengthways, into three equal strips, leaving the dough joined at one end. Braid the dough, then moisten the ends with water and press them together firmly. Carefully lift the dough braid on to the prepared baking sheet and return it to a warm place for 45 minutes to 1 hour or until the dough has almost doubled in bulk.

Preheat the oven to hot 425°F (Gas Mark 7, 220°C). Using a pastry brush, brush the dough with the egg and milk mixture and sprinkle with the poppy seeds.

Place the baking sheet in the centre of the oven and bake for 45 minutes.

Remove the baking sheet from the oven, tip the loaf off the baking sheet and rap the underside with your knuckles. If the bread sounds hollow, like a drum, it is cooked. If it does not sound hollow, reduce the oven temperature to warm 325°F (Gas Mark 3, 170°C), return the loaf to the oven and bake for a further 5 minutes.

Cool the loaf on a wire rack and serve.

Poppy Seed Cake

An adaptation of a traditional Middle-European cake, Poppy Seed Cake makes the ideal accompaniment to milk or coffee.

ONE 7-INCH CAKE

6 oz. [¾ cup] plus 1 teaspoon butter
10 oz. [2½ cups] plus 1 tablespoon flour
8 oz. [1 cup] sugar
1½ teaspoons vanilla essence
2 oz. [½ cup] poppy seeds
5 fl. oz. [⅝ cup] milk
2 tablespoons sour cream
½ teaspoon salt
1 teaspoon baking powder
3 egg whites

Preheat the oven to moderate 350°F (Gas Mark 4, 180°C).

With the teaspoon of butter, grease a 7-inch loose-bottomed cake tin. Dust the tin with the 1 tablespoon of flour and tip and rotate the tin to cover the sides and bottom. Knock out any excess. Set aside.

In a large mixing bowl, cream the remaining butter with a wooden spoon until it is light and fluffy. Add the sugar and beat until the mixture is smooth and creamy. Stir in the vanilla essence, poppy seeds, half the milk and the sour cream.

Sift in the remaining flour, salt and baking powder and fold them into the creamed mixture with a metal spoon. Stir in the remaining milk.

In a large mixing bowl, whisk the egg whites with a wire whisk or rotary beater until they form stiff peaks.

With the metal spoon, fold the egg whites into the cake batter. Spoon the batter into the cake tin. Place the tin in the oven and bake the cake for 1¼ to 1½ hours or until a skewer inserted into the centre comes out clean.

Remove the tin from the oven and allow the cake to cool in the tin for 5 minutes. Then turn the cake out on to a wire rack to cool completely before serving.

Poppy Seed Roll

These attractive sweet breads are filled with dried fruits, nuts and poppy seeds. Serve as a nourishing snack with milk, or spread thick slices with cream cheese as a dessert.

TWO 14-INCH ROLLS

4 oz. [½ cup] butter, softened
½ oz. fresh yeast
4 oz. [½ cup] plus ¼ teaspoon sugar
2 tablespoons lukewarm water
4 fl. oz. [½ cup] lukewarm milk
1 lb. [4 cups] flour
2 teaspoons salt
3 eggs, lightly beaten
2 teaspoons grated lemon rind
1 egg, beaten with 1 tablespoon milk

FILLING
6 oz. [1½ cups] poppy seeds, ground
2 oz. [½ cup] slivered almonds
6 oz. [1 cup] chopped dates
2 oz. [⅓ cup] currants
1 teaspoon grated orange rind
8 oz. [1 cup] sugar
1 tablespoon flour mixed to a paste

with 5 tablespoons single [light] cream

1 egg, lightly beaten

3 oz. [⅜ cup] butter, melted

Grease two large baking sheets with 2 teaspoons of the butter and set aside.

Crumble the yeast into a small bowl and mash in the ¼ teaspoon sugar with a kitchen fork. Add the water and half the milk, and cream the liquids and yeast together to form a smooth paste. Set the bowl aside in a warm, draught-free place for 15 to 20 minutes or until the yeast mixture is puffed up and frothy.

Sift the flour, remaining sugar and the salt into a warmed, large mixing bowl. Make a well in the centre of the flour mixture and pour in the yeast mixture, the remaining milk, the beaten eggs and lemon rind. Using your fingers or a spatula, gradually draw the flour into the liquid. Continue mixing until all the flour is incorporated and the dough comes away from the sides of the bowl.

Turn the dough out on to a floured board or marble slab and knead it for about 5 minutes, reflouring the surface if the dough becomes sticky. The dough

---

A rich fruit, nut and poppy seed sweetbread, Poppy Seed Roll tastes and looks very attractive.

should be smooth and elastic.

Rinse, thoroughly dry and lightly grease the large mixing bowl. Shape the dough into a ball and return it to the bowl. Dust the top of the dough with a little flour and cover the bowl with a clean damp cloth. Set the bowl in a warm, draught-free place and leave it for 1½ to 2 hours or until the dough has risen and has almost doubled in bulk.

Meanwhile, prepare the filling. In a medium-sized mixing bowl, combine the ground poppy seeds, almonds, dates, currants and orange rind.

In a small saucepan, dissolve the sugar in the flour mixture over low heat, stirring constantly. Increase the heat to moderate and bring the mixture to the boil, stirring constantly. Cook the sauce for 1 minute. Remove the pan from the heat. Pour the sauce into the bowl containing the poppy seeds. Add the egg and melted butter to the bowl and stir with a wooden spoon until the ingredients are well mixed. Set aside.

Turn the risen dough out on to a floured surface and knead it for 4 minutes. Roll the dough out into a rectangle 14-inches by 8-inches and about ½-inch thick. Spread the dough with the remaining butter. Fold the dough in three and turn it so that the open edges face you. Roll out again into an oblong shape and fold and turn as before. Divide the dough in half.

Roll one-half of the dough out into a rectangle 14-inches by 8-inches and ¼-inch thick. Spoon half the poppy seed mixture on to the dough and spread it out evenly, leaving a ½-inch border all round.

Carefully roll one of the short sides of the dough rectangle towards the centre, Swiss [jelly] roll style. Carefully roll the other short side of the dough rectangle towards the middle so that it meets the other 'roll'.

Repeat the shaping, filling and rolling process with the remaining dough. Trim the ends of the rolls and discard the trimmings.

Grasp one roll firmly with both hands, and turn it over and place it on one of the baking sheets, so that the smooth side is uppermost. Place the other roll on the second baking sheet in the same manner.

Cover the rolls with a cloth and return them to a warm place for 45 minutes, or until they have almost doubled in bulk.

Preheat the oven to fairly hot 400°F (Gas Mark 6, 200°C).

Brush the rolls with the beaten egg and milk mixture.

Place the baking sheets in the oven and bake for 40 minutes or until the rolls are a deep golden brown.

Remove the baking sheets from the oven. Transfer the rolls to a wire rack and set them aside to cool completely before serving.

Pork

Pork is the fresh meat from a pig, as opposed to ham and bacon which are cured before cooking. Before the advent of cold storage, pork was a very seasonal meat, but now it may be bought all the year round.

Pork that has been frozen should be cooked as soon as it is completely thawed. Ideally it should be thawed out overnight in the refrigerator, not in a warm place.

When buying good-quality pork the points to look for are fine-textured, firm, pink-coloured, smooth flesh, with no gristle (this only develops in older animals). The flesh should be 'marbled' with small specks of fat and the fat under the skin should be firm and white. The skin should be fine and springy to the touch (coarse, thick skin indicates an older animal) and the bones should be pinkish in colour.

All pork should be thoroughly cooked and never served underdone. This is because pork sometimes harbours a parasite which is dangerous to man.

Roast Loin of Pork with the skin scored into diamond shapes to produce crunchy crackling. The pork is served with fried pineapple rings.

Thorough cooking destroys the parasite. To test pork to see if it is cooked, pierce the flesh with a sharp knife; if the juices that run out are clear then the pork is cooked.

The amount of pork you buy depends on family requirements, but an approximate, if generous guide, is 6 to 8 ounces of boned meat or 8 to 12 ounces of meat with bone per person.

Pork is a rich meat which requires tart and refreshing accompaniments. Fruit such as apples, pineapples, apricots, and cranberries are ideal. Savoury, well spiced stuffings also help to moderate the richness of the meat.

The prime cuts of pork are the **leg**, which is sometimes divided into fillet and knuckle; **loin**, the best and most expensive joint from which loin chops are cut

and which is sometimes divided into hind and fore loin; **blade** or **blade bone**, which is a joint cut from the top part of the foreleg.

The medium cuts are the **hand and spring**; **belly**; **spare ribs** from which cutlets and neck chops are cut; and **chump chops**. **Fillet** is a fatless cut which is removed from either side of the backbone. The **head** is also cooked, usually whole, but sometimes split in half.

ROASTING

The leg, loin, blade, hand and spring, spare ribs, chops and head are all suitable for roasting. The only extra fat needed for roasting pork is 1 tablespoon of oil to grease the tin. To prepare a pork loin for roasting ask the butcher to chine it — this makes carving and serving simple. For a special occasion, two loins may be chined, bent outwards to form a 'crown' and the centre filled with a traditional stuffing — this is called CROWN ROAST OF PORK.

Pork may be roasted quickly or by the

slow method. To roast pork, preheat the oven to fairly hot 375°F (Gas Mark 5, 190°C). Allow 30 to 35 minutes per pound plus 30 minutes over; for joints without bone, i.e. boned and rolled, allow 40 minutes per pound plus 40 minutes over; for boned, rolled and stuffed joints allow 40 to 45 minutes per pound plus 40 to 45 minutes over.

If a meat thermometer is used the internal temperature for cooked pork should be 180°F.

If you wish to make crackling of the skin, it must be scored into parallel, thin slices $\frac{1}{4}$-inch apart, with a sharp knife. The butcher will do this if asked. Rub 1 tablespoon of coarse salt into the cuts in the skin and brush the skin with 1 tablespoon of vegetable oil. Increase the temperature to hot 425°F (Gas Mark 7, 220°C) for the last 20 minutes of the cooking time. Crackling tends to soften if the meat is kept warm.

Accompaniments for roast pork are thin brown gravy and apple sauce. However, cranberry sauce, fried apple rings and redcurrant jelly are also popular. Boned joints may be stuffed with a sage and onion stuffing, or with a dried or fresh fruit stuffing.

Roast pork is excellent cold, served with salads.

BRAISING

Pork is not usually braised, since it produces a lot of fat during cooking. If you wish to braise pork, use spare ribs or cutlets or neck chops. Allow 25 to 30 minutes per pound for spare ribs and 20 to 25 minutes for the chops.

STEWING

Although the cuts suggested for braising may be used in casseroles and stews, they give out so much fat that they should be cooked a day in advance, so that the stew may be cooled and the fat removed and discarded. However fillet, which has no fat, is ideal for casseroles and should be cooked for 45 to 55 minutes depending on the size of the meat cubes.

BOILING

All cuts of pork may be boiled for serving cold, although salt belly of pork is the cut most often boiled. Allow 30 minutes to the pound and 30 minutes over.

FRYING AND GRILLING [BROILING]

To fry pork chops, in a large frying-pan, melt a mixture of butter and oil, (1 ounce [2 tablespoons] of butter and 1 tablespoon of oil will be enough for 4 to 6 chops) over moderate heat. Add the chops, fry them for 5 minutes on each side or until they are well browned all over. Cover the pan, reduce the heat to low and cook for 25 to 35 minutes, depending on the thickness of the chops. Test the chops by piercing them with a sharp knife; if the juices run clear, the chops are done. To grill [broil] pork chops. Preheat the grill [broiler] to moderate. Trim the chops of excess fat, season them and lay them on the grill [broiler] rack. Place the pan beneath the heat and cook the chops for 15 to 20 minutes on each side — depending on the thickness of the chops.

If fillet pieces are to be grilled [broiled], brush them with melted butter frequently throughout the cooking time.

1 Spare Rib Chops, 2 Spare Rib, 3 Chump Chops, 4 Loin, 5 Loin Chops, 6 Leg, 7 Blade, 8 Hand and Spring, 9 Fillet, 10 Knuckle, 11 Belly, 12 Fillet End of Leg.

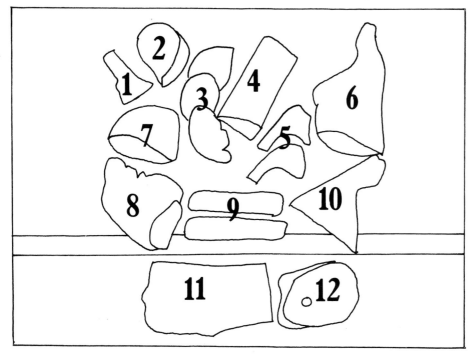

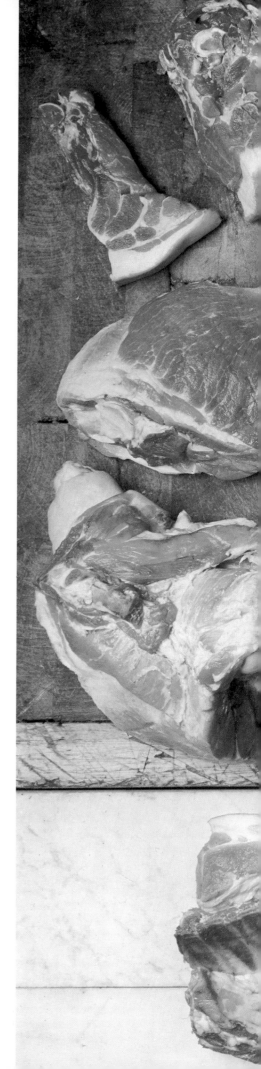

Pork and Apricot Salad

A colourful and tasty dish, Pork and Apricot Salad is a super way to use up leftover roast pork. Serve Pork and Apricot Salad with warm French bread and butter and a chilled Mateus Rosé wine.

4-6 SERVINGS

1½ lb. cooked roast pork, cut into 1-inch cubes
2 celery stalks, trimmed and finely chopped
1 small onion, finely chopped
1 large green pepper, white pith removed, seeded and finely chopped
1 large red pepper, white pith removed, seeded and finely chopped
10 oz. canned sweetcorn kernels, drained
5 oz. [2 cups] cooked rice
14 oz. canned apricot halves, drained
4 oz. [1 cup] slivered almonds
3 oz. [½ cup] sultanas or seedless raisins
6 fl. oz. [¾ cup] mayonnaise
1 tablespoon lemon juice
1 teaspoon salt
½ teaspoon black pepper
½ teaspoon curry powder

Serve Pork Balls with Ginger as part of a Chinese meal accompanied by jasmine tea. Alternatively, serve it on its own with boiled noodles.

In a large serving bowl, combine the pork, celery, onion, green and red peppers, sweetcorn, rice, apricots, almonds and sultanas or seedless raisins. Set aside.

In a small mixing bowl, beat the mayonnaise, lemon juice, salt, pepper and curry powder together with a fork until they are well blended.

Pour the mayonnaise mixture into the pork and rice mixture and mix well.

Place the bowl in the refrigerator to chill for 30 minutes before serving.

Pork Balls with Ginger

An adaptation of a Chinese recipe, Pork Balls with Ginger may be served as part of a Chinese meal or on its own with boiled rice or noodles.

4 SERVINGS

1½ lb. minced [ground] pork
1-inch piece fresh root ginger, peeled and finely chopped
4 canned water chestnuts, drained and finely chopped
1 egg
1 teaspoon salt
1 tablespoon soy sauce
5 tablespoons cornflour [cornstarch]
1 teaspoon sugar
8 dried mushrooms, soaked in warm water for 20 minutes
1 canned bamboo shoot
1 red pepper, white pith removed and seeded
1 green pepper, white pith removed and seeded
8 tablespoons vegetable oil
SAUCE
5 tablespoons wine vinegar
5 tablespoons dry sherry
2 tablespoons sugar
2 tablespoons tomato purée
1 teaspoon salt
¼ teaspoon pepper
1 teaspoon cornflour [cornstarch] dissolved in 2 tablespoons water

In a medium-sized mixing bowl, combine the pork, ginger, water chestnuts, egg, salt, soy sauce, 2 tablespoons of cornflour [cornstarch] and the sugar together. Using your hands, knead and mix the ingredients thoroughly. Shape the mixture into walnut-sized balls. Put the remaining cornflour [cornstarch] on a large plate. Roll the pork balls in the cornflour [cornstarch]. Set aside.

Remove the mushrooms from the water and squeeze them dry. Remove and discard the stalks. Put them, and the other vegetables, on a chopping board and cut them into small equal-sized dice. Set aside.

In a large frying-pan, heat 6 tablespoons of the oil over high heat. When the oil is hot, reduce the heat to moderately low. Add the pork balls and fry them, turning them frequently, for 15 minutes or until they are cooked through, and are crisp and golden brown. Transfer the pork balls, as they brown, to a warmed serving dish. Cover the dish and keep the pork balls hot while you cook the vegetables and make the sauce.

In a small mixing bowl, combine all the ingredients for the sauce except the cornflour [cornstarch]. Set aside.

Pour off and discard the oil in the frying-pan. Rinse the pan, wipe it dry with kitchen paper towels and return it to high heat for 30 seconds. Add the remaining oil. Reduce the heat to moderate and heat the oil for 30 seconds. Add the

vegetables and fry them, stirring constantly, for 3 minutes. Pour over the sauce mixture and cook, stirring constantly, for a further 3 minutes. Stir in the dissolved cornflour [cornstarch]. When the sauce thickens and becomes translucent, remove the pan from the heat and pour the sauce over the pork balls. Serve immediately.

Pork Balls in Wine Sauce

☆

This is a tasty dish of pork balls baked in a wine sauce. Serve it with buttered rice, leaf spinach and a lightly chilled Tavel rosé wine.

4 SERVINGS

1½ lb. minced [ground] pork
8 oz. lean bacon or gammon, minced [ground]
4 oz. [2 cups] fresh breadcrumbs
1 large egg
1 teaspoon salt
½ teaspoon black pepper
½ teaspoon ground allspice
2 tablespoons chopped fresh parsley
8 fl. oz. [1 cup] dry sherry
8 fl. oz. [1 cup] chicken stock
2 tablespoons wine vinegar
1 tablespoon sugar
1 teaspoon salt
4 teaspoons cornflour [cornstarch] dissolved in 3 tablespoons water

Preheat the oven to moderate 350°F (Gas Mark 4, 180°C).

In a large mixing bowl, combine the pork, bacon or gammon, breadcrumbs, egg, salt, pepper, allspice and parsley. Using your hands, mix and knead the ingredients until they are well combined. Shape the mixture into 12 balls. Place the balls, in one layer, in a large baking dish. Set aside.

In a small saucepan, combine the sherry, stock, vinegar, sugar and salt over low heat, stirring constantly. When the sugar has dissolved, increase the heat to high and bring the mixture to the boil. Reduce the heat to low and stir in the cornflour [cornstarch] mixture. Cook, stirring constantly, until the sauce has thickened slightly.

Remove the pan from the heat and pour the sauce over the meatballs.

Put the meatballs in the oven and bake them for 1½ hours, basting occasionally with the sauce.

Remove the baking dish from the oven and serve immediately, from the dish.

Succulent Pork Balls with Wine Sauce ready to be baked until crisp.

Pork Casserole with Lemon

The lemon flavouring in this recipe counter-acts the richness of the pork and enhances its flavour. Serve the casserole with jacket potatoes and steamed French beans. Pare the lemon rind in one piece so that it will be easy to remove.

8 SERVINGS

1 oz. [$\frac{1}{4}$ cup] seasoned flour, made with 1 oz. [$\frac{1}{4}$ cup] flour, $\frac{1}{2}$ teaspoon salt and $\frac{1}{2}$ teaspoon black pepper
4 lb. pork fillets, cut into 1-inch cubes
2 fl. oz. [$\frac{1}{4}$ cup] olive oil
2 garlic cloves, crushed
3 medium-sized onions, chopped
6 celery stalks, trimmed and cut into $\frac{1}{2}$-inch lengths
1$\frac{1}{2}$ pints [$3\frac{3}{4}$ cups] chicken stock
1 teaspoon dried marjoram
1 teaspoon dried chervil
$\frac{1}{2}$ teaspoon dried thyme
finely pared rind and juice of 2 lemons
2 lemons, peeled, white pith removed, segmented and chopped
1 tablespoon beurre manié

Placed the seasoned flour on a plate and coat the pork cubes in it, shaking off any excess. Set aside.

In a very large flameproof casserole, heat the oil over moderate heat. When the oil is hot, add the garlic and onions and cook them, stirring occasionally, for 5 to 7 minutes or until the onions are soft and translucent but not brown. Using a slotted spoon, transfer the onions and garlic to a plate. Set aside.

Add the pork cubes to the pan, a few at a time, and fry them, turning them frequently, for 6 to 8 minutes or until they are lightly and evenly browned. With a slotted spoon, transfer the cubes to a plate as they brown.

Return the onions and garlic to the casserole. Add the celery and pour in the chicken stock. Increase the heat to high and bring the stock to the boil, stirring constantly. Add the pork cubes and, when the mixture comes to the boil again, reduce the heat to low. Stir in the marjoram, chervil, thyme, lemon rind and juice. Cover the casserole and simmer the meat for 50 minutes or until it is tender when pierced with the point of a sharp knife.

Remove and discard the lemon rind. Increase the heat to moderate and stir in the lemon segments. Add the beurre manié, in small pieces, stirring constantly, making sure that each piece is absorbed before adding the next. Reduce the heat to low and simmer the sauce for 2 minutes, stirring frequently. Remove the casserole from the heat and serve immediately.

Pork Chilli

A simple, easy-to-prepare supper dish, Pork Chilli makes good use of convenience foods. Serve with potatoes or crusty bread and butter and a green vegetable.

4 SERVINGS

1 tablespoon butter
1 tablespoon olive oil
2 medium-sized onions, thinly sliced
1 green pepper, white pith removed, seeded and finely chopped
2 lb. boned pork shoulder, trimmed of excess fat and cut into 1-inch cubes
14 oz. canned condensed tomato soup
1 large celery stalk, trimmed and finely chopped
$\frac{1}{4}$ teaspoon hot chilli powder
14 oz. canned red kidney beans, drained
1 teaspoon salt
$\frac{1}{2}$ teaspoon black pepper

In a large saucepan, melt the butter with the oil over moderate heat. When the foam subsides, add the onions. Fry, stirring occasionally, for 8 to 10 minutes or until the onions are golden brown.

Add the green pepper and the pork cubes and cook, stirring frequently, for 6 to 8 minutes or until the pork cubes are lightly and evenly browned. Reduce the heat to low, cover the pan and cook for 35 minutes.

Add the soup, celery and chilli powder and stir well. Continue to cook, covered, for 15 minutes, or until the pork is tender when pierced with the point of a sharp knife.

Stir in the kidney beans, salt and pepper and increase the heat to moderate. Cook, uncovered and stirring occasionally, for 5 minutes. Remove the pan from the heat and serve immediately.

Pork Chops with Apples

This is probably the simplest, certainly the most traditional and, to many people, the best way of serving pork chops. They are seasoned, fried in a little butter and cooked with apples. Roast potatoes are the traditional accompaniment to Pork Chops with Apples and shredded cabbage or green beans may be served too.

4 SERVINGS

4 large pork chops
$\frac{1}{2}$ teaspoon salt
$\frac{1}{4}$ teaspoon black pepper
1 teaspoon dried rosemary
1 oz. [2 tablespoons] butter
3 cooking apples, peeled, cored and thinly sliced
1 tablespoon soft brown sugar

Place the pork chops on a board and rub them all over with the salt, pepper and rosemary. Set aside.

In a large frying-pan, melt the butter

over moderate heat. When the foam subsides, add the chops and cook them for 10 minutes on each side.

Add the sliced apples to the pan and sprinkle over the sugar. Cover the pan and cook for 20 to 30 minutes, or until the pork chops are thoroughly cooked and tender.

Using tongs, transfer the chops to a heated serving dish. Keep them hot while you finish cooking the apples.

Increase the heat to moderately high and cook the apples, stirring constantly, for 3 minutes.

Remove the pan from the heat. Spoon the apples over the pork.

Serve immediately.

Pork Chops Baked with Cabbage

An appetizing and nutritious dish, Pork Chops Baked with Cabbage is very easy to prepare. Serve with creamed potatoes and glazed carrots for a sustaining dinner for the family.

4 SERVINGS
1 oz. [2 tablespoons] butter
2 tablespoons vegetable oil
4 large pork chops
1 onion, finely chopped
1 garlic clove, crushed
½ teaspoon salt
¼ teaspoon black pepper
2 lb. cabbage, coarse outer leaves removed, washed, cut into julienne strips, cooked for 5 minutes and drained
8 fl. oz. [1 cup] chicken stock
1 tablespoon beurre manié
bouquet garni, consisting of 4 parsley sprigs, 1 thyme spray and 1 bay leaf tied together

In a large frying-pan, melt the butter with the oil over moderate heat. When the foam subsides, add the pork chops and fry for 5 minutes on each side or until they are well browned all over. Using tongs, transfer the chops to a plate. Set aside.

Add the onion, garlic, salt and pepper to the pan. Fry, stirring occasionally, for 5 to 7 minutes or until the onion is soft and translucent but not brown. Add the cabbage to the pan and cook the mixture, stirring frequently, for 5 minutes. Remove the pan from the heat and, using a slotted spoon, remove the onion and cabbage mixture from the pan. Set the pan aside.

Preheat the oven to moderate 350°F (Gas Mark 4, 180°C).

Arrange about one-third of the cabbage and onion mixture on the bottom of a large ovenproof casserole. Lay two pork chops on top and cover with half of the remaining cabbage. Make another layer with the remaining chops and finish with a layer of cabbage. Set aside.

Pour the chicken stock into the frying-pan and set the pan over high heat. Bring the stock to the boil, stirring frequently. Reduce the heat to low and stir in the beurre manié, a little at a time. Cook the sauce for 2 minutes or until it is fairly thick and smooth. Remove the pan from the heat. Taste the sauce and add more salt and pepper if necessary. Pour the sauce into the casserole and add the bouquet garni. Cover the casserole, place it in the oven and bake for 1 to 1½ hours or until the chops are thoroughly cooked and tender.

Remove the casserole from the oven. Remove and discard the bouquet garni, and serve at once.

Lemon-flavoured Pork Casserole in which you can almost taste the sunshine! Serve it with jacket potatoes and some crisply cooked vegetables.

Pork Chops Baked with Cream and Tarragon

The perfect dish for an informal dinner party, Pork Chops Baked with Cream and Tarragon is easy to prepare and you can just forget about it while it is cooking. Serve the chops wrapped in the foil, accompanied by croquette potatoes and minted peas. A chilled bottle of Liebfraumilch would be an excellent accompaniment.

6 SERVINGS

2 teaspoons vegetable oil
6 large pork chops
1 teaspoon salt
½ teaspoon black pepper
1 tablespoon finely chopped fresh tarragon or 1 teaspoon dried tarragon
2 oz. [¼ cup] butter
1 medium-sized onion, finely chopped
10 oz. button mushrooms, wiped clean and finely chopped
1 tablespoon flour
6 tablespoons double [heavy] cream

Preheat the oven to moderate 350°F (Gas Mark 4, 180°C).

Tasty toppings enhance the flavour of these Pork Chops with Cheese and Pork Chops Baked with Cream and Tarragon. Serve with glazed carrots.

Cut out 6 pieces of aluminium foil, approximately 6-inches by 10-inches, or large enough to completely wrap around a pork chop. Using a pastry brush, coat one side of each piece of foil with a little oil. Set aside.

Place the pork chops on a board and rub them all over with the salt, pepper and tarragon. Set aside.

Remove the pan from the heat and gradually add the cream, stirring constantly. Return the pan to moderate heat and cook the onion and mushroom mixture for 1 minute, stirring constantly. Remove the pan from the heat. Set aside.

Place one chop in the middle of each piece of aluminium foil. Cover each chop with two tablespoons of the mushroom mixture. Carefully bring together the edges of the foil and seal the parcel by folding the edges over.

Arrange the parcels on a baking sheet and bake in the oven for 1 to 1¼ hours or until the chops are thoroughly cooked and tender. Remove the baking sheet from the oven. Serve the pork immediately in the aluminium foil.

Pork Chops Braised with Onions and Wine

   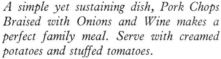

A simple yet sustaining dish, Pork Chops Braised with Onions and Wine makes a perfect family meal. Serve with creamed potatoes and stuffed tomatoes.

6 SERVINGS

1 tablespoon butter
6 large pork chops
1 teaspoon salt
½ teaspoon black pepper
1 garlic clove, crushed
1 tablespoon grated orange rind
1 teaspoon dried sage
1 teaspoon dried marjoram
2 large onions, thinly sliced
4 fl. oz. [½ cup] chicken stock
6 fl. oz. [¾ cup] dry white wine
1 tablespoon beurre manié
2 tablespoons double [heavy] cream

Using the butter, generously grease a large shallow, flameproof baking dish. Set aside.

Preheat the oven to moderate 350°F (Gas Mark 4, 180°C).

Place the pork chops on a board and rub them all over with the salt, pepper, garlic, orange rind, sage and marjoram.

Place the chops, in one layer, on the bottom of the baking dish. Cover the chops with the onion slices. Pour over the chicken stock and wine.

Place the dish in the centre of the oven and bake the chops for 1 to 1½ hours or until the chops are thoroughly cooked and tender. Remove the baking dish from the oven. With a slotted spoon, transfer the chops and the onions to a warmed serving dish. Keep hot while you prepare the sauce.

Place the baking dish over moderate heat and bring the liquid to the boil. Continue to boil, stirring frequently, for

5 minutes or until the liquid has reduced by about a third. Stir in the beurre manié, a little at a time, and cook, stirring constantly, for 2 minutes or until the sauce is smooth and fairly thick. Stir in the cream and cook for a further 30 seconds, or until the sauce is heated through.

Remove the dish from the heat. Pour the sauce over the pork chops and onions. Serve immediately.

Pork Chops with Cheese

This is an easy and delicious way to cook pork chops. Serve Pork Chops with Cheese with baked potatoes and glazed carrots and, to drink, a lightly chilled Tavel rosé wine.

4 SERVINGS

1 teaspoon salt
½ teaspoon black pepper
¼ teaspoon cayenne pepper
1 garlic clove, crushed
4 large pork chops
1 tablespoon butter
1 tablespoon olive oil
1 oz [¼ cup] Gruyère cheese, grated
1 oz. [¼ cup] Parmesan cheese, grated
2 teaspoons prepared French mustard
1 egg
1 tablespoon milk

In a small saucer, combine the salt, black pepper, cayenne and garlic. Rub the mixture all over the pork chops. Set aside.

In a large frying-pan, melt the butter with the oil over moderate heat. When the foam subsides, add the pork chops and cook them for 3 minutes on each side or until they are lightly browned all over. Reduce the heat to low, cover the pan and cook the chops for 25 to 40 minutes, depending on the thickness of the chops, or until they are thoroughly cooked and tender.

Meanwhile, in a small mixing bowl, combine the Gruyère, Parmesan, mustard, egg and milk, beating with a spoon until the mixture forms a smooth paste. Set aside.

Preheat the grill [broiler] to high. Line the grill [broiler] pan with aluminium foil.

Remove the frying-pan from the heat and transfer the pork chops to the rack in the pan. Using a table knife, spread the cheese paste over the pork chops. Place the pan under the heat. Grill [broil] the chops for 2 minutes or until the cheese is golden brown. Remove the pan from under the heat.

Transfer the chops to a warmed serving dish and serve immediately.

In a large frying-pan, melt the butter over moderate heat. When the foam subsides, add the pork chops, three at a time, and cook for 5 minutes on each side, or until they are golden brown all over.

With tongs, transfer the chops to a plate and set aside.

Pour off all but 2 tablespoons of the fat in the frying-pan. Place the pan over moderate heat. Add the onion and fry, stirring occasionally, for 5 to 7 minutes or until it is soft and translucent but not brown. Add the mushrooms and cook for 3 minutes, stirring occasionally. Stir in the flour and cook for 30 seconds.

Pork Chops with Cranberry Sauce

The sour-sweet taste of cranberries enhances the flavour of the meat in delicious Pork Chops with Cranberry Sauce. Served on a bed of creamed potatoes, with green beans or courgettes [zucchini]. A chilled white Zilavka wine would go well with this dish — and may also be used in the sauce.

4 SERVINGS

1 oz. [¼ cup] seasoned flour, made with 1 oz. [¼ cup] flour, 1 teaspoon salt, ¼ teaspoon cayenne pepper and ½ teaspoon dried rosemary
4 large boned pork chops
1 tablespoon butter
1 tablespoon vegetable oil
4 tablespoons canned cranberries
5 fl. oz. [⅝ cup] dry white wine
¼ teaspoon salt
¼ teaspoon black pepper
2 tablespoons double [heavy] cream

Place the seasoned flour on a plate and dip each chop into it, coating thoroughly on all sides. Shake off any excess flour. Set aside.

In a large frying-pan, melt the butter with the oil over moderate heat. When the foam subsides, add the pork chops and fry them for 5 minutes on each side

Tangy flavoured Pork Chops with Cranberry Sauce are served with courgettes [zucchini] and potatoes.

or until they are well browned all over. Reduce the heat to moderately low and continue cooking the chops for 20 to 30 minutes or until they are thoroughly cooked and tender. Using tongs, transfer the pork chops to a warmed serving dish. Cover the dish and keep the chops hot while you finish making the sauce.

Remove the pan from the heat and pour off all but a tablespoon of the cooking fat. Return the pan to the heat and stir in the cranberries, wine, salt and pepper. Bring the mixture to the boil.

Stirring constantly with a wooden spoon, cook the sauce for 5 minutes. Stir in the cream and cook for 30 seconds more. Remove the pan from the heat and pour the sauce over the chops. Serve immediately.

Pork Chops with Morello Cherries

Pork chops marinated in Marsala and flavoured with cherries is a delightful dish to look at and delicious to eat. Serve with

green beans and new potatoes. If Morello cherries are not available ordinary black cherries may be used instead.

6 SERVINGS

6 large pork chops
1 teaspoon salt
½ teaspoon black pepper
1 small onion, thinly sliced
14 oz. canned Morello cherries, drained and 4 tablespoons of the can juice reserved
3 tablespoons Marsala
6 spring onions [scallions], trimmed and finely chopped
4 parsley stalks
½-inch piece fresh root ginger, peeled and finely chopped
1 oz. [2 tablespoons] butter
1 tablespoon vegetable oil

Place the pork chops on a board and rub them all over with the salt and pepper. Arrange the chops in a shallow dish and cover them with onion slices.

In a small mixing bowl, combine the reserved cherry can juice, the Marsala, spring onions [scallions], parsley stalks and ginger. Spoon the mixture over the chops and set aside to marinate for 45 minutes, turning them occasionally.

Remove the chops from the marinade and pat them dry with kitchen paper towels. Reserve the marinade.

Cherries are an ideal, but different, accompaniment to pork. Pork Chops with Morello Cherries are delicious served with beans and potatoes.

Pork Chops with Mushroom and Parsley Stuffing

  ①

The delicate flavour of this dish is enhanced by Maître d'Hôtel Butter. Glazed carrots and button onions are an ideal accompaniment, together with a glass of chilled white wine.

4 SERVINGS

4 double loin pork chops
1 tablespoon chopped fresh parsley
1 oz. [½ cup] fresh white
    breadcrumbs
¼ teaspoon cayenne pepper
¼ teaspoon black pepper
½ teaspoon salt
1 oz. [2 tablespoons] butter
1 small onion, finely chopped
1 garlic clove, crushed
2 oz. mushrooms, wiped clean and
    finely chopped
1 tablespoon vegetable oil
2 oz. [¼ cup] Maître d'Hôtel
    Butter, sliced

Preheat the oven to warm 325°F (Gas Mark 3, 170°C).

Place the pork chops flat on a wooden board. With a sharp knife, cut horizontal slits into the meaty part of the chops to make pockets. Set aside.

In a small bowl, combine the parsley,

Pork Chops Stuffed with Mushrooms and Parsley will grace any table accompanied by carrots and onions.

breadcrumbs, cayenne, black pepper and salt. Set aside.

In a small saucepan, melt the butter over moderate heat. When the foam subsides, add the onion and garlic and cook, stirring occasionally, for 5 to 7 minutes or until the onion is soft and translucent but not brown. Add the mushrooms and cook, stirring occasionally, for 3 minutes.

Remove the pan from the heat and, with a wooden spoon, stir the onion and mushroom mixture into the parsley mixture. Stir to blend.

Spoon the stuffing into the pockets in the chops until all the stuffing has been used. Close each pocket by pushing a cocktail stick through the two layers of meat. Place the chops in a large ovenproof casserole and brush them with the oil.

Cover the casserole and place it in the centre of the oven. Bake the chops for 1 hour. Uncover the casserole and continue cooking for a further 30 minutes.

Remove the casserole from the oven and remove and discard the cocktail sticks. Place the chops on a warmed serving dish, top them with slices of the maître d'hôtel butter and serve at once.

In a large frying-pan, melt the butter with the oil over moderate heat. When the foam subsides, add three of the chops to the pan and fry them for 5 minutes on each side or until they are well browned all over. Reduce the heat to moderately low and cook for 20 to 30 minutes or until they are thoroughly cooked and tender. With tongs, transfer the chops to a warmed serving plate. Keep warm while you cook the remaining chops in the same way, adding a little more butter and oil if necessary.

(If you have two large frying-pans, cook all of the chops at the same time dividing the butter and oil between the two pans and adding a little more if necessary.)

Remove the pan from the heat and pour off and discard the fat.

Remove and discard the onion slices and the parsley stalks from the marinade. Pour the marinade and the cherries into the frying-pan and return it to moderate heat. Bring the mixture to the boil, stirring constantly. Remove the pan from the heat and pour the sauce over the pork chops. Serve immediately.

Pork Chops with Mushrooms and Tomatoes

A succulent and simple dish to prepare, Pork Chops with Mushrooms and Tomatoes is ideal for an informal dinner party. Serve with roast potatoes. For the tastiest result, ask the butcher to bone and roll a pork loin and then cut 4 chops each about $\frac{3}{4}$-inch thick.

4 SERVINGS

Low Cal

4 boned loin pork chops
2 tablespoons vegetable oil
1 teaspoon dried thyme
1 teaspoon salt
$\frac{1}{2}$ teaspoon black pepper
1 tablespoon butter
4 oz. mushrooms, wiped clean and sliced
14 oz. canned peeled tomatoes, chopped
1 teaspoon dried sage
1 tablespoon chopped fresh parsley

Preheat the grill [broiler] to high. Using a pastry brush, brush the pork chops with the oil. Sprinkle with the thyme, half the salt and half the pepper. Lay the chops on the rack in the grill [broiler] pan and place the pan under the heat. Grill [broil] the chops for 5 minutes on each side. Reduce the heat to moderately low and cook for a further 15 to 20 minutes on each side, depending on the thickness of the chops, or until they are thoroughly cooked and tender.

Meanwhile, make the sauce. In a large frying-pan, melt the butter over moderate heat. When the foam subsides, add the mushrooms and fry, stirring occasionally, for 3 minutes. Add the tomatoes with the can juice, the sage, parsley and the remaining salt and pepper. Cover the pan, reduce the heat to low and cook the sauce, stirring occasionally, for 25 minutes. Remove the pan from the heat.

Remove the grill [broiler] pan from under the heat. Using tongs, transfer the chops to a warmed serving dish. Arrange the meat in the dish and spoon the sauce over and around the meat. Serve at once.

Pork Chops with Mustard Sauce

An easy-to-make dish, Pork Chops with Mustard Sauce makes an excellent main course for a dinner or formal lunch. Serve with puréed potatoes and Brussels sprouts.

4 SERVINGS

4 large pork chops
1 teaspoon salt
1 teaspoon black pepper
2 teaspoons paprika

3 oz. [$\frac{3}{8}$ cup] butter
3 shallots, finely chopped
1 garlic clove, crushed
8 oz. button mushrooms, wiped clean and sliced
3 fl. oz. [$\frac{3}{8}$ cup] brandy
2 tablespoons prepared French mustard
8 fl. oz. double cream [1 cup heavy cream]
1 tablespoon cornflour [cornstarch] dissolved in 2 tablespoons double [heavy] cream

Place the pork chops on a board and rub them all over with the salt, pepper and paprika. Set aside.

In a large frying-pan, melt 2 ounces [$\frac{1}{4}$ cup] of the butter over moderate heat.

When the foam subsides, add the chops and cook them for 3 minutes on each side or until they are lightly browned all over. With tongs, transfer the chops to a plate. Set aside.

Add the remaining butter to the pan and melt it over moderate heat. When the foam subsides, add the shallots and garlic and cook, stirring occasionally, for 3 to 4 minutes or until the shallots are soft and translucent but not brown. Add the mushrooms and stir well to mix. Cook the mixture, stirring occasionally, for 3 minutes.

Reduce the heat to low and return the chops to the pan, basting them well. Cover the pan and simmer the chops, turning once or twice, for 20 minutes. Remove the pan from the heat.

*Both Pork Chops with Mushrooms
and Tomatoes and Pork Chops with
Pistachio Nut Stuffing are super!*

8 fl. oz. [1 cup] dry white wine
2 tablespoons double [heavy] cream
STUFFING
  1 tablespoon butter
  2 bacon slices, chopped
  1 small onion, finely chopped
  1 garlic clove, crushed
  2 chicken livers, chopped
  1 tablespoon pistachio nuts,
    chopped
  2 tablespoons fresh breadcrumbs
  $\frac{1}{2}$ small egg, lightly beaten
  $\frac{1}{4}$ teaspoon salt
  $\frac{1}{8}$ teaspoon black pepper
  1 tablespoon brandy

First, make the stuffing. In a small frying-pan, melt the butter over moderate heat. When the foam subsides, add the bacon to the pan and fry for 5 minutes, or until it is crisp and has rendered most of its fat. Add the onion and garlic and fry, stirring occasionally, for 5 to 7 minutes or until the onion is soft and translucent but not brown. Add the chicken livers and cook for a further 2 minutes, stirring frequently.

Remove the pan from the heat. Stir in the pistachio nuts, breadcrumbs and egg. Season with the salt and pepper and stir in the brandy. Stir well until the mixture is thoroughly combined. Set aside.

Place the chops on a board. Using a sharp knife, cut horizontal slits into the meaty part of the chops to make pockets. Spoon the stuffing into the pockets in the chops until all the stuffing has been used. Close each pocket by pushing a cocktail stick through the two layers of meat.

In a large, flameproof casserole, heat the oil over moderate heat. When the oil is hot, add the chops and fry them for 7 minutes on each side. Pour over the wine and, when it comes to the boil, reduce the heat to low. Cover the casserole and simmer for 1 hour or until the chops are thoroughly cooked and tender.

Remove the casserole from the heat. Using a slotted spoon, transfer the chops to a warmed serving dish. Remove and discard the cocktail sticks. Set aside and keep hot while you finish the sauce.

Return the casserole to the heat. Increase the heat to high and bring the sauce to the boil. Reduce the heat to low and stir in the cream.

Cook the sauce for 30 seconds or until it is heated through.

Remove the casserole from the heat, pour the sauce over the chops and serve at once.

Meanwhile, in a small saucepan, heat the brandy over low heat until it is hot but not boiling.

Pour the brandy into the frying-pan and ignite. When the flames have died down, return the pan to low heat and cook, uncovered, for a further 10 to 20 minutes, depending on the thickness of the chops, or until they are thoroughly cooked and tender.

Using tongs or a fork, transfer the chops to a warmed serving dish. Keep warm while you finish making the sauce.

Bring the liquid to the boil over high heat. Reduce the heat to moderate and boil for 5 minutes or until it has reduced by about one-third.

Add the mustard, cream and the corn-flour [cornstarch] mixture and stir well to mix. Cook the mixture, stirring occasionally, for 3 minutes or until the sauce has thickened and is smooth.

Remove the pan from the heat and pour the mixture over the chops. Serve at once.

Pork Chops with Pistachio Nut Stuffing

An unusual and tasty way to cook pork, Pork Chops with Pistachio Nut Stuffing may be accompanied by steamed cauliflower, petits pois and sautéed potatoes.

6 SERVINGS

6 double loin pork chops
2 tablespoons vegetable oil

Pork Chops with Rosemary

Pork chops flavoured with rosemary, basil and marjoram and cooked in cider, Pork Chops with Rosemary may be served with a green vegetable and sautéed potatoes.

6 SERVINGS

1 oz. [$\frac{1}{4}$ cup] seasoned flour, made with 1 oz. [$\frac{1}{4}$ cup] flour, $\frac{1}{4}$ teaspoon salt and $\frac{1}{8}$ teaspoon black pepper
6 large loin pork chops
1$\frac{1}{2}$ oz. [3 tablespoons] butter
1 tablespoon vegetable oil
1 large onion, finely chopped
1 teaspoon dried rosemary
$\frac{1}{2}$ teaspoon dried basil
$\frac{1}{2}$ teaspoon dried marjoram
$\frac{1}{4}$ teaspoon salt
$\frac{1}{8}$ teaspoon black pepper
10 fl. oz. [1$\frac{1}{4}$ cups] dry cider

Preheat the oven to moderate 350°F (Gas Mark 4, 180°C).

Place the seasoned flour on a plate and dip each chop into it, coating thoroughly on both sides. Shake off any excess flour.

In a large flameproof casserole, melt the butter with the oil over moderate heat. When the foam subsides, add the chops to the casserole and fry for 5 minutes on each side or until they are well browned all over. Using tongs, transfer the chops to a plate.

Add the onion to the casserole and fry, stirring occasionally, for 5 to 7 minutes or until it is soft and translucent but not brown.

Return the chops to the casserole and sprinkle with the rosemary, basil, marjoram, salt and pepper. Pour over the cider.

Cover the casserole and place it in the oven. Bake for 1 to 1$\frac{1}{2}$ hours or until the chops are thoroughly cooked and tender.

Remove the casserole from the oven and serve immediately, from the casserole.

Pork Curry

This is a spicy, pungent curry which is best served with plain boiled rice, Old-Fashioned Date Chutney and an onion and tomato salad. Reduce the number of chillis and chilli powder if you prefer a milder curry.

6 SERVINGS

1 tablespoon ground coriander
1 teaspoon ground cumin
1 teaspoon hot chilli powder
1$\frac{1}{2}$ teaspoons turmeric
$\frac{1}{2}$ teaspoon ground cinnamon
$\frac{1}{2}$ teaspoon ground cardamom
$\frac{1}{2}$ teaspoon ground cloves
$\frac{1}{2}$ teaspoon black pepper

3 tablespoons vinegar
4 tablespoons vegetable oil
3 medium-sized onions, finely chopped
3 garlic cloves, crushed
2-inch piece fresh root ginger, peeled and finely chopped
2 to 3 green chillis, finely chopped
3 lb. pork fillets, cut into 2-inch cubes
1$\frac{1}{2}$ teaspoons salt
1 teaspoon sugar
1$\frac{1}{2}$-inch slice creamed coconut dissolved in 1 pint [2$\frac{1}{2}$ cups] boiling water

In a small mixing bowl, combine the coriander, cumin, chilli powder, turmeric, cinnamon, cardamom, cloves and black pepper. Pour over the vinegar and stir until the mixture forms a smooth paste. Set aside.

In a large saucepan, heat the oil over moderate heat. When the oil is hot, add the onions and fry, stirring occasionally, for 8 to 10 minutes or until they are golden brown.

Add the garlic, ginger and chillis and fry, stirring frequently, for 3 minutes. Add the spice paste and fry, stirring constantly, for 10 minutes. If the mixture gets too dry add a spoonful of vinegar or water. Add the pork cubes and fry, stirring frequently, for 6 to 8 minutes or until the pork no longer looks raw. Add the salt and sugar and pour over the coconut mixture. Stir the mixture and bring it to the boil. Cover the pan, reduce the heat to low and simmer the curry for 1 to 1$\frac{1}{4}$ hours or until the pork is very tender when pierced with the point of a sharp knife.

Taste the curry and add more salt if necessary. Spoon the curry into a warmed serving dish and serve immediately.

Pork Fillets in Cream Sauce

A delightful and flavoursome dish, Pork Fillets in Cream Sauce may be served with a border of thickly piped Duchess Potatoes and garnished with lemon slices and parsley sprigs.

8 SERVINGS

4 lb. pork fillets, cut into 1-inch cubes
3 medium-sized onions, sliced
4 medium-sized carrots, scraped and sliced
3 celery stalks, trimmed and chopped
juice of 1 lemon
10 fl. oz. [1$\frac{1}{4}$ cups] dry white wine
1$\frac{1}{2}$ pints [3$\frac{3}{4}$ cups] water

1 teaspoon salt
bouquet garni, consisting of 4 parsley sprigs, 1 thyme spray and 1 bay leaf tied together
1$\frac{1}{2}$ oz. [3 tablespoons] butter
6 tablespoons flour
4 egg yolks
10 fl. oz. single cream [1$\frac{1}{4}$ cups light cream]

Place the pork cubes, onions, carrots, celery, lemon juice, wine, water, salt and bouquet garni in a large flameproof casserole. Set the casserole over high heat and bring the liquid to the boil. When the mixture boils, cover the pan and reduce the heat to low. Simmer the mixture for 50 minutes or until the pork cubes are tender when pierced with the point of a sharp knife.

Remove the casserole from the heat. Using a slotted spoon, transfer the pork cubes and vegetables to a plate and keep warm. Remove and discard the bouquet garni. Measure the cooking liquid and reserve 1$\frac{1}{2}$ pints [3$\frac{3}{4}$ cups] of it. Discard the remaining cooking liquid, if any.

In a large saucepan, melt the butter over moderate heat. When the foam subsides, reduce the heat to low. Stir in the flour with a wooden spoon and cook, stirring frequently, for 1 minute. Remove the pan from the heat. Gradually add the reserved cooking liquid, stirring constantly, being careful to avoid lumps. Return the pan to the heat and, stirring constantly, bring the sauce to the boil. Reduce the heat to low and cook for 5 minutes, stirring frequently.

Meanwhile, in a small mixing bowl, combine the egg yolks and cream. Set aside. Remove the pan from the heat. If the sauce is lumpy, which may happen when making such a large quantity of sauce, pour it through a strainer into a clean saucepan before continuing.

Add 2 tablespoons of the sauce to the egg mixture and beat until the ingredients are well blended. Pour the egg and sauce mixture back into the saucepan and stir well. Return the pan to low heat and stir in the meat and vegetables. Cook them, stirring frequently, for 8 minutes. Do not allow the sauce to boil or the egg yolks will scramble.

Remove the pan from the heat. Pour the contents of the pan into a large, warmed serving dish and serve immediately.

An attractive dish for a dinner party, Pork Fillets in Cream Sauce are garnished with spirals of Duchess Potato, lemon slices and parsley. Serve with a well-chilled white Burgundy.

Pork Fillets, Korean-Style

An adaptation of a traditional dish, Pork Fillets, Korean-Style is simple to prepare — and delicious to eat! Serve with puréed potatoes, Courgettes Grillées and a tossed salad for a nourishing meal.

4 SERVINGS

2 lb. pork fillets, thinly sliced
2 tablespoons sesame oil

MARINADE

4 fl. oz. [$\frac{1}{2}$ cup] soy sauce
2 fl. oz. [$\frac{1}{4}$ cup] water
3 tablespoons sugar
2 spring onions [scallions], finely chopped
2 garlic cloves, crushed
1-inch piece fresh root ginger, peeled and finely chopped
$\frac{1}{8}$ teaspoon salt
10 black peppercorns, crushed

(Low Cal)

First, make the marinade. In a large mixing bowl, combine all of the marinade ingredients together, stirring to mix well. Arrange the pork slices in the marinade and baste to coat the meat thoroughly. Marinate the meat, at room temperature, for 2 hours, basting occasionally.

Preheat the oven to fairly hot 375°F (Gas Mark 5, 190°C).

Remove the pork slices from the marinade and pat them dry with kitchen paper towels. Reserve the marinade.

With a pastry brush, generously coat the bottom and sides of a large baking dish with the sesame oil. Arrange the pork slices in the baking dish, in one layer if possible. Cover the dish and bake the meat for 45 minutes to 1 hour or until it is very tender when pierced with the point of a sharp knife.

Meanwhile, pour the marinade into a small saucepan. Place the saucepan over high heat and bring the liquid to the boil. Reduce the heat to low and simmer the sauce for 10 to 15 minutes or until it has reduced slightly.

When the meat is cooked, remove it from the oven and arrange the slices on a large, warmed serving dish.

Pour the pork cooking juices into the reduced marinade and bring the mixture to the boil over high heat. Remove the pan from the heat and strain the sauce into a sauceboat. Serve the pork at once, with the sauce.

Pork Fillets with Red Wine

Pork Fillets with Red Wine is a Danish dish, usually served with horseradish and apple sauce. It makes an excellent and filling meal accompanied by sautéed potatoes and broccoli.

Spicy Pork Fillets, Korean-Style are so simple to prepare! Serve them with a crisp green salad for a quick and tasty lunch or dinner.

6 SERVINGS

4 oz. [$\frac{1}{2}$ cup] butter
2 fl. oz. [$\frac{1}{4}$ cup] olive oil
3 lb. pork fillets, cut into thick slices
2 large onions, chopped
1 teaspoon salt
$\frac{1}{2}$ teaspoon black pepper
12 fl. oz. [1$\frac{1}{2}$ cups] red wine
10 oz. mushrooms, wiped clean and sliced
2 tablespoons flour
12 fl. oz. double cream [1$\frac{1}{2}$ cups heavy cream]

Preheat the oven to moderate 350°F (Gas Mark 4, 180°C).

In a large, heavy frying-pan, melt 2 ounces [$\frac{1}{4}$ cup] of the butter with the oil over moderate heat. When the foam subsides, add the pork slices and fry them for 1 to 2 minutes on each side or until they are lightly and evenly browned. With a slotted spoon, remove the pork slices from the pan and place them in a large, ovenproof casserole. Set aside.

Add the onions to the frying-pan and fry them, stirring occasionally, for 5 to 7 minutes or until they are soft and translucent but not brown. With a slotted spoon, transfer the onions to the casserole, arranging them on top of the meat. Sprinkle over the salt and pepper and pour over the wine.

Place the casserole in the oven and cook the meat for 1½ hours or until it is tender when pierced with the point of a sharp knife.

Fifteen minutes before the end of the cooking time, in a small saucepan, melt the remaining butter over moderate heat. When the foam subsides, add the mushrooms and cook them, stirring occasionally, for 3 minutes. With a slotted spoon, transfer the mushrooms to the casserole for the remainder of the cooking time.

Remove the casserole from the oven. With a pair of tongs, remove the meat slices and place them on a warmed, large serving dish. Keep them warm while you make the sauce.

In a small saucepan, combine the flour

Be sure to give generous servings of Pork Fried Rice, as it disappears like magic and people are sure to come back for more. Serve with a tomato and cucumber salad.

and cream, beating with a wooden spoon until they form a smooth paste. Add the casserole juices and set the pan over low heat. Cook, stirring constantly, for 3 minutes or until the sauce is thick and smooth and hot but not boiling.

Remove the pan from the heat and pour the sauce over the meat. Serve immediately.

Pork Fried Rice

This is a wonderful way to use up leftover roast pork. Serve Pork Fried Rice on its own as a light luncheon dish, or for supper accompanied by a salad. Chicken or beef may be substituted for the pork if you prefer.

4 SERVINGS

3 tablespoons vegetable oil
1 small onion, finely chopped
2 celery stalks, trimmed and finely chopped
2 small carrots, scraped and finely chopped
8 oz. cooked roast pork, cut into strips 1-inch long
½ small cabbage, coarse outer leaves removed, washed and finely shredded

½ teaspoon black pepper
2 tablespoons soy sauce
8 oz. [3 cups] cooked long-grain rice
2 eggs, lightly beaten
¼ teaspoon salt

In a large frying-pan, heat 2 tablespoons of the oil over moderate heat. When the oil is hot, add the onion, celery and carrots and cook, stirring constantly, for 5 minutes. Stir in the pork, cabbage, pepper, soy sauce and rice and cook, stirring constantly, for a further 2 to 3 minutes or until the mixture is hot. Moisten with a little water or chicken stock if the mixture is dry. Set aside and keep hot while you make the garnish.

In a small frying-pan, heat the remaining oil over moderate heat. When the oil is hot, add the beaten eggs and salt and cook for 2 minutes. When the bottom is set and lightly browned turn the omelet over, using a fish slice. Cook for a further 2 to 3 minutes or until the omelet is completely set. Remove the pan from the heat and, using the fish slice, remove the omelet from the pan. Cut the omelet into strips 1-inch by ¼-inch.

Spoon the rice mixture on to a warmed serving dish. Garnish with the omelet strips and serve at once.

Pork with Ginger and Pineapple

This is just the dish for an informal dinner party. It is easy to make, can be made in advance and reheated when needed and will not spoil if it cooks a little longer than necessary. Use fresh pineapple if possible. Serve with buttered rice or noodles and accompany with a chilled Rosé d'Anjou wine.

8 SERVINGS

1 oz. [2 tablespoons] butter
3 tablespoons vegetable oil
4 lb. pork fillets, cut into 1-inch cubes
3-inch piece fresh root ginger, peeled and chopped
2 garlic cloves, crushed
2 tablespoons tomato purée
2 tablespoons wine vinegar
1 tablespoon soft brown sugar
1½ teaspoons salt
½ teaspoon black pepper
2 tablespoons flour
15 fl. oz. [1⅞ cups] dry white wine
15 fl. oz. [1⅞ cups] chicken stock
2 red peppers, white pith removed, seeded and cut into pieces
2 green peppers, white pith removed, seeded and cut into pieces
1 medium-sized pineapple, peeled, cored and cubed

In a large saucepan, melt the butter with the oil over moderate heat. When the foam subsides, add the pork cubes, a few at a time, and fry them, turning them frequently, for 6 to 8 minutes or until they are lightly and evenly browned. With a slotted spoon, transfer the cubes to a plate as they brown. Set aside.

Add the ginger and garlic to the pan and fry, stirring constantly, for 2 minutes. Stir in the tomato purée, vinegar, sugar, salt, pepper and flour. Pour in the wine and stock and, stirring constantly, bring the mixture to the boil. When the mixture comes to the boil, add the pork cubes. Cover the pan, reduce the heat to low and simmer the pork for 40 minutes.

Uncover the pan and add the peppers and pineapple. Increase the heat to moderate and cook for a further 10 minutes, or until the pork is tender when pierced with the point of a sharp knife. Taste the sauce and add more salt and pepper if necessary.

Remove the pan from the heat and spoon the mixture into a warmed serving dish.

Serve immediately.

Pork Goulasch

A delicious stew with a Hungarian flavour, Pork Goulasch is a tasty combination of pork, sauerkraut, sour cream and caraway seeds. Serve with buttered noodles and tomato salad and, to drink, a well-chilled Hungarian Riesling.

4 SERVINGS

2 oz. [¼ cup] butter
2 lb. pork fillets, cut into 2-inch cubes
3 medium-sized onions, thinly sliced

2 garlic cloves, crushed
1½ lb. canned sauerkraut, drained
½ teaspoon dried dill
1 teaspoon caraway seeds
1 teaspoon salt
1 teaspoon black pepper
8 fl. oz. [1 cup] chicken stock
8 fl. oz. [1 cup] sour cream

In a large, flameproof casserole, melt the butter over moderate heat. When the foam subsides, add the pork cubes, a few at a time, and cook them, turning occasionally, for 6 to 8 minutes or until they are lightly and evenly browned. With a slotted spoon, transfer the cubes, as they brown, to a plate.

Add the onions and garlic to the casserole and cook, stirring occasionally, for 5 to 7 minutes or until the onions are soft and translucent but not brown. Stir in the sauerkraut, dill, caraway seeds, salt, pepper and stock and bring to the boil.

Return the pork cubes to the casserole and stir well to mix. Reduce the heat to low, cover the casserole and simmer the goulasch for 1 to 1¼ hours or until the

pork is very tender when pierced with the point of a sharp knife.

Remove the pan from the heat and stir in the sour cream. Transfer the goulasch to a warmed serving dish and serve it at once.

Pork with Grapes

A most unusual dish, Pork with Grapes is served with a slightly sweet yet peppery sauce and is garnished with green grapes. The ingredients used — coriander, juniper berries, Worcestershire sauce, grapes and gin — may seem strange, but the combination of flavours is sensational!

6-8 SERVINGS

2½ lb. seedless green grapes
1 x 5 lb. boned loin of pork, trimmed of excess fat and rolled
1 teaspoon salt
½ teaspoon black pepper
1 teaspoon ground coriander
16 juniper berries, crushed
1 garlic clove, crushed
2 shallots, finely chopped
1 tablespoon plus 1 teaspoon Worcestershire sauce
2 oz. [¼ cup] butter
5 fl. oz. [⅝ cup] dry white wine
⅛ teaspoon cayenne pepper
2 fl. oz. [¼ cup] gin
1 tablespoon cornflour [cornstarch] dissolved in 1 tablespoon white wine
GARNISH
2 oz. [¼ cup] butter
2 lb. seedless green grapes

Pass the grapes through a food mill or juice extractor. Alternatively, purée the grapes in an electric blender and strain the juice, discarding the pulp. Set the juice aside.

Place the pork in a large shallow dish. Rub it with the salt and pepper. Pour over the grape juice and add the coriander, juniper berries, garlic, half the shallots and 1 tablespoon of the Worcestershire sauce. Leave the pork to marinate, at room temperature, for 8 hours or overnight.

Remove the pork from the marinade and dry it with kitchen paper towels. Set aside. Reserve the marinade.

In a large flameproof casserole, melt the butter over moderate heat. When the foam subsides, add the remaining shallot and cook, stirring occasionally, for 3 to 4 minutes or until it is soft and translucent

An aromatic sauce accompanies this splendid Pork with Grapes.

but not brown. Place the pork in the casserole and cook, turning it with two large spoons, for 6 to 8 minutes or until it is lightly browned on all sides.

Add half the reserved marinade with all of the juniper berries, the wine, cayenne and remaining Worcestershire sauce. Discard the remaining marinade.

Bring the liquid to the boil, stirring frequently. Cover the casserole and reduce the heat to low. Cook for 2½ hours, or until the pork is well cooked. Test the meat by piercing it with the point of a sharp knife. The juices that run out should be clear.

Ten minutes before the pork has finished cooking, prepare the garnish. In a large frying-pan, melt the butter over moderate heat. When the foam subsides, add the grapes. Cook, stirring frequently, for 6 to 8 minutes or until they are lightly and evenly browned. Remove the pan from the heat. Set aside and keep warm.

In a small saucepan, warm the gin over low heat for 2 minutes. Remove the pan from the heat and pour the gin over the pork. Ignite it. When the flames die down, using two large spoons, transfer the pork to a warmed serving dish. Arrange the grapes around the pork. Set aside and keep warm.

Skim the excess fat off the surface of the cooking liquid in the casserole. Stir the dissolved cornflour [cornstarch] into the liquid and increase the heat to moderate. Cook, stirring frequently, for 10 minutes. Taste the sauce and add more salt and pepper if necessary.

Remove the casserole from the heat and strain the sauce into a warmed sauceboat. Pour a little of the sauce over the pork and serve immediately, with the remaining sauce.

Pork with Gruyère

An unusual and rich main dish, Pork with Gruyère has a sauce with a Fondue Suisse flavour. It needs only very simple accompaniments such as buttered noodles or boiled rice and a green salad.

4 SERVINGS

1 x 3 lb. boned loin of pork, trimmed of excess fat
6 oz. Gruyère cheese, cut into strips
1 oz. [2 tablespoons] butter
1 medium-sized onion, finely chopped
8 fl. oz. [1 cup] dry white wine
½ teaspoon black pepper
2 tablespoons cornflour [cornstarch] dissolved in 2 tablespoons kirsch
1 oz. [¼ cup] Gruyère cheese, grated
1 tablespoon chopped fresh parsley

Preheat the oven to fairly hot 375°F (Gas Mark 5, 190°C).

Lay the pork out on a flat surface and cover it with the strips of Gruyère cheese. Roll up the pork and tie it securely at 1-inch intervals with string. Set the pork aside.

In a large flameproof casserole, melt the butter over moderate heat. When the foam subsides, add the onion. Cook, stirring occasionally, for 5 to 7 minutes or until it is soft and translucent but not brown.

Place the pork in the casserole and cook, turning it with two large spoons, for 8 to 10 minutes, or until it is well browned all over.

Pour in the wine and add the pepper. Bring the liquid to the boil. Cover the casserole and place it in the oven. Braise for 1½ to 2 hours, or until the pork is well cooked. Stir the cooking liquid in the casserole from time to time as some of the cheese will run out of the pork and may stick to the pan. Test the meat by piercing it with the point of a sharp knife. The juices that run out should be clear.

When the pork is cooked, remove the casserole from the oven. Using two large

A hot dish of spiced meat, Pork Korma may be served with a raita and naan as part of an Indian meal or as a luncheon meal with boiled rice.

spoons, transfer the pork to a warmed dish. Remove and discard the string. Set aside and keep warm while you make the sauce.

With a metal spoon, skim all the fat off the surface of the cooking liquid. Strain the skimmed liquid into a medium-sized saucepan, pressing down on the cheese and onion in the strainer to extract all the liquid. Discard the contents of the strainer.

With a wooden spoon, stir the cornflour [cornstarch] mixture into the liquid in the saucepan and place it over moderate heat. Cook, stirring constantly, for 2 to 3 minutes or until the sauce thickens slightly. Stir in the grated Gruyère cheese. As soon as the cheese has melted and the sauce is smooth remove the pan from the heat.

Replace the pork in the casserole. Pour over the sauce. Sprinkle over the parsley and serve.

Pork Korma
BRAISED SLICED PORK

An aromatic dish of pork cooked with yogurt and cream, Pork Korma (kohr-mah) may be served as part of an Indian meal with Chapattis or naan. Unlike most curries this dish requires a little care in the cooking.

4 SERVINGS

2 oz. [¼ cup] butter
1½-inch piece fresh root ginger, peeled and finely chopped
3 garlic cloves, crushed
2 medium-sized onions, finely chopped
½ teaspoon hot chilli powder
2 tablespoons ground coriander
2 lb. pork fillets, cut into 1½-inch cubes
1 teaspoon salt
10 fl. oz. [1¼ cups] yogurt
4 oz. [⅔ cup] ground almonds
10 fl. oz. double cream [1¼ cups heavy cream]
½ teaspoon ground cinnamon
¼ teaspoon ground mace
½ teaspoon ground cardamom

$\frac{1}{4}$ teaspoon saffron threads soaked in 2 tablespoons boiling water for 10 minutes

GARNISH

2 medium-sized onions, thinly sliced, pushed out into rings and fried until crisp

In a large saucepan, melt the butter over moderate heat. When the foam subsides, add the ginger, garlic and onions and fry, stirring constantly, for 8 to 10 minutes or until the onions are golden brown.

Stir in the chilli powder and coriander and fry for 1 minute. Add the pork cubes and fry, turning them constantly, for 6 to 8 minutes or until they are lightly and evenly browned.

Increase the heat to high and cook, stirring constantly, for a further 8 to 10 minutes or until all the cooking juices in the pan have evaporated.

Reduce the heat to moderate. Add the salt and 4 tablespoons of the yogurt, stirring vigorously until the yogurt evaporates. Add 4 more tablespoons of yogurt and stir it until it evaporates. Continue in this manner until all the yogurt is used up and there is no liquid in the pan.

Remove the pan from the heat while you mix the ground almonds and the cream together in a small mixing bowl. Return the pan to moderate heat, and stir in the almond and cream mixture. Add the cinnamon, mace and cardamom and stir well to mix. Bring the korma to the boil. Reduce the heat to low, cover the pan and simmer the pork for 25 minutes, stirring occasionally to prevent the mixture from sticking to the pan.

Meanwhile, preheat the oven to moderate 350°F (Gas Mark 4, 180°C).

Transfer the pork mixture to an oven-proof casserole, stir in the saffron mixture, cover and place the casserole in the oven for 15 minutes. Remove the pan from the oven. Spoon the korma into a warmed serving dish. Garnish with the fried onions and serve immediately.

Pork with Mixed Vegetables

A colourful and mouth-watering dish, Pork with Mixed Vegetables is an adaptation of a traditional Chinese dish. It is easy to prepare and makes an impressive dinner party dish. Serve Pork with Mixed Vegetables with Fried Rice and warm rice wine.

4 SERVINGS

1½ lb. pork fillets, cut into thin strips 2-inches x ¼-inch
10 dried mushrooms, soaked in warm water for 20 minutes

5 tablespoons vegetable oil
1 medium-sized onion, thinly sliced
2 celery stalks, trimmed and cut into thin strips
1 medium-sized green pepper, white pith removed, seeded and cut into thin strips
10 water chestnuts, thinly sliced
1 lb. fresh bean sprouts
1 teaspoon salt
1 teaspoon sugar
2 tablespoons soy sauce
2 tablespoons rice wine

MARINADE

2 tablespoons soy sauce
1-inch piece fresh root ginger, peeled and finely chopped
1 teaspoon salt
$\frac{1}{8}$ teaspoon monosodium glutamate (optional)
2 teaspoons sugar
2 garlic cloves, crushed
2 tablespoons rice wine

(Low Cal)

First, make the marinade. In a medium-sized mixing bowl, combine the soy sauce, ginger, salt, monosodium glutamate if you are using it, sugar, garlic and rice wine. Mix the ingredients thoroughly with a spoon. Add the pork strips and stir well until the meat is thoroughly coated. Set aside to marinate for 30 minutes.

Drain the mushrooms and squeeze them dry. Remove and discard the stalks. With a sharp knife, cut the mushrooms into thin slices. Set aside.

In a large wok or deep 12-inch frying-pan, heat 2 tablespoons of the oil over high heat. When the oil is very hot, reduce the heat to moderate and add the mushrooms, onion, celery, green pepper and water chestnuts. Fry, stirring constantly, for 2 minutes. With a slotted spoon, transfer the vegetables to a plate and keep hot.

Add the remaining oil to the wok or frying-pan and increase the heat to high. When the oil is very hot, reduce the heat to moderate and add the pork slices and the marinade and fry, stirring constantly, for 5 minutes or until the pork is well browned. Stir in the reserved vegetables and the bean sprouts. Season with the salt, sugar, soy sauce and rice wine. Cook for a further 3 minutes, stirring constantly, or until the vegetables are thoroughly hot.

Remove the wok or frying-pan from the heat. Spoon the pork and vegetables on to a warmed serving dish. Serve immediately.

Pork with Mixed Vegetables is a colourful Chinese dish.

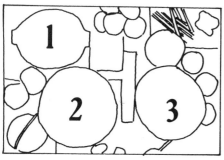

1 Colourful Pork with Sweet and Sour Sauce, 2 inexpensive and tasty Pork Ribs with Juniper Berries and 3 a really hot curry, Pork Vindaloo, show the versatility of pork.

Pork Pie

Pork Pie is a traditional British raised pie. Many different combinations of herbs and flavourings can be added to the pork and it is said that each county in England has its own special filling.

4-6 SERVINGS

1 teaspoon vegetable oil
12 oz. [3 cups] Hot Water Crust Pastry dough
1½ lb. pork fillets, cut into ¾-inch cubes
1 onion, grated
1 tart apple, peeled, cored and grated
⅛ teaspoon ground mace
¼ teaspoon dried sage
½ teaspoon dried marjoram
½ teaspoon salt
½ teaspoon black pepper
1 large egg, lightly beaten
½ oz. gelatine
10 fl. oz. [1¼ cups] home-made chicken stock

Preheat the oven to moderate 350°F (Gas Mark 4, 180°C).

Grease the base and sides of a 2-pound jam jar with the oil. Set aside.

Place one-quarter of the dough on a plate. Keep warm. Pat the remaining dough into a circle. Stand the jam jar, upside-down, on a flat surface and put the circle of dough on the base. Press the dough from the bottom down the sides of the jar, until the dough covers two-thirds of the jar and is about ½-inch thick all over. Set aside for 10 minutes or until the dough has cooled and become firm.

Cut out a double thickness of greaseproof or waxed paper in a strip long enough to go round the jar, leaving a little extra. Place the strip of paper round the dough and secure it with 2 paper clips. Turn the jam jar over on to its base and place it on a baking sheet. Gently ease the jam jar out of the dough case. Set aside.

In a medium-sized mixing bowl, combine the pork cubes, onion, apple, mace, sage, marjoram, salt and pepper. Put the mixture in the dough shell, being careful not to disturb the shape of the shell. Trim the shell so that it is nearly level with the meat filling.

Press the remaining dough into a circle slightly larger than the top of the shell. Place the dough circle on top and trim it to fit. Dampen the edges with water and press them together to seal. Cut the dough trimmings into small leaves. Make a rosette ½-inch in diameter out of the remaining dough trimmings. Set the rosette aside. Dampen the leaves with water and decorate the top of the pie with them. With a sharp knife, cut a 1-inch slit in the centre of the pie. Brush the top of the pie and the rosette with a little of the beaten egg.

Place the rosette on the baking sheet with the pie. Place the baking sheet in the centre of the oven and bake for 1½ hours. Remove the rosette after 30 minutes.

Remove the baking sheet from the oven. Remove and discard the greaseproof or waxed paper and paper clips. Brush the sides of the pie with the remaining beaten egg. Return the baking sheet to the oven and bake for a further 45 minutes or until a skewer inserted into the pie pierces the meat with ease. Remove the baking sheet from the oven and set the pie aside to cool completely. Place the cooled pie on a plate.

In a small saucepan, dissolve the gelatine in 4 tablespoons of the chicken stock over moderate heat, stirring constantly. When the gelatine mixture is clear, remove the pan from the heat. Pour the gelatine mixture into a small jug and stir in the remaining chicken stock. Pour the stock mixture through the slit in the pie, and place the rosette over the slit.

Place the pie in the refrigerator and chill for 3 hours or until the stock mixture has set. Remove the pie from the refrigerator at least 2 hours before serving.

Pork Ribs with Juniper Berries

An inexpensive and tasty dish, Pork Ribs with Juniper Berries is ideal for an informal supper party or a family meal. Serve with fried rice and a crisp green salad and accompany with a chilled bottle of Mateus Rosé wine.

4-6 SERVINGS

3 lb. lean spareribs of pork, cut into individual ribs
2 garlic cloves, crushed
24 juniper berries, crushed
1 teaspoon salt
1 teaspoon black pepper
1 tablespoon vegetable oil
12 fl. oz. [1½ cups] dry white wine
1 tablespoon beurre manié
2 tablespoons chopped fresh parsley

Preheat the oven to fairly hot 375°F (Gas Mark 5, 190°C).

Place the ribs on a board and rub them all over with the garlic, juniper berries, salt and pepper.

In a large, heavy-bottomed frying-pan, heat the oil over moderate heat. When the oil is hot, add the ribs, a few at a time, and fry them for 5 to 7 minutes or until they are golden brown. With tongs, transfer the ribs to a large roasting tin as they brown.

Pour over the wine and place the roasting tin over high heat. When the wine begins to bubble, remove the tin from the heat and place it in the oven. Cook for 1¼ hours or until the ribs are thoroughly cooked and tender.

Remove the tin from the oven. Transfer the ribs to a warmed serving dish and keep hot while you prepare the sauce.

Place the tin over moderate heat and bring the contents of the tin to the boil. Stir in the beurre manié, a little at a time, and cook, stirring frequently, for 2 minutes or until the sauce is fairly thick and smooth. Strain the sauce over the ribs. Sprinkle with the chopped parsley and serve immediately.

Pork with Sweet and Sour Sauce

This is an adaptation of a traditional Chinese dish, so well-known that it has become international. Serve with fried, or plain, rice or noodles.

4 SERVINGS

4 tablespoons soy sauce
1-inch piece fresh root ginger, peeled and grated
1½ lb. pork fillets, cut into small cubes
2 eggs
3 tablespoons cornflour [cornstarch]
sufficient vegetable oil for deep-frying

SAUCE

2 tablespoons vegetable oil
1-inch piece fresh root ginger, peeled and finely chopped
2 large carrots, scraped and thinly sliced on the diagonal
1 large red pepper, white pith removed, seeded and thinly sliced

1 large green pepper, white pith removed, seeded and thinly sliced
1 lb. canned pineapple chunks
1 tablespoon soy sauce
3 tablespoons wine vinegar
3 tablespoons soft brown sugar
$\frac{1}{4}$ teaspoon salt
2 tablespoons cornflour [cornstarch] dissolved in 6 tablespoons water

In a cup, combine the soy sauce and the ginger together. Put the pork cubes into a medium-sized mixing bowl and pour over the soy sauce mixture. Using a large spoon, turn the pork cubes over in the marinade. Cover the bowl and set it aside for 1 hour.

In a small mixing bowl, mix the eggs and cornflour [cornstarch] together, stirring until they are well blended and the mixture is smooth. Pour the batter over the pork cubes and mix well with a spoon.

Preheat the oven to moderate 350°F (Gas Mark 4, 180°C).

Fill a deep-frying pan one-third full with the oil. Place the pan over moderately high heat and heat the oil until it registers 360°F on a deep-fat thermometer or until a small cube of stale bread dropped into the oil browns in 50 seconds.

Reduce the heat to moderate and add the pork cubes. Fry them for 5 to 6 minutes or until they are crisp and dark brown. Using a slotted spoon, transfer the pork cubes to an ovenproof dish. Cover the dish with aluminium foil and place it in the oven while you make the sauce.

In a large frying-pan, heat the oil over moderate heat. When the oil is hot, add the ginger, carrots and the peppers and fry, stirring constantly, for 3 minutes. Stir in the pineapple chunks with the can juice, soy sauce, vinegar, sugar and salt and bring the mixture to the boil. Boil the sauce for 1 minute, stirring constantly. Remove the pan from the heat and stir in the cornflour [cornstarch] mixture. Return the pan to the heat and cook, stirring, until the sauce is thick and translucent.

Remove the pork cubes from the oven. Pour the sauce over the pork and serve immediately.

Pork Vindaloo
PORK VINEGAR CURRY

A pungent, strongly flavoured curry from the west coast of India, Pork Vindaloo is for those who like really hot curries. If you do not have the whole spices and an electric blender, use ground spices. Serve the vindaloo with plain boiled rice, yogurt and an onion and tomato salad.

4-6 SERVINGS

2-inch piece fresh root ginger, peeled and chopped
4 garlic cloves, chopped
1½ teaspoons hot chilli powder
2 teaspoons turmeric
1 teaspoon salt
seeds of 6 whole cardamom
6 cloves
6 peppercorns
1 x 2-inch cinnamon stick
2 tablespoons coriander seed
1 tablespoon cumin seed
5 fl. oz. [$\frac{5}{8}$ cup] wine vinegar
2 lb. pork fillets, cut into large cubes
4 curry leaves (optional)
3 tablespoons vegetable oil
1 teaspoon mustard seed
5 fl. oz. [$\frac{5}{8}$ cup] water

Put the ginger, garlic, chilli powder, turmeric, salt, cardamom seeds, cloves, peppercorns, cinnamon stick, coriander seed, cumin seed and the vinegar into an electric blender. Blend the mixture at high speed for 30 seconds. Scrape down the sides of the blender and blend for another 30 seconds. Add more vinegar if necessary and blend until the mixture forms a smooth liquid paste.

Place the pork in a large mixing bowl and mix in the spice paste. Cover the bowl and set it aside to marinate for 1 hour at room temperature. Lay the curry leaves, if you are using them, on top. Re-cover the bowl and place it in the refrigerator for 24 hours, turning the meat 2 or 3 times during that time.

Two hours before cooking time, remove the bowl from the refrigerator and set aside at room temperature.

In a large saucepan, heat the oil over moderate heat. When the oil is hot, add the mustard seed. Cover the pan to stop the seeds from spattering and when they stop popping, add the pork, all the marinade and the water. Stir to mix and bring the mixture to the boil. When the curry boils, reduce the heat to low, cover the pan and simmer for 30 minutes. Uncover the pan and continue cooking for a further 30 minutes or until the pork is very tender and the sauce is neither too thick nor too thin.

Remove the pan from the heat. Spoon the vindaloo into a warmed serving dish. Serve immediately.

Pork and Walnut Casserole

A warming dish for colder days, Pork and Walnut Casserole may be served with rice for a delicious informal lunch.

6 SERVINGS

6 tablespoons seasoned flour, made with 6 tablespoons flour, 1 teaspoon salt and ½ teaspoon black pepper
3 lb. pork fillets, cut into 1-inch cubes
2 fl. oz. [$\frac{1}{4}$ cup] olive oil
2 medium-sized onions, sliced
2 garlic cloves, crushed
2 green chillis, seeded and chopped
4 medium-sized potatoes, peeled and cut into 1-inch cubes
1 tablespoon chopped fresh coriander leaves
14 oz. canned peeled tomatoes
1 teaspoon salt
½ teaspoon black pepper
1 teaspoon sugar
1 teaspoon dried thyme
10 fl. oz. [1¼ cups] chicken stock
4 oz. [1 cup] walnuts, halved

Place the seasoned flour on a plate and dip the pork cubes in it to coat them thoroughly. Shake off any excess flour and set aside.

In a large flameproof casserole, heat the oil over moderate heat. When the oil is hot, add the pork cubes, a few at a time, and cook them, turning frequently, for 6 to 8 minutes or until they are lightly and evenly browned. With a slotted spoon, transfer the pork to a large plate. Set aside while you fry the remaining pork in the same way.

Add the onions and garlic to the casserole and cook, stirring occasionally, for 5 to 7 minutes or until the onions are soft and translucent but not brown. Stir in the chillis, potatoes, coriander leaves and tomatoes with the can juice, and cook for a further 5 minutes. Stir in the salt, pepper, sugar, thyme and chicken stock and return the pork cubes to the casserole.

Increase the heat to high and bring the liquid to the boil. Cover the casserole, reduce the heat to low and simmer the stew for 1 hour or until the pork is very tender when pierced with the point of a sharp knife. Stir in the walnuts.

Cook the stew, uncovered, for a further 5 to 7 minutes or until the walnuts are hot.

Remove the casserole from the heat and transfer the stew to a warmed serving dish. Serve immediately.

Pork with Wine and Orange Sauce

Pork with Wine and Orange Sauce may be served with roast potatoes and a good dry white wine, such as Meursault for a very special meal.

4-6 SERVINGS

1 x 4 lb. boned loin of pork, trimmed of excess fat and rolled
1 garlic clove, halved
½ teaspoon salt
½ teaspoon black pepper
5 fl. oz. [⅝ cup] chicken stock
2 fl. oz. [¼ cup] dry white wine
juice of 1 large orange
1 orange
1 tablespoon beurre manié

Preheat the oven to fairly hot 400°F (Gas Mark 6, 200°C).

Rub the pork all over with the garlic halves. Discard the garlic. Then rub it all over with the salt and pepper.

Place the meat on a rack in a roasting tin and place the tin in the oven. Roast the pork for 2 hours or until it is well cooked. Test the meat by piercing it with the point of a sharp knife. The juices that run out should be clear.

Remove the pork from the oven and transfer it to a carving board or heated serving dish and set aside.

Pour off all the fat from the roasting tin. Place the tin over moderate heat and scrape up all the brown bits that have adhered to the bottom and sides. Add the stock, wine and orange juice and boil, stirring occasionally, for 5 to 7 minutes or until the sauce has reduced slightly.

Meanwhile, wash and dry the orange and, using a sharp knife, cut it into thin, even slices. Arrange the slices decoratively around the pork.

Add the beurre manié to the sauce, a small piece at a time. Cook the sauce, stirring constantly, for 3 minutes or until it is thick and smooth.

Remove the tin from the heat and strain the sauce into a warmed sauceboat. Serve the pork immediately, with the sauce.

Porridge

This famous Scottish breakfast dish is made from OATMEAL and, traditionally, water, milk or a combination of both. Coarse oatmeal gives a particularly delicious nutty flavour to porridge, but medium-ground is more commonly used. The porridge should be soft enough to drop off a spoon easily, but not too runny.

The traditional Scottish way to serve porridge is piping hot in an individual serving bowl, with an individual bowl of cold milk or cream to each person. A spoonful of porridge is then dipped into the cold milk or cream before eating rather than pouring the milk over. Porridge should be served sprinkled with salt, although outside Scotland something sweet, such as brown or white sugar, or honey is generally preferred.

Porridge

A traditional Scottish breakfast dish, Porridge is a warming and filling cereal made from oatmeal and water. Serve sprinkled with salt and a bowl of cold milk or cream. For those with a sweet tooth, sugar or honey may be served with porridge instead of salt.

2-4 SERVINGS

1 pint [2½ cups] water
4 oz. [1 cup] oatmeal
1 teaspoon salt

In a medium-sized saucepan, bring the water to the boil over moderate heat. Gradually sprinkle over the oatmeal, stirring constantly. Reduce the heat to low and simmer the porridge for 15 minutes, stirring frequently. Add the salt and cook, stirring constantly, for a further 5 minutes.

Remove the pan from the heat, pour the porridge into individual warmed serving bowls and serve immediately.

Porridge and Chocolate Biscuits [Cookies]

Very quick and economical to make, Porridge and Chocolate Biscuits [Cookies] taste delicious served slightly warm from the oven with hot tea or coffee.

ABOUT 15 BISCUITS

4 oz. [1 cup] self-raising flour
½ teaspoon salt
1 tablespoon cocoa powder
4 oz. [½ cup] butter
4 oz. [½ cup] castor sugar
3 oz. [¾ cup] plus 2 tablespoons rolled oats
2 tablespoons strong black coffee

Preheat the oven to moderate 350°F (Gas Mark 4, 180°C). Line two medium-sized baking sheets with non-stick silicone paper and set them aside.

Sift the flour, salt and cocoa powder into a medium-sized mixing bowl. Add the butter and cut it into small pieces with a table knife. Using your fingertips, rub the butter into the flour mixture until it resembles very coarse breadcrumbs. Stir in the sugar, 3 ounces [¾ cup] of the rolled oats and the coffee. Mix and knead the dough lightly with your hands until it is smooth.

Place the remaining oats on a plate. Break off walnut-sized pieces of the dough and roll them into balls. Roll the balls in the oats to coat them evenly, shaking off any excess. Place them on the prepared baking sheets, spaced well apart. Using the palm of your hand, flatten the balls

Richly flavoured and coloured, Port and Raspberry Kissel is a delightful dessert for any dinner party.

into disc shapes approximately ¼-inch thick.

Place the baking sheets in the centre of the oven and bake the biscuits [cookies] for 15 minutes or until they are crisp and golden.

Remove the baking sheets from the oven. Using a spatula or a fish slice, carefully transfer the biscuits [cookies] to a wire rack to cool slightly before serving.

Port

Port is a fortified wine produced in the Douro district of Portugal. It is made by adding brandy to red wine about halfway through the fermentation period — thus stopping fermentation and ensuring that the finished product will be sweet and rather strong, alcoholically.

There are two main types of port: vintage port and wood port. A port is 'vintage' when it is considered to possess special merit. Only the shippers have the authority to make a 'declaration of vintage' and this declaration is based on their judgement of the wine.

All port is a blend of several wines but vintage port is made from wines of one year while wood port is a blend of wines of a number of years. Vintage port is stored, in casks, in Portugal for two years, then shipped to Britain and other countries where it is bottled and laid down. At this point, vintage port is quite undrinkable and it should remain, on its side, in a cellar for a minimum of 15 years before being decanted and drunk. It is generally thought to be at its best when it is around 20 years old, although it seems to mature indefinitely and never 'goes off'.

Wood port is the general description given to the port most usually bought (there are few who can afford to pay the price demanded for vintage port) and it indicates that the wine is aged exclusively in wooden casks. Wood port, in its turn, is divided into two categories: ruby and tawny port. Ruby is the cheaper of the two and is drunk young (although a reputable ruby will have matured in casks for at least five or six years). It is deep, rich red in colour and sweet and heavy to taste. Tawny port is matured longer — a good one will be in casks for anywhere between 12 and 15 years while its colour changes from its original deep red to the deep gold its name suggests. It is mellow and very smooth to taste.

A third 'type' of port gaining in popularity is so-called white port. White port

is made in exactly the same way as other port except that white grapes are used instead of red. It can be somewhat drier than ruby or tawny and tends to be served as an appetizer rather than as a dessert or after-dinner wine.

Port is an essentially English drink, despite its origins. There is evidence to suggest, in fact, that the interruption of the fermenting process which produces the beverage was first thought up by an Englishman anxious to make the rather harsh, dry red wines of Portugal more palatable to the English, with their perennial sweet tooth. Even today a vast percentage of the port trade remains in the hands of British companies and it is to the British Isles that most of it is exported. And, despite the fact that those British gentlemen who immortalized port with their after-dinner cigars do not seem quite so plentiful as they once were, it continues to be a popular drink among the British.

Port may be drunk as a rich, subtle dessert wine, or with cheese and biscuits, or as an after-dinner drink for those who do not enjoy the taste of liqueur.

Port Flip

An almost festive drink, Port Flip is made with egg yolk, sugar and port. Traditionally, a flip has nutmeg sprinkled over the top, but this may be omitted if preferred.

1 SERVING

4 ice-cubes, crushed
1 egg yolk
1 teaspoon castor sugar
3 fl. oz. [$\frac{3}{8}$ cup] port
$\frac{1}{8}$ teaspoon grated nutmeg

Half-fill a cocktail shaker or large screw-top jar with the ice-cubes. Add the egg yolk, sugar and port and screw the lid on tightly. Shake the jar vigorously until the mixture is well blended.

Pour the mixture through a fine wire

strainer held over a wine glass. Discard the ice-cubes. Sprinkle with the nutmeg and serve.

Port and Raspberry Kissel

Serve this delicious Port and Raspberry Kissel with castor sugar and lots of whipped cream for a super dinner party dessert.

4-6 SERVINGS

1 lb. fresh raspberries, hulled
6 fl. oz. [$\frac{3}{4}$ cup] port
4 oz. [$\frac{1}{2}$ cup] sugar
2 tablespoons arrowroot, dissolved in 4 tablespoons water
10 fl. oz. [$1\frac{1}{4}$ cups] boiling water
2 teaspoons grated orange rind

Place the raspberries and port in a medium-sized saucepan. Place the pan over high heat and bring the mixture to

Low Cal

Port Wine Steaks are accompanied by a rich mushroom and wine sauce.

the boil, stirring constantly. Reduce the heat to low and simmer for 15 minutes or until the raspberries are beginning to pulp.

Remove the pan from the heat and pour the fruit through a fine wire strainer held over a medium-sized mixing bowl. Using the back of a wooden spoon, rub the raspberries through the strainer until only the seeds are left. Discard the seeds in the strainer and return the purée to the saucepan. Stir in the sugar and bring the mixture to the boil over moderate heat, stirring constantly. Remove the pan from the heat and set it aside.

Place the dissolved arrowroot in a medium-sized mixing bowl. Gradually add the boiling water, stirring constantly until the liquid thickens. Stir the mixture into the raspberry purée and add the orange rind. Return the pan to the heat and cook the mixture, stirring constantly, until it is thick and smooth.

Remove the pan from the heat and pour the mixture into a serving dish. Serve immediately, or chill before serving.

Port-Salut

A semi-hard, mild-flavoured French cheese, Port-Salut is made in a flat, round shape about 2-inches thick and 8- to 10-inches in diameter. One Port-Salut cheese usually weighs between 3 and 4 pounds.

The cheese was originally made by Trappist monks of Port-du-Salut for their own consumption. Later production was expanded and the name Port-Salut registered. The cheese is now made in many parts of France.

Port-Salut is best eaten as an after-dinner cheese. It is rarely used in cooking.

Port Wine Steaks

This is a fabulous way to cook rump steak. Serve with sautéed potatoes and steamed, buttered French beans and, to drink, a good claret such as St. Emilion. The cooking time of the steaks depends on the amount of heat applied, the thickness of the frying-pan and the quality of the meat. We have given an approximate timing and suggest you test the steaks half way through the cooking time.

4 SERVINGS

4 x 8 oz. rump steaks
1 teaspoon salt
½ teaspoon black pepper
3 oz. [⅜ cup] butter
8 oz. mushrooms wiped clean and sliced
2 fl. oz. [¼ cup] port wine
5 fl. oz. [⅝ cup] Brown Sauce

Rub the steaks all over with the salt and pepper. Set aside.

In a small frying-pan, melt 1 ounce [2 tablespoons] of the butter over moderate heat. When the foam subsides, add the mushrooms and cook them, stirring frequently, for 2 minutes. Remove the pan from the heat and set aside.

In a large frying-pan, melt 1½ ounces [3 tablespoons] of the remaining butter over moderately high heat. When the foam subsides, add the steaks and cook them for 2 minutes on each side.

Reduce the heat to low and cook the steaks for a further 2 minutes on each side. This will produce rare steaks. Double the cooking time for well-done steaks.

Remove the steaks from the pan and transfer them to a warmed serving dish. Set aside and keep hot while you make the sauce.

Increase the heat to moderately high. Add the port wine and the brown sauce to the pan and, stirring constantly, bring the sauce to the boil. Add the mushrooms and the remaining butter, swirling the pan carefully.

When the butter has melted and the sauce comes to the boil again, remove the pan from the heat and pour the sauce over the steaks. Serve immediately.

Porter

Porter is a traditional British beer which gets its dark brown colour and distinctive flavour from roasted malt and, sometimes, from the addition of burnt sugar to the beer.

Porterhouse Steak

Porterhouse Steak is a thick slice of beef, on the bone and including the fillet, which weighs anywhere between $\frac{3}{4}$ to $1\frac{1}{2}$ pounds. The term also applies to a thick fillet, or entrecôte steak. (See the entry under CHATEAUBRIAND.)

The name porterhouse is thought to have originated from the days when this succulent steak was served at porter, or beer, houses.

Porterhouse steak is usually grilled [broiled] but it can also be pan-fried in butter or oil. A steak weighing approximately 1 pound should serve 2 people.

To grill [broil] porterhouse steak, brush with a little melted butter and then rub a little salt and pepper into the meat. Preheat the grill [broiler] to high. Cook for 2 minutes on each side, reduce the heat to low and cook for a further 2 minutes on each side. This will produce rare steak. Double the cooking times for well-done steak.

To fry porterhouse steak, melt about 1 tablespoon of butter or oil in a frying-pan over moderate heat. When the foam subsides, add the steak and cook for 2 minutes on each side. Reduce the heat to low and cook for a further 2 minutes on each side. This will produce rare steak. Double the cooking times for well-done steak.

All cooking times are approximate and depend on the quality of the meat, the strength of the heat and the thickness of the pan.

Porterhouse Steak with Red Wine Sauce

A sophisticated dinner party dish, Porterhouse Steak with Red Wine Sauce may be served with Pommes de Terre à la Lyonnaise and a tossed mixed salad. A mellow Nuits St. Georges wine would go beautifully with this dish.

4 SERVINGS

3 tablespoons black peppercorns
4 x 6 oz. porterhouse steaks
2 garlic cloves, crushed
1 teaspoon salt
2 oz. [$\frac{1}{4}$ cup] butter
2 medium-sized onions, thinly sliced
4 oz. mushrooms, wiped clean and thinly sliced
4 fl. oz. [$\frac{1}{2}$ cup] red wine

Porterhouse Steak with Red Wine Sauce is steak covered with crushed peppercorns and a delicious sauce.

$\frac{1}{4}$ teaspoon dried thyme
1 tablespoon beurre manié

Using a mortar and pestle, or rolling pin, crush the peppercorns coarsely and set them aside on a plate.

Rub the steaks all over with the garlic and salt, then press each steak into the crushed peppercorns, coating both sides. Shake off any excess pepper and set the steaks aside.

In a large frying-pan, melt half of the butter over moderate heat. When the foam subsides, add the onions and cook, stirring occasionally, for 5 to 7 minutes or until they are soft and translucent but not brown. Stir in the mushrooms and cook, stirring occasionally, for 3 minutes. With a slotted spoon, transfer the onions and mushrooms to a plate. Set aside while you cook the steaks.

Add the remaining butter to the pan and melt it over moderate heat. When the foam subsides, add the steaks and cook them for 2 minutes on each side. Reduce the heat to low and cook them for a further 2 minutes on each side. This will produce rare steaks. Double the cooking time for well-done steaks.

Remove the steaks from the pan and transfer them to a warmed serving dish. Keep them hot while you finish making the sauce.

Return the onion and mushroom mixture to the pan and pour over the red wine. Stir in the thyme. Boil the mixture, stirring occasionally, for 2 minutes or until the liquid has reduced slightly. Stir in the beurre manié, a little at a time, and cook, stirring frequently, for a further 2 minutes or until the sauce is hot and has thickened.

Remove the pan from the heat and pour the sauce over the steaks. Serve at once.

Porterhouse Steak with Roquefort Cheese

An absolutely extravagant dish that is well worth every penny, Porterhouse Steak with Roquefort Cheese may be served with crisp French-fried potatoes and garnished with thin slices of tomato.

4 SERVINGS

2 x 1 lb. porterhouse steaks, on the bone and 1-inch thick
2 oz. [¼ cup] butter
½ teaspoon salt
¼ teaspoon black pepper
1 tablespoon sour cream
3 oz. Roquefort cheese, crumbled

Preheat the grill [broiler] to high and line the grill [broiler] pan with aluminium foil. Using a sharp knife, cut each steak in half, crosswise.

In a small saucepan, melt half the butter over moderate heat. Remove the pan from the heat. With a pastry brush, brush the steaks with the butter, then season with the salt and pepper.

Place the steaks on the rack in the grill [broiler] pan and place the pan under the heat. Grill [broil] for 2 minutes on each side. Reduce the heat to low and cook for a further 2 minutes on each side. This will produce rare steaks. Double the cooking times for well-done steaks. Remove the pan from under the heat and transfer the steaks to a warmed serving dish.

In a small mixing bowl, mash the remaining butter, sour cream and cheese together with a fork. Place a spoonful of the mixture on top of each steak and serve at once.

Porterhouse Steak with Spices

A very simple and quick-to-make recipe,

Porterhouse Steak with Spices is steak coated with a tasty spice and butter mixture, then grilled [broiled]. *This dish may be served with a tossed green salad and saffron rice.*

4 SERVINGS

1 teaspoon salt
4 black peppercorns, crushed
1 large garlic clove, crushed
1 teaspoon turmeric
2 cardamom seeds, crushed
¼ teaspoon cayenne pepper
½ teaspoon ground cumin
1 oz. [2 tablespoons] butter, melted
1 tablespoon soy sauce
4 x 6 oz. porterhouse steaks

Preheat the grill [broiler] to high and line the grill [broiler] pan with aluminium foil.

In a small mixing bowl, combine the salt, peppercorns, garlic, turmeric, cardamom, cayenne and cumin. Using a small wooden spoon, stir in the butter and soy sauce, stirring until the mixture is smooth.

Place the steaks on the rack in the grill [broiler] pan and, using a pastry brush, brush the upper sides of the steaks with half of the spice mixture.

Place the steaks under the grill [broiler] and grill [broil] for 2 minutes. Turn the steaks over and brush them with the remaining spice mixture. Grill [broil] for a further 2 minutes.

Reduce the heat to low and grill [broil] the steaks for a further 2 minutes on each side. This will produce rare steaks. Double the cooking times for well-done steaks.

Remove the steaks from the grill [broiler] and transfer them to a warmed serving dish. Serve immediately.

Porterhouse Steak with Watercress Butter

One of the classic ways to serve steak is with parsley butter and this delicious recipe for Porterhouse Steak with Watercress Butter is a variation of that theme. Serve the steaks very hot so that the butter will melt instantly.

4 SERVINGS

2 x 1 lb. porterhouse steaks, on the bone and 1-inch thick
1 tablespoon Tabasco sauce
½ teaspoon salt
¼ teaspoon black pepper

Porterhouse Steak with Watercress Butter and Porterhouse Steak with Roquefort Cheese.

2 oz. [¼ cup] butter
2 tablespoons finely chopped fresh
   watercress

Preheat the grill [broiler] to high and line the grill [broiler] pan with aluminium foil.

Using a sharp knife, cut each steak in half, crosswise.

Rub each steak with the Tabasco sauce and season with the salt and pepper. Place the steaks on the rack in the grill [broiler] pan and place the pan under the heat. Grill [broil] for 2 minutes on each side.

Reduce the heat to low and cook for a further 2 minutes on each side. This will produce rare steaks. Double the cooking time for well-done steaks.

Remove the pan from under the heat. Transfer the steaks to a warmed serving dish.

In a small mixing bowl, mash the butter and watercress together with a fork. Place a spoonful of the watercress butter on top of each steak and serve at once.

Portuguese Custard

A smooth, creamy dessert, Portuguese Custard is flavoured with a hint of port and nutmeg. Serve with whipped cream and any fresh fruit in season.

4-6 SERVINGS

1 teaspoon vegetable oil
10 fl. oz. single cream [1¼ cups
   light cream]
5 fl. oz. [⅝ cup] milk
4 oz. [½ cup] sugar
10 fl. oz. [1¼ cups] warm water
3 egg yolks
2 eggs
1 tablespoon port
¼ teaspoon grated nutmeg

Preheat the oven to warm 325°F (Gas Mark 3, 170°C). Using the teaspoon of oil, grease a 1½-pint [1-quart] heatproof mould.

Place the cream and milk in a medium-sized saucepan and heat over low heat until the mixture is just tepid. Remove the pan from the heat and set the pan aside.

Meanwhile, make the caramel. Place the sugar in a small saucepan. Pour in half the water and set the pan over low heat. Stirring constantly, heat the mixture until the sugar has dissolved. Increase the heat to moderately high and boil until the caramel is a deep brown colour. Remove the pan from the heat and gradually stir in the remaining water until the mixture is smooth. Very gradually pour the caramel into the warm milk and cream mixture, stirring constantly.

In a medium-sized mixing bowl, using a wire whisk or rotary beater, beat the egg yolks and eggs together until they are light and fluffy. Beat in the port and nutmeg. Gradually pour the cream and caramel mixture on to the egg mixture, stirring constantly with a wooden spoon.

Pour the mixture through a fine wire strainer into the prepared mould. Cover the mould with aluminium foil and place the mould in a roasting tin. Pour in enough hot water to half-fill the tin. Place the tin in the centre of the oven and bake for 45 minutes to 1 hour or until the custard has set.

Remove the tin from the oven and lift the mould out of the tin. Remove and discard the foil. Set the custard aside to cool in the mould and then place the mould in the refrigerator to chill for 1 hour.

Remove the mould from the refrigerator. Run a sharp knife around the edge of the mould to loosen the sides. Quickly dip the bottom of the mould in boiling water. Place a chilled serving plate, inverted, over the top of the mould and reverse the two, giving the mould a sharp shake. The custard should slide out easily. Serve at once.

Portuguese Kebabs

Succulent pieces of pork and lamb marinated in garlic, herbs and sherry, Portuguese Kebabs makes a delicious meal for an informal dinner party. Serve Portuguese Kebabs with boiled rice and a crisp green salad.

4-6 SERVINGS

1 lb. pork fillets, cut into 1-inch
   cubes
1 lb. boned shoulder of lamb, cut
   into 1-inch cubes
MARINADE
4 garlic cloves, crushed
1 tablespoon paprika
1 teaspoon dried oregano
2 teaspoons grated orange rind
1 teaspoon salt
½ teaspoon black pepper
1 teaspoon sugar
1 tablespoon finely chopped fresh
   mint
1 tablespoon olive oil
2 tablespoons dry sherry

First prepare the marinade. In a medium-sized mixing bowl, combine the garlic, paprika, oregano, orange rind, salt, pepper, sugar, mint, oil and sherry together. With a kitchen fork, beat the ingredients until they are thoroughly combined. Add the meat pieces and baste them thoroughly with the marinade. Set aside to marinate for 2 hours, basting occasionally.

Preheat the grill [broiler] to high and line the grill [broiler] pan with aluminium foil.

With a slotted spoon, lift the meat cubes from the marinade and thread them on skewers, alternating the pork and lamb. Reserve the marinade.

Place the skewers on the rack in the grill [broiler] pan and, using a pastry brush, brush the meat with the marinade. Place the pan under the grill [broiler] and grill [broil] the meat for 10 to 15 minutes, turning the skewers two or three times and basting occasionally with the remaining marinade.

Slide the meat off the skewers on to a serving dish and serve immediately.

Portuguese Potatoes

A filling potato accompaniment to grilled [broiled] meat or fish, Portuguese Potatoes are ideal to serve at an informal dinner.

4-6 SERVINGS

3 large potatoes, peeled
1 teaspoon salt
2 tablespoons olive oil
1 medium-sized onion,
   chopped
1 garlic clove, crushed
14 oz. canned peeled tomatoes

Place the potatoes in a large saucepan. Pour over enough water just to cover and add the salt. Place the pan over high heat and bring the water to the boil. Reduce the heat to moderately low and cook the potatoes for 10 minutes. Remove the pan from the heat and drain the potatoes in a colander. Slice the potatoes and set aside.

In a large frying-pan, heat the oil over moderate heat. When the oil is hot, add the onion and garlic and fry, stirring occasionally, for 5 to 7 minutes or until the onion is soft and translucent but not brown. Add the tomatoes with the can juice to the pan and cook for 5 minutes, stirring occasionally.

Stir in the potato slices. Increase the heat to high and bring the mixture to the boil. Reduce the heat to low, cover the pan and cook for 10 to 15 minutes or until the potatoes are tender.

Remove the pan from the heat. Spoon the mixture into a warmed serving dish and serve at once.

Appetizing Portuguese Kebabs and tasty Portuguese Potatoes.

Portuguese Wines

Portugal is an important supplier of everyday wine to the world — and will become increasingly so as French and German wines continue to escalate in price and become, relatively at least, less available in the cheaper price ranges.

White, rosé and red wines are all produced in Portugal, and abundantly. Of the three, the rosés seem to be most important at the moment although that may change as wine-drinking habits become more sophisticated (most wine experts consider rosé to be the drink of the non-wine drinker!). Whatever might happen, the fact remains that, at the moment, Mateus Rosé, the single biggest seller among the Portuguese rosés, is one of the three or four most popular wines in the British Isles. In the United States, its considerable popularity is almost rivalled by Lancer's Rosé, a wine, like Mateus, which is pleasant, sparkling and light to taste. Both are attractively packaged in the sort of bottle that looks pretty, makes an attractive lamp after the contents have been drunk and contributes nothing at all to the storage powers of the wine. A third Portuguese rosé wine, gaining in popularity and considerably cheaper than either of the two mentioned above, is Isabel Rosé. It is described on the label as being light and slightly sparkling — and the label does not lie.

Portugal also makes great quantities of both white and red wines — the best of which, unfortunately, do not seem to travel well. Which may, of course, be an excellent excuse for incipient wine tasters to visit Portugal! Most Portuguese wine is blended, either at source or by shippers, and is sold abroad under brand or shippers names. When the shippers consider a wine to be of particularly good quality they label it *reserva* or *garrafeira* and give it a 'vintage'. Any wine so marked will be an excellent buy and an enjoyable wine to drink — and will still be markedly less expensive than an equivalent French, Italian or German wine.

Vinho Verde, or green wine, (a description which applies less to the colour of the drink than to the fact that it is bottled young, when it has barely fermented) is weak alcoholically and seems to have a slight 'fizz' to it. Although it comes in white, rosé and red, the whites are by far the best and, at their best, can be very delicate and lovely to drink.

The Dão region of Portugal is perhaps best-known to Portuguese wine drinkers outside the country. It produces both red and white wines of somewhat varying quality but again even the cheap wines are a good buy. The Dão reds, at their best, are big, full wines which age very well indeed. The whites are dry, clean to taste and should be drunk fairly young.

The province of Estremadura produces perhaps the best single wine of Portugal, Colares — if you can find a Colares Reserva, or even better, a Colares Garrafeira, it is something to be snapped up and treated with respect.

Portuguese white wine, especially vinho verde, makes an excellent summer thirst quencher or goes well with a salad and picnic foods. The rosés make marvellous accompaniments to chicken and veal dishes and to cold salads or buffet plates. The reds go well with almost any of the more highly spiced Iberian foods, and biscuits and cheese.

Posset

Posset is an old-fashioned British drink made from spiced milk or cream, curdled with wine, sherry, beer, treacle, or molasses. The drink, which may be thickened with egg yolks or white bread, is traditionally served hot in special china posset dishes.

Possets were considered beneficial to health in the olden days — they were often taken to cure colds.

Pot Au Feu

Pot au Feu (poh-toh-fer) is a classic French broth of which there are many varieties. It is made from mixed vegetables and meat (traditionally beef) and served in the pot in which it is made, or in a cocotte dish.

Pot au Feu is served in two stages — the cooking liquid is served as a clear broth, and the meat and vegetables follow as a main course. The broth is traditionally served with rice, pasta or bread and the meat and vegetables with pickled gherkins, mustard and, sometimes, a hot tomato sauce.

Pot au Feu à la Béarnaise

CHICKEN AND VEGETABLES IN BROTH

Also called Poule au Pot (pool oh poh), meaning literally hen in the pot, Pot au Feu à la Béarnaise (poh-toh-fer ah lah bair-nayz) is a filling dish for a dinner party. Serve the broth as the first course and the stuffed chicken and vegetables as the main course, with potatoes or French bread.

8-10 SERVINGS

½ beef marrow bone, sawn into 2 pieces
1 small veal knuckle, sawn into 2 pieces
6 pints [7½ pints] water
1 head of celery, trimmed, and cut into 1-inch lengths
4 medium-sized onions, thickly sliced and pushed out into rings
1 garlic clove, crushed
2 large carrots, scraped and thickly sliced
2 small parsnips, peeled and thickly sliced
large bouquet garni, consisting of 8 parsley sprigs, 2 thyme sprays and 2 bay leaves tied together
1 tablespoon salt
1 teaspoon black pepper
1 x 4 lb. chicken

STUFFING
1 oz. [2 tablespoons] butter
1 shallot, finely chopped
1 garlic clove, crushed
8 oz. pork sausage meat
2 oz. lean cooked ham, finely chopped
4 tablespoons dry white breadcrumbs
½ teaspoon salt
¼ teaspoon black pepper
1 teaspoon dried marjoram
½ teaspoon dried thyme
1 tablespoon finely chopped fresh parsley

(Low Cal)

Place the beef bone and veal knuckle in a very large, heavy-based saucepan and pour over the water. Set the pan over moderately high heat and bring the water to the boil. Boil for 4 minutes, skimming off the scum as it rises to the surface with a metal spoon.

Add the celery, onions, garlic, carrots, parsnips, bouquet garni, salt and pepper. When the liquid comes to the boil again, reduce the heat to very low, cover the pan tightly and simmer for 1 hour.

Meanwhile, make the stuffing. In a medium-sized saucepan, melt the butter over moderate heat. When the foam subsides, add the shallot and garlic and fry, stirring, for 3 to 4 minutes or until the shallot is soft and translucent but not brown.

Add the sausage meat and cook, stirring to break up the meat, for 8 to 10 minutes or until the pork has lost its pink colour. Stir in the ham, breadcrumbs, salt, pepper, marjoram, thyme and parsley. Cook the stuffing, stirring constantly, for a further 5 minutes.

Remove the pan from the heat. Spoon the stuffing into the cavity of the chicken

Serve the broth from Pot au Feu à la Béarnaise as a first course and the meat and vegetables as a main course.

and secure the cavity with a trussing needle and thread or skewers.

Place the chicken in the saucepan containing the vegetables. Increase the heat to moderately high and bring the mixture to the boil. Reduce the heat to very low, re-cover the pan and simmer for a further 1½ hours.

Remove the pan from the heat. Remove and discard the beef bone and veal knuckle, or reserve the knuckle for future use.

Using two large forks, lift the chicken out of the pan and transfer it to a warmed serving dish. Remove and discard the trussing thread or skewers.

Pour the broth through a large, fine wire strainer held over a warmed soup tureen. Remove and discard the bouquet garni and arrange the vegetables around the meat. Keep the meat and vegetables hot while you serve the broth.

Pot Roast

Pot roasting is a method of cooking meat or poultry with vegetables in a heavy saucepan or casserole with a tightly fitting lid on top of the stove. Traditionally, meat and vegetables are browned in fat and then covered and cooked slowly over low heat, the cooking time depending on the weight of the meat.

Liquids, such as stock or water, and

herbs may be included to give flavour to the meat. This method of cooking is especially recommended for meat which benefits from long, slow cooking. If a large enough saucepan or casserole is not available, the meat and liquid may be cooked in the oven and the vegetables cooked in a separate saucepan.

Pot Roast with Brandy

A splendidly different pot roast in a brandy sauce, Pot Roast with Brandy may be served with French bread or new potatoes.

6 SERVINGS

1 x 4 lb. top rump [bottom round] of beef
1 teaspoon salt
½ teaspoon black pepper
2 fl. oz. [¼ cup] vegetable oil
2½ lb. shallots, peeled
1½ pints [3¾ cups] beef stock
2 bay leaves
    pared rind of 1 lemon
2 oz. [¼ cup] butter
12 oz. button mushrooms, wiped clean
3 fl. oz. [⅜ cup] brandy
    very finely grated rind of ¼ lemon
1 tablespoon beurre manié

Rub the meat all over with salt and

Thick slices of beef, served with a rich sauce, Pot Roast with Brandy makes a superb dinner party dish.

pepper. Set aside.

In a large flameproof casserole, heat the vegetable oil over moderate heat. When the oil is hot, add the beef and, turning frequently, cook for 10 to 12 minutes or until it is evenly browned on all sides.

Place 1 pound of the shallots around the meat and cook, stirring occasionally, for 3 to 4 minutes, or until the shallots are soft and translucent but not brown.

Pour the stock over the beef and add the bay leaves and lemon rind. Bring the liquid to the boil. Cover the casserole, reduce the heat to low and cook for 2½ to 3 hours or until the meat is very tender when pierced with a sharp knife.

Preheat the oven to warm 325°F (Gas Mark 3, 170°C).

Remove the casserole from the heat. Using two large forks, remove the meat from the casserole and place it on an oven-proof plate. Cover with aluminium foil and put it in the oven to keep hot.

With a slotted spoon, remove and discard the bay leaves, shallots and lemon rind from the juices in the casserole. Using a metal spoon, skim off any fat from the surface of the liquid.

Add the remaining shallots to the

casserole. Place the casserole over moderately high heat and boil the liquid in the casserole, stirring frequently, for 20 to 30 minutes or until it has reduced by about half.

Meanwhile, in a medium-sized frying-pan, melt the butter over moderate heat. When the foam subsides, add the mushrooms and cook them for 3 minutes, or until they are just tender. Remove the frying-pan from the heat and keep the mushrooms warm.

When the liquid in the casserole has reduced, remove the shallots with a slotted spoon and place them on the plate with the meat.

Pour the liquid through a fine wire strainer into a medium-sized saucepan. Add the brandy and the grated lemon rind. Place the pan over moderate heat and bring the liquid to the boil. Reduce the heat to low and stir in the beurre manié, a little at a time, until the sauce is thick and smooth. Remove the pan from the heat and keep warm.

Remove the meat from the oven and remove and discard the foil. Place the meat on a carving board. Carve it into thick slices and place the slices on a warmed serving dish. Pour over half the sauce and put the remainder into a warmed sauceboat. Arrange the mushrooms and shallots around the meat and serve immediately, with the sauce.

Pot Roast with Brewer's Gravy

A warming variation of traditional pot roast, Pot Roast with Brewer's Gravy makes a delicious family meal. Serve it with potatoes baked in their jackets.

6 SERVINGS

1 x 4 lb. top rump [bottom round] of beef
1 teaspoon salt
$\frac{1}{2}$ teaspoon black pepper
2 fl. oz. [$\frac{1}{4}$ cup] vegetable oil
4 medium-sized leeks, cleaned and thinly sliced
6 medium-sized parsnips, peeled and sliced
1$\frac{1}{2}$ pints [3$\frac{3}{4}$ cups] beef stock
bouquet garni, consisting of 4 parsley sprigs, 1 thyme spray and 1 bay leaf tied together
8 fl. oz. [1 cup] light beer
1 tablespoon beurre manié
4 parsley sprigs

Rub the meat all over with salt and pepper. Set aside.

In a large flameproof casserole, heat the vegetable oil over moderate heat. When the oil is hot, add the beef to the casserole and, turning frequently, cook for 10 to 12 minutes or until it is evenly browned on all sides. Put half of the sliced leeks and

Pot Roast with Brewer's Gravy is served with the leeks and parsnips which are cooked with the beef.

half of the parsnips around the meat and cook for 8 minutes.

Pour the stock into the casserole and bring it to the boil. Add the bouquet garni. Cover the casserole, reduce the heat to low and cook for 2$\frac{1}{2}$ to 3 hours or until the meat is very tender when pierced with the point of a sharp knife.

Preheat the oven to warm 325°F (Gas Mark 3, 170°C).

Remove the casserole from the heat. Using two large forks, remove the meat from the casserole and transfer it to a warmed ovenproof plate. Cover with aluminium foil and put in the oven to keep hot.

With a metal spoon, skim off any fat from the liquid in the casserole. Pour the liquid through a fine wire strainer held over a medium-sized saucepan. Discard the contents of the strainer. Add the remaining vegetables to the liquid in the pan and set the pan over moderately high heat. Boil the liquid for 20 to 25 minutes, or until it has reduced by about one-half. Stir in the beer and bring the sauce to the boil again. Reduce the heat to low and stir in the beurre manié, a little at a time, until the gravy is thick and smooth.

Pot

Remove the pan from the heat and keep warm.

Remove the meat from the oven and remove and discard the foil. Place the meat on a carving board. Carve it into thick slices. Place the meat on a warmed serving dish and pour over the gravy and vegetables. Garnish with the parsley sprigs. Serve immediately.

Pot Roast with Garlic and Wine

This is a splendid dish which is ideal for a dinner party. Serve Pot Roast with Garlic and Wine with crusty bread or potatoes. A red Provençal or Rhône wine would be an excellent accompaniment.

10 SERVINGS

1 x 6 lb. top rump [bottom round] of beef
1½ teaspoons salt
½ teaspoon black pepper
4 oz. salt pork, diced
2 medium-sized onions, thinly sliced
3 garlic cloves, crushed
2 large carrots, scraped and sliced
5 oz. canned tomato purée
10 fl. oz. [1¼ cups] dry red wine
1½ pints [3¾ cups] beef stock
bouquet garni, consisting of 4 parsley sprigs, 1 thyme spray and 1 bay leaf tied together
1 tablespoon beurre manié
1 lb. tomatoes, blanched, peeled and roughly chopped
2 oz. [½ cup] stoned olives, chopped

Rub the meat all over with the salt and pepper. Set aside.

Place the salt pork in a large flameproof casserole and set the casserole over moderate heat. Fry the diced pork, stirring frequently, for 8 to 10 minutes or until the pork has rendered its fat. With a slotted spoon, remove and discard the salt pork.

Add the beef to the casserole and, turning frequently, cook for 10 to 12 minutes or until it is evenly browned on all sides. Add the onions, garlic and carrots and cook, stirring around the meat, for 8 minutes or until the onions are beginning to brown.

In a small mixing bowl, combine the tomato purée and the wine together. Pour the wine mixture and the stock over the beef and add the bouquet garni. Bring the liquid to the boil. Cover the casserole, reduce the heat to low and cook the meat for 3 to 3½ hours or until it is very tender when pierced with the point of a sharp knife.

Preheat the oven to warm 325°F (Gas Mark 3, 170°C).

Using two large forks, remove the meat from the casserole and place it on an ovenproof plate. Cover with aluminium foil and put it in the oven to keep hot while you finish making the sauce.

With a large metal spoon, skim off the fat from the cooking liquid. Increase the heat to moderately high and boil the liquid for 15 to 20 minutes or until it is reduced by about one-third. Remove the casserole from the heat and strain the liquid into a medium-sized saucepan, pressing down on the vegetables with the back of a wooden spoon to extract all the juices. Discard the contents of the strainer.

Place the pan over moderate heat and bring the liquid to the boil. Reduce the heat to low and stir in the beurre manié, a little at a time, until the sauce is thick and smooth. Stir in the tomatoes and cook, stirring frequently, for a further 8 minutes or until the tomatoes are beginning to pulp. Remove the pan from the heat and keep the sauce hot.

Remove the meat from the oven and remove and discard the foil. Place the meat on a carving board and carve it into thick slices. Transfer the meat slices to a warmed serving dish and scatter the olives on top.

Strain half of the sauce over the meat. Strain the remaining sauce into a warmed sauceboat.

Serve the meat immediately, with the sauce.

Pot Roast with Peppers and Garlic

Pot Roast with Peppers and Garlic is a colourful and appetizing meal for the family. Serve with baked potatoes or crusty bread to absorb all the delicious sauce.

6 SERVINGS

1 x 4 lb. top rump [bottom round] of beef
1 teaspoon salt
½ teaspoon freshly ground black pepper
2 fl. oz. [¼ cup] vegetable oil
2 large green peppers, white pith removed, seeded and sliced
2 large red peppers, white pith removed, seeded and sliced
1 medium-sized onion, thinly sliced and pushed out into rings
1½ pints [3¾ cups] beef stock
2 garlic cloves, crushed
½ teaspoon dried oregano
1 tablespoon beurre manié
2 tablespoons chopped fresh parsley

Rub the meat all over with the salt and pepper and set aside.

In a large flameproof casserole, heat the oil over moderate heat. When the oil is hot, add the beef to the casserole and, turning frequently with two large forks, cook it for 10 to 12 minutes or until it is evenly browned on all sides. Put half of the sliced green and red peppers and the onion around the meat and cook, stirring occasionally, for 5 to 7 minutes, or until the onion is soft and translucent but not brown.

Pour the stock into the casserole and add the garlic and oregano. Bring the liquid to the boil. Cover the casserole, reduce the heat to low and cook for 2½ to 3 hours or until the meat is very tender when pierced with the point of a sharp knife.

Preheat the oven to warm 325°F (Gas Mark 3, 170°C).

Remove the casserole from the heat. Using two large forks, remove the meat from the casserole and transfer it to a warmed ovenproof plate. Cover with aluminium foil and put in the oven to keep hot.

With a metal spoon, skim off any fat from the liquid in the casserole. Pour the liquid through a fine wire strainer held over a medium-sized saucepan. Discard the vegetables in the strainer. Add the remaining peppers and set the pan over high heat. Boil the liquid, stirring frequently, for 15 to 20 minutes or until the peppers are soft and the sauce has reduced by about one-third. Reduce the heat to low and stir in the beurre manié, a little at a time, until the sauce is thick and smooth. Remove the pan from the heat and keep the sauce warm.

Remove the meat from the oven and remove and discard the foil. Place the meat on a carving board. Carve it into thick slices, and transfer them to a warmed serving dish. Pour over half the sauce and vegetables and pour the remainder into a warmed sauceboat. Sprinkle the parsley over the meat and serve immediately, with the sauce.

Pot Roast with Vegetables

A traditional combination of meat, vegetables and herbs gives a special flavour to Pot Roast with Vegetables. Serve with mashed potatoes and a red Burgundy wine.

6 SERVINGS

1 x 4 lb. top rump [bottom round] of beef
1 teaspoon salt
½ teaspoon black pepper
2 fl. oz. [¼ cup] vegetable oil

4 oz. lean raw ham, diced

1½ lb. baby carrots, scraped and sliced

8 celery stalks, trimmed and chopped

4 medium-sized onions, thinly sliced and pushed out into rings

1½ pints [3¾ cups] beef stock

bouquet garni, consisting of 4 parsley sprigs, 1 thyme spray and 1 bay leaf tied together

1 tablespoon beurre manié

4 parsley sprigs

Rub the meat all over with the salt and pepper and set aside.

In a large flameproof casserole, heat the vegetable oil over moderate heat. When the oil is hot, add the beef to the casserole and, turning frequently, cook for 10 to 12 minutes or until it is evenly browned on all sides. Put the ham, half the carrots, half the celery and half the onions around

the meat and cook, stirring occasionally, for 8 to 10 minutes or until the onions are golden brown.

Pour the stock over the beef and add the bouquet garni. Bring the liquid to the boil. Cover the casserole, reduce the heat to low and cook for 2½ to 3 hours or until the meat is very tender when pierced with the point of a sharp knife.

Preheat the oven to warm 325°F (Gas Mark 3, 170°C).

Remove the casserole from the heat. Using two large forks, remove the meat from the casserole and place it on an oven-proof plate. Cover with aluminium foil and put in the oven to keep hot.

Pour the contents of the casserole through a fine wire strainer held over a medium-sized saucepan. Discard the contents of the strainer.

With a metal spoon, skim off and discard any fat from the liquid in the pan. Add the remaining vegetables to the pan.

A colourful and appetizing dish, Pot Roast with Peppers and Garlic has a thick, beefy sauce.

Bring the liquid to the boil over high heat and boil, stirring frequently, for 15 to 20 minutes or until it has reduced by about one-third and the vegetables are tender.

Reduce the heat to low and stir in the beurre manié, a little at a time, until the sauce is thick and smooth. Remove the pan from the heat and keep the sauce warm.

Remove the meat from the oven and remove and discard the foil. Place the meat on a carving board. Carve it into thick slices. Transfer the meat slices to a warmed serving dish and pour over half the sauce. Arrange the vegetables around the meat and garnish with the parsley sprigs. Pour the remaining sauce into a warmed sauceboat. Serve immediately.

Potage

Potage (poh-tahj) is the French word for soup.

Potage au Brocoli

CREAM OF BROCCOLI SOUP

Potage au Brocoli (poh-tahj oh broh-koh-lee) is an economical and warming soup, delicious served with crusty bread. In this recipe a short, cooked, pasta such as macaroni may be substituted for the rice and leeks may be used instead of spring onions [scallions] when these are not easily obtainable.

4-6 SERVINGS

12 spring onions [scallions], washed and finely chopped
 2 large carrots, scraped and sliced
 2 celery stalks, trimmed and diced
 2 garlic cloves, crushed
 1 bay leaf
 8 fl. oz. [1 cup] water
12 oz. broccoli, cooked, drained and coarsely chopped
 1 teaspoon salt
 ½ teaspoon white pepper
 ½ teaspoon paprika
1½ pints [3¾ cups] chicken stock
 8 fl. oz. single cream [1 cup light cream]
2½ oz. [1 cup] cooked long-grain rice
 4 tablespoons sour cream

Place the spring onions [scallions], carrots, celery, garlic, bay leaf and water in a large, heavy-based saucepan. Place the pan over moderate heat and bring the water to the boil, stirring constantly. Cover the saucepan, reduce the heat to low and simmer for 15 to 20 minutes or until the vegetables are tender.

Remove the pan from the heat and add the broccoli, salt, pepper, paprika and chicken stock. Stir well and return the pan to the heat. Cook the soup, stirring constantly, for 10 minutes.

Remove the pan from the heat. Pour the soup through a fine wire strainer held over a large mixing bowl. With the back of a wooden spoon, rub the vegetables through the strainer. Discard any pulp remaining in the strainer.

Alternatively, remove and discard the

bay leaf and blend the soup in an electric blender until the vegetables form a fine purée.

Pour the soup back into the saucepan and return the pan to low heat. Stir in the single [light] cream and the rice. Cook the soup, stirring constantly, for 5 minutes or until it has heated through.

Remove the pan from the heat and pour the soup into a warmed soup tureen or individual soup bowls. Spoon over the sour cream and serve immediately.

Potage au Chou-Fleur
CREAM OF CAULIFLOWER SOUP

A creamy and filling soup, Potage au Chou-Fleur (poh-tahj oh shoo-fler) should be served as a first course for an informal meal.

4-6 SERVINGS

2 oz. [¼ cup] butter
1 large onion, finely chopped
2 celery stalks, trimmed and finely chopped
2 oz. [½ cup] flour
1 teaspoon salt
½ teaspoon black pepper
2 pints [5 cups] chicken stock
1 medium-sized cauliflower, cleaned, separated into flowerets and 4 small leaves reserved
4 tablespoons double [heavy] cream
¼ teaspoon grated nutmeg
1 tablespoon finely chopped fresh parsley

In a large, heavy-based saucepan, melt the butter over moderate heat. When the foam subsides, add the onion and celery and cook, stirring occasionally, for 5 to 7 minutes or until the onion is soft and translucent but not brown.

Remove the pan from the heat and, with a wooden spoon, stir in the flour, salt and pepper. Gradually pour in the chicken stock, stirring constantly and being careful to avoid lumps. Add the cauliflower and the reserved cauliflower leaves.

Return the pan to the heat and bring the soup to the boil, stirring constantly. Reduce the heat to low, cover the pan and simmer for 30 minutes, stirring occa-sionally.

Remove the pan from the heat and pour the soup through a fine strainer held over a large mixing bowl. Using the back of a wooden spoon, rub the vegetables through the strainer into the bowl. Discard any pulp left in the strainer.

Alternatively, blend the soup in an electric blender until the vegetables form a fine purée.

Return the soup to the pan and place the pan over low heat. Stir in the cream and cook the soup, stirring constantly, for 5 minutes or until it is hot but not boiling.

Remove the pan from the heat and pour the soup into a warmed soup tureen. Sprinkle over the grated nutmeg and chopped parsley and serve immediately.

Potage Crécy
CARROT SOUP

A delicate and very easy-to-make soup, Potage Crécy (poh-tahj kreh-see) makes a delicious first course. Serve with crusty French bread and butter.

4-6 SERVINGS

1½ oz. [3 tablespoons] butter
1 large onion, finely chopped
1 lb. carrots, scraped and finely chopped
2 tablespoons long-grain rice, washed, soaked in cold water for 30 minutes and drained
1 teaspoon salt
½ teaspoon black pepper
½ teaspoon sugar
2 pints [5 cups] veal stock

4 tablespoons double [heavy] cream
1 medium-sized carrot, scraped and cut into julienne strips

In a large saucepan, melt the butter over moderate heat. When the foam subsides, add the onion and cook, stirring occasionally, for 5 to 7 minutes or until it is soft and translucent but not brown. Add the carrots, rice, salt, pepper and sugar and cook for a further 3 minutes, stirring frequently. Pour over the veal stock and bring the liquid to the boil, stirring constantly. Reduce the heat to low, cover the pan and simmer the mixture for 35 minutes or until the carrots are very tender.

Remove the pan from the heat and pour the soup through a fine wire strainer held over a large mixing bowl. Using the back of a wooden spoon, rub the vegetables through the strainer until only a dry pulp is left. Discard the pulp in the strainer.

Alternatively, blend the soup in an electric blender until the vegetables form a fine purée.

Return the soup to the saucepan. Stir in the cream. Place the pan over low heat and cook the soup, stirring constantly, for 5 minutes or until it is hot but not boiling.

Remove the pan from the heat. Pour the soup into a warmed soup tureen or individual soup bowls. Sprinkle over the carrot strips and serve immediately.

Potage d'Hiver
WINTER VEGETABLE SOUP

A classic soup, Potage d'Hiver (poh-tahj d'ee-vair) is made with dried beans and split peas which are puréed with fresh vegetables. The necessity of using dried vegetables in the winter is thought to have given this soup its name.

4 SERVINGS

2¼ pints [5⅝ cups] water
6 oz. [¾ cup] dried kidney beans, soaked overnight in cold water and drained
8 oz. [1 cup] dried yellow split peas, soaked overnight in cold water and drained
6 oz. dried butter beans [1 cup

A fabulous, tempting variety of warming soups, all the Potage recipes are really delicious.

dried lima beans] soaked overnight
in cold water and drained

2 oz. [$\frac{1}{4}$ cup] butter

3 onions, finely chopped

3 carrots, scraped, parboiled,
drained and finely chopped

$\frac{1}{2}$ teaspoon dried thyme

1 teaspoon salt

$\frac{1}{2}$ teaspoon black pepper

1$\frac{1}{2}$ pints [3$\frac{3}{4}$ cups] chicken stock
bouquet garni, consisting of 4
parsley sprigs, 1 thyme spray
and 1 bay leaf tied together

8 oz. spinach, cooked, drained
and puréed

In a large saucepan, bring the water to
the boil over high heat. Add the kidney
beans, split peas and butter [lima] beans
to the water, a few at a time, so that the
boiling does not stop. Reduce the heat to
low, cover the pan and simmer the beans
and peas for 1$\frac{1}{2}$ to 2 hours or until they
are tender. Remove the pan from the heat
and set aside.

In a large frying-pan, melt the butter
over moderate heat. When the foam subsides, add the onions to the pan and fry,
stirring occasionally, for 5 to 7 minutes or
until they are soft and translucent but not
brown. Add the carrots to the pan and
fry, stirring frequently, for 5 minutes or
until they are tender. Remove the pan
from the heat. Purée the onions, carrots,
beans and peas in food mill.

Alternatively, blend the vegetables in

an electric blender until they form a fine
purée.

Transfer the mixture to a large saucepan and stir in the thyme, salt, pepper and
stock. Add the bouquet garni.

Place the pan over high heat and, stirring frequently, bring the soup to the
boil. Reduce the heat to low, cover the
pan and simmer for 15 minutes. Remove
and discard the bouquet garni. Stir in the
puréed spinach and cook, stirring occasionally, for a further 5 minutes or until
the soup is hot.

Remove the pan from the heat. Ladle
the soup into a warmed soup tureen or
individual soup bowls and serve immediately.

Potage Parmentier

POTATO SOUP

  ①

*A warm soup, easy-to-make and inexpen-
sive, Potage Parmentier (poh-tahj pahr-
mahn-tee-ay) makes a tasty lunch. Garnish
with parsley and serve with crusty bread.*

4-6 SERVINGS

2 oz. [$\frac{1}{4}$ cup] butter

2 tablespoons vegetable oil

1 large onion, finely chopped

3 medium-sized leeks, white parts
only, trimmed and thinly sliced

6 medium-sized potatoes, peeled
and finely chopped

1 teaspoon salt

$\frac{1}{2}$ teaspoon black pepper

1 pint [2$\frac{1}{2}$ cups] chicken stock

10 fl. oz. [1$\frac{1}{4}$ cups] milk

In a medium-sized saucepan, melt the
butter with the oil over moderate heat.
When the foam subsides, add the onion
and cook, stirring occasionally, for 5 to 7
minutes or until the onion is soft and
translucent but not brown. Add the leeks
and potatoes and cook, stirring and turning occasionally, for 10 to 12 minutes or
until the potatoes are lightly and evenly
browned. Season with the salt and pepper
and pour over the chicken stock and milk.
Increase the heat to high and bring the
liquid to the boil, stirring constantly.
Reduce the heat to low, cover the pan and
simmer for 20 to 25 minutes or until the
potatoes are very tender.

Remove the pan from the heat and pour
the soup through a fine wire strainer held
over a large mixing bowl. Using the back
of a wooden spoon, rub the vegetables
through the strainer. Discard the pulp
left in the strainer.

Alternatively, blend the soup in an
electric blender until the vegetables form
a fine purée.

Return the soup to the saucepan and
place the pan over low heat. Cook the
soup, stirring occasionally, for 5 minutes
or until it is hot.

Remove the pan from the heat. Pour
the soup into a warmed soup tureen or
individual soup bowls and serve.

Potage Paysanne

FRENCH VEGETABLE SOUP

Potage Paysanne (poh-tahj pay-zahn) *is a classic French vegetable soup, warming and filling and suitable for a light lunch or snack. Serve it with thin slices of French bread.*

6-8 SERVINGS

2 oz. [¼ cup] butter
4 medium-sized carrots, scraped and finely shredded
1 medium-sized turnip, peeled and shredded
1 large leek, white part only, finely shredded
4 celery stalks, trimmed and finely chopped
1 small cabbage, coarse outer leaves removed, washed and shredded
1 teaspoon salt
½ teaspoon black pepper
½ teaspoon sugar
3 pints [7½ cups] chicken stock
4 small potatoes, peeled and thinly sliced
4 tablespoons fresh or frozen peas
1 tablespoon chopped fresh chervil or 1½ teaspoons dried chervil

In a large, heavy-based saucepan, melt the butter over moderate heat. When the foam subsides, add the shredded carrots, turnip, leek, celery and cabbage. Sprinkle over the salt, pepper and sugar. Fry the vegetables, stirring frequently, for 7 minutes.

Add the stock and bring the soup to the boil, stirring constantly. Reduce the heat to low, cover the pan and simmer for 35 minutes. Add the potatoes, peas and chervil and continue cooking for a further 15 to 20 minutes or until the potatoes are tender when pierced with the point of a sharp knife.

Remove the pan from the heat, pour the soup into a warmed soup tureen or individual soup bowls and serve immediately.

Potage de Poireaux et Cresson

LEEK AND CRESS SOUP

This hearty leek, potato and cress soup, flavoured with bacon, makes a warming lunch served with hot buttered rolls and cheese. Potage de Poireaux et Cresson (poh-tahj d' pwah-roh eh creh-sawn) is also delicious served with hot croûtons.

6-8 SERVINGS

4 streaky bacon slices, diced

1 tablespoon butter
1 lb. trimmed leeks, washed and thinly sliced
1 lb. potatoes, peeled and chopped
2 tablespoons flour
1 teaspoon salt
½ teaspoon black pepper
¼ teaspoon cayenne pepper
¼ teaspoon grated nutmeg
2 pints [5 cups] home-made chicken stock
10 fl. oz. [1¼ cups] milk
1 bunch watercress, washed, shaken dry and coarsely chopped
8 tablespoons chopped mustard and cress
1 bay leaf
5 fl. oz. [⅝ cup] sour cream
1 tablespoon chopped fresh chives (optional)

In a large saucepan, fry the bacon over moderate heat for 5 minutes or until it is crisp and has rendered most of its fat, scraping the bottom of the pan frequently with a wooden spoon to prevent the bacon from sticking. With a slotted spoon, remove the bacon from the pan and drain

on kitchen paper towels. Crumble the bacon and keep warm.

Add the butter to the pan and melt it with the bacon fat. When the foam subsides, add the leeks and potatoes. Fry the vegetables, stirring constantly, for 6 to 8 minutes or until they are golden.

Remove the pan from the heat. Sprinkle over the flour, salt, pepper, cayenne and nutmeg. Stir well with a wooden spoon to coat the vegetables with the flour and seasonings. Gradually pour in the chicken stock, stirring constantly and being careful to avoid lumps. Stir in the milk, cress and bay leaf.

Return the pan to the heat and bring the soup to the boil, stirring constantly. Reduce the heat to low, cover the pan and simmer for 30 minutes, stirring occasionally.

Remove the pan from the heat. Remove and discard the bay leaf. Pour the soup through a fine wire strainer held over a large mixing bowl. Using the back of a wooden spoon, rub the vegetables through the strainer until only a dry pulp is left. Discard the pulp in the strainer.

Alternatively, blend the soup in an

electric blender until the vegetables form a fine purée.

Return the soup to the saucepan and stir in the sour cream. Set the pan over moderately low heat and cook, stirring constantly, for 2 to 3 minutes or until the soup has heated through.

Remove the pan from the heat and pour

haricot bean soup, *Potage de Tomate à la Paysanne* (poh-tahj d'toh-maht ah lah pay-zahn) *is almost a meal in itself. Accompany it with bread, butter and cheese.*

6 SERVINGS

3 tablespoons olive oil
2 medium-sized onions, finely chopped

occasionally, for 5 to 7 minutes or until the onions are soft and translucent but not brown.

Add the tomatoes, bay leaf, thyme, salt and pepper and stir well. Reduce the heat to low. Cook, stirring occasionally, for 20 minutes or until the tomato mixture is very thick.

Add the stock. Cover the pan and simmer the soup for 15 minutes or until it is quite thick. Add the beans and heat until the beans are heated through.

Remove the pan from the heat. Ladle the soup into a warmed tureen or individual soup bowls. Sprinkle over the parsley and serve.

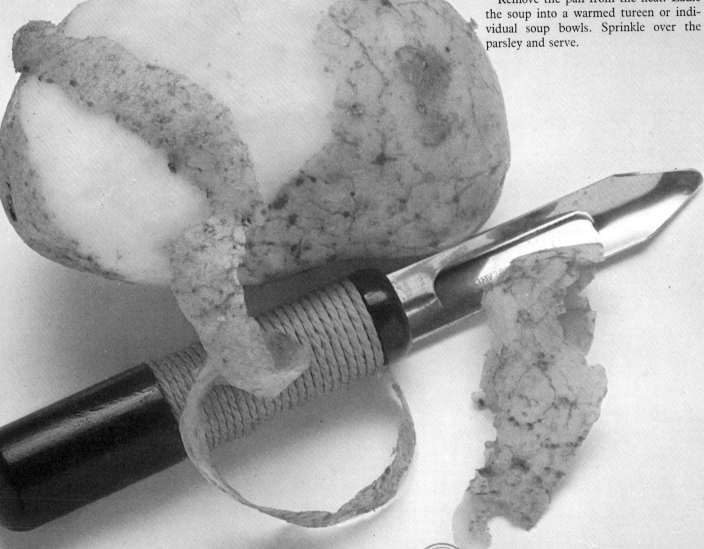

the soup into a large, warmed tureen or individual soup bowls. Sprinkle over the chopped chives, if you are using them, and the fried bacon. Serve immediately.

Potage de Tomate à la Paysanne

TOMATO SOUP PEASANT-STYLE

A thick and hearty tomato and white

Potage de Tomate à la Paysanne is a thick and hearty tomato soup.

2 garlic cloves, crushed
2½ lb. tomatoes, blanched, peeled and quartered
1 bay leaf
1 tablespoon chopped fresh thyme or 1 teaspoon dried thyme
1 teaspoon salt
½ teaspoon black pepper
1 pint [2½ cups] chicken stock
1 lb. dried white haricot beans, soaked, cooked and drained
1 tablespoon chopped fresh parsley

(Low Cal)

In a large saucepan, heat the oil over moderate heat. When the oil is hot, add the onions and garlic and fry, stirring

Potato

The potato is one of the most important food plants in the world.

The Irish or white potato, *solanum tuberosum*, which now grows commonly in Europe and North America, is the descendant of a plant which originated in the Andes in South America.

The plant is a perennial of the *solanacene* family. It grows to one to three feet in height, with branching stems and many leaves. The flowers are white or bluish with yellow centres and sometimes produce a berry. None of the above-ground parts of the potato are eaten because they contain poisonous alkaloids.

Pot

The potato was probably brought to Europe by Spaniards returning from their conquest of South America during the latter half of the sixteenth century. Those early potatoes had irregular and deep-eyed skins and, perhaps because of this, took a long time to become established — they .were only grown experimentally in Europe for over half a century.

The eighteenth century saw an increase in popularity and the potato came to be widely grown in Europe, especially in Ireland. And, by the beginning of the nineteenth century, the potato was established as a staple food in the British Isles and in most countries in Europe.

Today potatoes are grown prolifically in northern temperate zones, but are also cultivated, with a lesser yield, in Scandinavian latitudes and in sub-tropical regions.

Potatoes are generally oval or kidney-shaped, and vary greatly in size and regularity of shape.

There are numerous varieties of potato and each potato-producing country grows 'early' varieties and 'maincrop' varieties, thus ensuring supplies all the year round. The best varieties are those with a high yield per acre and freedom from disease, with shallow 'eyes' and good keeping properties.

Potatoes have a high water content (about 77 per cent) and contain small amounts of minerals, vitamins B and C and about 2 per cent protein. However, as they are generally eaten in comparatively large quantities, the sum total of the nutrients can be an important contribution to the diet.

Potatoes should always be eaten cooked, when they make an easily digestible and palatable food. They may be cooked in many different ways.

All potatoes may be cooked and eaten unpeeled, in their jackets, and this is recommended as most of the nutrients lie immediately beneath the skin. If you must peel potatoes, and some dishes require this, peel only old potatoes; new potatoes need only be scrubbed.

To boil potatoes, choose potatoes of uniform size or cut them to size so that they all cook in the same amount of time.

Place the potatoes in a saucepan large enough to take them comfortably, pour over enough water just to cover them and bring the water to the boil over high heat. Add salt, cover the pan, reduce the heat to low and simmer the potatoes for 15 to 20 minutes or until they are tender. Remove the pan from the heat, drain the potatoes, being careful not to damage them and place them in a warmed serving dish. The potatoes may be dotted with a little butter and sprinkled with a tablespoon of chopped fresh parsley.

To mash boiled potatoes, cook and drain the potatoes as above and mash and stir the potatoes to a rough purée with a potato masher or a kitchen fork. Mashed potatoes should not be beaten.

To cream boiled potatoes, cook and drain the potatoes as above and beat in 1 ounce [2 tablespoons] of butter and 2 tablespoons of milk or single [light] cream to every 2 pounds of potatoes. Beat until the mixture is light and fluffy. Alternatively, put the potatoes through a food mill or beat them with an electric mixer.

To make potatoes for piping, see DUCHESS POTATOES.

Steaming is a particularly good way of cooking new potatoes. To steam potatoes, place the prepared potatoes in the upper half of the steamer. Half-fill the lower pan with boiling water and place it over high heat. Place the upper half of the steamer over the water, cover and reduce the heat to low. Steam the potatoes for 15 to 20 minutes or until they are tender. Remove the pan from the heat and transfer the potatoes to a heated serving dish. The potatoes may be sprinkled with a little salt and melted butter. Toss the potatoes with a spoon to coat them with the butter.

To sauté potatoes, prepare the potatoes and cut them into slices about $\frac{1}{3}$-inch thick. In a large frying-pan, heat enough butter and oil together to cover the bottom of the pan. Place the pan over moderately high heat. When the foam subsides, add enough potato slices to make a single layer on the bottom of the frying-pan. Fry the potato slices, turning them frequently, for 10 to 15 minutes or until they are tender and golden brown. Transfer the potatoes to kitchen paper towels to drain.

Cooked or parboiled potatoes may also be sautéed. Cut them into slices and fry them for 5 to 8 minutes or until they are golden brown. Transfer the slices to kitchen paper towels to drain.

To cook French-fried potatoes, first cut peeled potatoes into fingers, $\frac{1}{3}$- to $\frac{1}{2}$-inch thick and pat them dry with kitchen paper towels. Fill a deep-frying pan one-third full with vegetable oil and heat it over moderate heat until the temperature registers 360°F on a deep-fat thermometer or until a small cube of stale bread dropped into the oil turns golden brown in 50 seconds. Place about two handfuls of the potato fingers in a deep-frying basket, which has first been dipped in the hot oil, and lower the basket into the oil. Fry the potatoes for 5 minutes or until they are golden brown. Lift the basket out of the oil and allow the excess oil to run back into the pan. Drain the potatoes on kitchen paper towels and keep them hot while you cook the remaining potato fingers in the same way. French-fried potatoes should be crisp on the outside and floury inside.

To bake potatoes in their jackets, preheat the oven to fairly hot 375°F (Gas Mark 5, 190°C). Choose uniform-sized, unblemished potatoes. Scrub the skins to remove any soil and prick the skins, in several places, with the prongs of a fork. Distribute the potatoes over the rungs of the oven shelves, being careful to arrange them so that they do not touch. Bake the potatoes for 45 minutes to 1½ hours, depending on the size of the potatoes. The potatoes are cooked if they feel soft when you pinch them. Remove the potatoes from the oven. Cut a cross on one of the flat sides of each potato. Pinch the lower part of each potato with both hands so that the 'cross' opens out. Place a little butter in the 'opening' and sprinkle with a little salt and pepper.

To roast potatoes, either leave them whole if they are small or medium-sized, or cut them into large cubes if they are large. Preheat the oven to fairly hot 400°F (Gas Mark 6, 200°C). Heat a $\frac{1}{4}$-inch layer of vegetable oil in a baking tin in the oven for 8 minutes or until it is very hot. Remove the tin from the oven and place the potatoes in the oil. Brush them all over with some of the hot oil. Return the tin to the oven and roast the potatoes for 1 hour, brushing occasionally with the oil and turning once, or until the potatoes are deep golden brown. Remove the tin from the oven and transfer the potatoes to kitchen paper towels. Set the potatoes aside to drain.

To roast potatoes with meat, parboil the potatoes, drain and add them to the pan in which the meat is roasting, for the last hour of cooking time.

Potato Bread

This is a light, smooth-textured bread which cuts well if kept for one day. Potato Bread may be used for open sandwiches or savoury gâteaux. It is also delicious eaten on its own, spread with butter.

ONE 2-POUND LOAF

2 oz. [¼ cup] plus 1 teaspoon butter
½ oz. fresh yeast
1 tablespoon plus ¼ teaspoon sugar
2 tablespoons lukewarm water
3 medium-sized potatoes, cooked and mashed
10 fl. oz. [1¼ cups] lukewarm milk
1 lb. [4 cups] flour
1 teaspoon salt
1 tablespoon finely chopped fresh chives

Grease a 2-pound loaf tin with the teaspoon of butter and set aside.

Crumble the yeast into a small bowl and mash in the ¼ teaspoon of sugar with a kitchen fork. Add the water and cream the water and yeast together to form a smooth paste. Place the potatoes in a warmed, large mixing bowl. Stir in the yeast mixture and 2 tablespoons of the lukewarm milk. Set the bowl aside in a warm, draught-free place for 20 minutes.

In a small saucepan, scald the remaining milk over moderately low heat (bring it to just below boiling point). Remove the pan from the heat and add the remaining butter, cut into small pieces. Stir until the butter has melted. Allow the milk and butter mixture to cool to lukewarm.

Sift the flour, the remaining sugar and the salt into the large mixing bowl. Stir in the chives. Make a well in the centre of the flour mixture and pour in the milk and butter mixture.

Using your fingers or a spatula, gradually draw the flour mixture into the liquid. Continue mixing until all the flour mixture is incorporated and the dough comes away from the sides of the bowl.

Turn the dough out on to a floured board or marble slab and knead for about 10 minutes, reflouring the surface if the dough becomes sticky. The dough should be elastic and smooth.

Rinse, thoroughly dry and lightly grease the large mixing bowl. Shape the dough into a ball and return it to the bowl. Cover with a clean, damp cloth. Set the bowl in a warm, draught-free place and leave it for 1½ to 2 hours or until the dough has risen and has almost doubled in bulk.

Turn the risen dough out of the bowl on to a floured surface and knead for about 4 minutes. Roll and shape the dough into a loaf. Place the dough in the prepared tin, cover with a damp cloth and return to a warm place for 45 minutes to 1 hour or until the dough has risen to the top of the tin.

Preheat the oven to very hot 450°F (Gas Mark 8, 230°C).

Place the tin in the centre of the oven and bake for 15 minutes. Reduce the oven temperature to fairly hot 375°F (Gas Mark 5, 190°C) and bake for a further 45 minutes.

After removing the bread from the oven, tip the loaf out and rap the underside with your knuckles. If the bread sounds hollow, like a drum, it is cooked. If the bread does not sound hollow, reduce the oven temperature to moderate 350°F (Gas Mark 4, 180°C), return the loaf, upside-down, to the oven and bake for a further 10 minutes.

Place the loaf on a wire rack to cool.

Potato Casserole

A hearty and warming meal for the family, Potato Casserole is ideal for cold winter nights.

4 SERVINGS

1 oz. [2 tablespoons] butter
2 shallots, coarsely chopped
2 celery stalks, trimmed and coarsely chopped
1 garlic clove, crushed
2 lb. potatoes, peeled and thinly sliced
8 oz. carrots, scraped and thinly sliced
4 streaky bacon slices, chopped
14 oz. canned peeled tomatoes
8 fl. oz. [1 cup] brown stock
1 teaspoon salt
½ teaspoon black pepper
2 teaspoons paprika
¼ teaspoon dried basil

Low Cal

In a large frying-pan, melt the butter over moderate heat. When the foam subsides, add the shallots, celery and garlic and cook, stirring occasionally, for 3 to 4 minutes or until the shallots are soft and translucent but not brown.

Add the potatoes, carrots and bacon and cook, stirring frequently, for 15 minutes or until the potatoes are golden brown.

Pour in the tomatoes with the can juice, the stock, salt, pepper, paprika and basil. Bring the liquid to the boil over moderate heat, stirring frequently. Reduce the heat to low. Cover the pan and simmer for 10 minutes or until the potatoes are tender.

Remove the pan from the heat. Turn the mixture out into a warmed serving dish and serve immediately.

Potato and Cheese Pie

An economical supper dish, this Potato and Cheese Pie is a favourite with children and is very easy to make. The mixture may also be served as a vegetable accompaniment to plain fish dishes.

4 SERVINGS

2 oz. [¼ cup] plus 1 teaspoon butter
1½ lb. potatoes, cooked, peeled, mashed and kept warm
2 medium-sized onions, finely chopped
1 oz. [¼ cup] flour
1 teaspoon salt
½ teaspoon freshly ground black pepper
½ teaspoon dried mixed herbs
12 fl. oz. [1½ cups] milk
8 oz. [2 cups] Cheddar cheese, finely grated

Preheat the oven to moderate 350°F (Gas Mark 4, 180°C).

With the teaspoon of butter, lightly grease a medium-sized baking dish. Set aside. Place the potatoes in a medium-sized mixing bowl and set them aside.

In a medium-sized saucepan, melt the remaining butter over moderate heat. When the foam subsides, add the onions and cook, stirring occasionally, for 5 to 7 minutes or until they are soft and translucent but not brown.

Remove the pan from the heat. With a wooden spoon, stir in the flour, salt, pepper and mixed herbs to make a smooth paste. Gradually add the milk, stirring constantly and being careful to avoid lumps.

Set the pan over low heat and cook the sauce, stirring constantly, for 4 to 5 minutes or until it is smooth and has thickened.

Add 6 ounces [1½ cups] of the cheese and cook, stirring constantly, for 3 to 4 minutes or until it has melted.

Gradually pour the cheese sauce over

the potatoes, beating constantly with a wooden spoon until the mixture is smooth. Turn the mixture into the prepared baking dish and smooth the mixture down with the back of a spoon. Sprinkle over the remaining cheese.

Place the dish in the centre of the oven and bake for 20 to 25 minutes or until the top is golden brown.

Remove the dish from the oven and serve immediately.

Potato Croquettes

Delicious served with almost any meat, fish or vegetable dish, Potato Croquettes are quick and easy to make.

3-4 SERVINGS

1½ lb. potatoes, cooked, peeled and mashed
1 egg yolk
2 oz. [¼ cup] butter
2 fl. oz. [¼ cup] hot milk
1 teaspoon salt
½ teaspoon black pepper
1 teaspoon chopped fresh parsley
1 egg, lightly beaten
4 oz. [1⅓ cups] dry white breadcrumbs
3 tablespoons vegetable oil

Place the mashed potatoes in a medium-

Potato Croquettes and Potato Fritters go well with any meat or fish.

sized mixing bowl and, using a wooden spoon, beat in the egg yolk, half the butter and enough of the hot milk to make a firm consistency. Add the salt, pepper and parsley and beat until the mixture is smooth.

With floured hands, break off pieces of the mixture and roll them into sausage shapes. Place the croquettes, in one layer, on a plate and chill them in the refrigerator for 30 minutes, or until they are firm.

Put the lightly beaten egg on one plate and the breadcrumbs on another.

Remove the croquettes from the refrigerator and dip them first in the egg, then roll them in the breadcrumbs, coating them thoroughly and shaking off any excess. Set aside.

In a large frying-pan, heat the remaining butter with the oil over moderate heat. When the foam subsides, add the croquettes to the pan, a few at a time, and fry them for 3 to 4 minutes or until they are crisp and lightly browned all over.

Remove the croquettes from the pan and drain them well on kitchen paper towels. Transfer the croquettes to a warmed serving dish. Keep them hot while you fry the remaining croquettes in the same way. Serve the croquettes hot.

Potato Fritters

Potato Fritters, potatoes fried in crispy batter, tastes delicious served as an accompaniment to meat or fish dishes.

2 SERVINGS

1 lb. potatoes, peeled, parboiled and cut into ½-inch thick slices
4 tablespoons flour
sufficient vegetable oil for deep-frying
10 fl. oz. [1¼ cups] Fritter Batter II

Dry the potato slices thoroughly with kitchen paper towels. Place the flour on a plate and pour the batter into a small, shallow bowl.

Dip the potato slices, a few at a time, in the flour, coating them thoroughly and shaking off any excess. Set aside.

Fill a medium-sized deep-frying pan one-third full with the vegetable oil. Place the pan over moderate heat and heat the oil until it registers 360°F on a deep-fat thermometer, or until a small cube of stale bread dropped in the oil turns golden brown in 50 seconds.

Dip a few of the potato slices into the batter, coating them thoroughly. Carefully lower the slices into the hot oil and fry them for 4 to 5 minutes, or until they are cooked and the batter is crisp and golden.

Using a slotted spoon, remove the potatoes from the oil and drain them thoroughly on kitchen paper towels. Transfer the potatoes to a warmed serving dish and keep them hot while you fry and drain the remaining potatoes in the same way.

Serve hot.

Potato and Herring Salad

This is an adaptation of a popular Danish dish. Rollmop herrings may be used, but Scandinavian pickled herrings have a more subtle flavour.

4 SERVINGS

1 lb. potatoes, cooked, peeled and sliced
4 pickled herrings, cut into strips
2 cooking apples, peeled, cored and cut into julienne strips
1 pickled cucumber, cut into julienne strips
1 tablespoon fruit chutney
4 fl. oz. [½ cup] sour cream
1 tablespoon sugar
1 hard-boiled egg, chopped
1 tablespoon chopped fresh dill

In a medium-sized mixing bowl, combine the potatoes, herrings, apples, cucumber, chutney, sour cream and sugar. Cover the

Subtly-flavoured Potato and Herring Salad and a savoury vegetable accompaniment, Potato Kugel.

bowl and place it in the refrigerator to chill for 1 hour.

Remove the bowl from the refrigerator and transfer the potato mixture to a glass salad bowl.

In a small mixing bowl, combine the chopped egg and dill together. Sprinkle the mixture over the salad and serve immediately.

Potato Kugel

This savoury potato cake may be served with grilled [broiled] pork chops or with grilled [broiled] bacon and sautéed mushrooms. If you cannot buy potato flour, cornflour [cornstarch] may be substituted.

6 SERVINGS

1 tablespoon butter
4 eggs, lightly beaten
2 lb. potatoes, cooked, mashed and kept warm
1 oz. [¼ cup] potato flour
½ teaspoon baking powder
1 teaspoon salt
½ teaspoon black pepper
1 small onion, finely chopped

1 tablespoon chopped fresh parsley
1½ oz. [3 tablespoons] butter, melted

Preheat the oven to moderate 350°F (Gas Mark 4, 180°C).

With the tablespoon of butter, generously grease a 2½-pint [1½-quart] ovenproof dish. Set aside.

In a large mixing bowl, combine the eggs and the potatoes together, beating until they form a smooth paste.

Add the potato flour, baking powder, salt, pepper, onion and parsley and beat well with a wooden spoon until all the ingredients are thoroughly combined. Stir in the melted butter. Spoon the potato mixture into the buttered dish.

Place the dish in the oven and bake for 30 to 35 minutes or until the top of the potato mixture is deep golden brown.

Remove the kugel from the oven and serve immediately.

Potatoes with Peppers and Olives

This dish has a distinctively Italian flavour and is an appetizing and colourful way of serving potatoes. Serve it as a delicious accompaniment to garlic sausage or salami.

4 SERVINGS

2 oz. [¼ cup] butter

Two unusual salads — Potato, Egg and Anchovy Salad and Potato and Cheese Salad.

2 tablespoons vegetable oil
2 lb. potatoes, peeled and thinly sliced
2 medium-sized onions, coarsely chopped
2 garlic cloves, crushed
1 teaspoon salt

$\frac{1}{2}$ teaspoon freshly ground black pepper
1 small green pepper, white pith removed, seeded and diced
1 small red pepper, white pith removed, seeded and diced
1 oz. [$\frac{1}{4}$ cup] black olives, halved and stoned
1 oz. [$\frac{1}{4}$ cup] stuffed olives, halved

In a large frying-pan, melt the butter with the oil over moderate heat. When the

foam subsides, reduce the heat to low and add the potatoes, onions, garlic, salt and pepper. Cook, stirring frequently, for 15 minutes or until the potatoes are golden brown.

Add the green and red peppers and cook, stirring frequently, for 5 to 10 minutes or until the potatoes are tender. Add the olives and continue cooking for 5 minutes.

Remove the pan from the heat. Turn the mixture into a warmed serving dish

and serve immediately.

Potato Puffs

Delicious and unusual, Potato Puffs are best served with grilled [broiled] steak or chops.

4 SERVINGS

2 oz. [¼ cup] plus 1 teaspoon butter, melted

2 lb. potatoes, cooked, peeled and mashed
2 eggs, well beaten
3 tablespoons flour
6 spring onions [scallions], trimmed and finely chopped
1 teaspoon salt
½ teaspoon black pepper
1 tablespoon finely chopped fresh parsley

Using the teaspoon of butter, lightly grease two medium-sized baking sheets and set aside.

Preheat the oven to fairly hot 375°F (Gas Mark 5, 190°C).

In a large mixing bowl, combine all the remaining ingredients, beating well with a wooden spoon until they are thoroughly combined.

Place heaped tablespoons of the mixture, slightly spaced, on the prepared baking sheets. Place the baking sheets in the oven and bake for 10 minutes or until the puffs are golden.

Remove the baking sheets from the oven. Using a spatula or fish slice, transfer the puffs to a warmed serving dish and serve immediately.

Potato Salad

This simple Potato Salad with mayonnaise dressing may be served with cold meat or as one of a selection of salads. Use the green part of the leeks for this recipe and save the white parts for future use.

4 SERVINGS

1 lb. potatoes, cooked, peeled and sliced
4 fl. oz. [½ cup] mayonnaise
1 tablespoon lemon juice
1 tablespoon olive oil
½ teaspoon salt
½ teaspoon black pepper
2 tablespoons chopped fresh chives
4 tablespoons chopped leeks

Place three-quarters of the potatoes in a medium-sized mixing bowl. Pour over the mayonnaise and sprinkle with the lemon juice, oil, salt, pepper and 1 tablespoon of chives. Using two large spoons, carefully toss the potatoes until they are thoroughly coated with the mayonnaise mixture.

Spoon the mixture into a serving bowl. Arrange the remaining potato slices over the top of the salad. Sprinkle with the remaining chives and scatter the leeks around the edge of the bowl.

Cover the bowl and place it in the refrigerator to chill for 30 minutes before serving.

Potato and Cheese Salad

This dish is adapted from a Northern Italian recipe and may be served as a light luncheon dish, accompanied by lettuce salad.

4 SERVINGS

1 lb. potatoes, cooked and peeled
4 fl. oz. [½ cup] mayonnaise
½ teaspoon black pepper
⅛ teaspoon cayenne pepper
1 garlic clove, crushed
3 oz. Gruyère cheese, cut into ¼-inch cubes
2 oz. Gorgonzola cheese, crumbled
4 slices proscuitto, halved and rolled

Place the potatoes on a board and cut them into ½-inch cubes. Transfer the potatoes to a medium-sized mixing bowl. Add the mayonnaise, pepper, cayenne, garlic, Gruyère and Gorgonzola to the bowl and toss with two large spoons until the ingredients are well mixed.

Transfer the salad to a glass salad bowl. Garnish with the rolled proscuitto and serve immediately.

Potato, Egg and Anchovy Salad

This strongly flavoured salad may be served with cold chicken or turkey.

4 SERVINGS

1 lb. new potatoes, cooked, peeled and sliced
½ head of fennel, trimmed and thinly sliced
1 tablespoon chopped fresh chives
2 hard-boiled eggs, chopped
10 anchovy fillets, chopped
1 tablespoon red wine vinegar
2 tablespoons olive oil
½ teaspoon salt
½ teaspoon freshly ground black pepper
4 fl. oz. [½ cup] mayonnaise
1 tablespoon capers

In a medium-sized mixing bowl, combine the potatoes, fennel, chives, eggs and anchovies together.

In a small mixing bowl, beat the vinegar, oil, salt and pepper together with a kitchen fork. Stir the mayonnaise into the dressing. Pour the mayonnaise mixture over the potato mixture and toss well with two forks until the ingredients are well mixed. Transfer the salad to a glass salad bowl. Sprinkle the capers over the salad.

Serve immediately or chill the salad until it is required.

Potato Salad with Herbs

Potato Salad with Herbs should be made with fresh herbs for the best result.

4 SERVINGS

1 lb. potatoes, cooked and peeled
8 spring onions [scallions], trimmed and chopped
1 tablespoon chopped fresh parsley
2 teaspoons chopped fresh basil
1 teaspoon chopped fresh marjoram
½ teaspoon chopped fresh lemon thyme
½ teaspoon chopped fresh fennel leaves
6 tablespoons olive oil
2 tablespoons wine vinegar
1 teaspoon salt
½ teaspoon black pepper
½ teaspoon sugar

Place the potatoes on a board and cut them into ½-inch cubes. Transfer the potato cubes to a medium-sized serving bowl. Add the spring onions [scallions], parsley, basil, marjoram, lemon thyme and fennel leaves.

In a small mixing bowl, combine the olive oil, vinegar, salt, pepper and sugar together, beating with a fork until they are well mixed.

Pour the dressing over the potatoes and herbs and serve immediately or chill in the refrigerator before serving.

Potato Scones [Biscuits]

Potato Scones [Biscuits] are cooked on a griddle and served hot with butter. They are also excellent served with bacon for breakfast.

ABOUT 8 SCONES

1 lb. potatoes, cooked and peeled
4 oz. [1 cup] plus 1 tablespoon flour
1 teaspoon salt
⅛ teaspoon cayenne pepper
1 oz. [2 tablespoons] butter, softened
1 tablespoon cold water

Drain the potatoes and mash them with a potato masher or fork until they are absolutely smooth and free from lumps.

Place the potatoes in a large mixing bowl, add 4 ounces [1 cup] of the flour, the salt and cayenne and mix well.

Beat in the butter with a wooden spoon, then add the water. Beat until the mixture forms a firm dough. Add more flour if the dough is too soft.

On a lightly floured board, roll out the dough to ½-inch thick. Using a 3-inch pastry cutter, cut the dough into circles.

Prick the dough circles all over with a fork.

Dredge the griddle with the remaining flour and heat over moderate heat until the flour turns light brown.

Place the scones on the griddle and cook them for 4 to 6 minutes on each side or until they are golden brown and well cooked. Serve immediately.

Potatoes with Spices and Mustard

New potatoes cooked with mustard and spices in the creole style, Potatoes with Spices and Mustard makes a delicious accompaniment to grilled [broiled] lamb chops.

4 SERVINGS

sufficient vegetable oil for deep-frying
2 lb. small new potatoes, parboiled and drained
2 teaspoons prepared French or German mustard
1½ oz. [3 tablespoons] butter, melted
¼ teaspoon cayenne pepper
¼ teaspoon hot chilli powder
¾ teaspoon salt
¼ teaspoon black pepper
2 teaspoons chilli vinegar

Fill a medium-sized deep-frying pan one-third full with the vegetable oil. Place the pan over moderate heat and heat the oil until it reaches 360°F on a deep-fat thermometer or until a small cube of stale bread dropped into the oil turns golden brown in 50 seconds.

Fry the potatoes in the oil, a few at a time, for 3 to 4 minutes or until they turn golden brown. Using a slotted spoon, remove the potatoes from the oil and drain them on kitchen paper towels. Fry and drain the remaining potatoes in the same way.

In a medium-sized saucepan, combine the mustard, melted butter, cayenne, chilli powder, salt, pepper and vinegar together. Add the potatoes and stir to coat them with the mixture. Set the pan over moderate heat and cook for 5 minutes, shaking the pan frequently to prevent the potatoes from sticking.

Remove the pan from the heat and turn the mixture into a warmed serving dish. Serve immediately.

Potatoes Stuffed and Baked

Baked potatoes are doubly delicious when the flesh is scooped out, mixed with savoury ingredients, returned to the potato shell and

reheated in the oven or under the grill [broiler] *until the top is golden brown.*

Allow one potato per person. The quantities of savoury fillings given below are sufficient to fill four potatoes.

To prepare the potatoes, bake the potatoes in their jackets, remove them from the oven and place them on a board. With a sharp knife remove a ½-inch slice from the top flat side of the potato. Using a teaspoon, scoop out the inside of each potato to within ¼-inch of the shell, being careful not to pierce the skin. Place the flesh in a medium-sized mixing bowl and arrange the potato shells in a roasting tin or in the grill [broiler] pan. Prepare the filling and spoon it into the potato shells, piling it up and rounding the top. Place the potatoes in an oven preheated to fairly hot 375°F (Gas Mark 5, 190°C) and bake them for 10 to 12 minutes or until the top of the filling is golden brown. Alternatively, place the potatoes under the grill [broiler], preheated to hot, and grill [broil] for 5 to 8 minutes or until they are golden brown. Serve immediately.

FILLING 1

the flesh from 4 potatoes baked in their jackets
2 oz. Brie cheese
½ teaspoon dried chives
½ teaspoon salt
1 egg yolk
2 oz. [¼ cup] butter, softened

In a medium-sized mixing bowl, combine the potato flesh, Brie, chives, salt, egg yolk and butter. Beat them with a wooden spoon until they are all thoroughly mixed.

FILLING 2

the flesh from 4 potatoes baked in their jackets
2 oz. Gorgonzola cheese, crumbled
1 tablespoon single [light] cream
2 teaspoons tomato purée
½ teaspoon black pepper
½ teaspoon dried basil
2 oz. [¼ cup] butter, softened

In a medium-sized mixing bowl, combine the potato flesh, Gorgonzola, cream, tomato purée, pepper, basil and butter. Beat them with a wooden spoon until they are thoroughly mixed.

FILLING 3

the flesh from 4 potatoes baked in their jackets

A simple but tasty Potato Salad sprinkled with chives and leeks.

4 oz. [1 cup] Cheshire cheese, crumbled

1 small eating apple, peeled, cored and finely chopped

1 teaspoon prepared mustard

$\frac{1}{2}$ teaspoon salt

2 oz. [$\frac{1}{4}$ cup] butter, softened

In a medium-sized mixing bowl, combine the potato flesh, Cheshire, apple, mustard, salt and butter. Beat them with a wooden spoon until they are thoroughly mixed.

FILLING 4

the flesh from 4 potatoes baked in their jackets

4 oz. [1 cup] Cheddar cheese, grated

2 teaspoons sour sweet chutney

1 small celery stalk, trimmed and finely chopped

2 oz. [$\frac{1}{4}$ cup] butter softened

In a medium-sized mixing bowl, combine the potato flesh, Cheddar, chutney, celery

and butter. Beat them vigorously with a wooden spoon until they are thoroughly mixed.

FILLING 5

the flesh from 4 potatoes baked in their jackets

4 slices streaky bacon, grilled [broiled] until golden brown and crumbled

1 oz. [2 tablespoons] butter

4 oz. mushrooms, wiped clean and chopped

$\frac{1}{2}$ teaspoon salt

$\frac{1}{4}$ teaspoon black pepper

In a medium-sized mixing bowl, combine the potato flesh and the bacon. Set aside.

In a small frying-pan, melt the butter over moderate heat. When the foam subsides, add the mushrooms and fry, stirring constantly, for 3 minutes. Remove the pan from the heat and pour the contents of the pan into the mixing bowl. Add the

A selection of tempting fillings for Potatoes Stuffed and Baked.

salt and pepper. Beat the ingredients with a wooden spoon until they are mixed.

FILLING 6

the flesh from 4 potatoes baked in their jackets

4 oz. shrimps or prawns, shelled

4 spring onions [scallions], chopped

$\frac{1}{2}$ teaspoon grated lemon rind

$\frac{1}{2}$ teaspoon chopped fresh parsley

$\frac{1}{4}$ teaspoon cayenne pepper

2 oz. [$\frac{1}{4}$ cup] butter, softened

In a medium-sized mixing bowl, combine the potato flesh, shrimps or prawns, spring onions [scallions], lemon rind, parsley, cayenne and butter. Beat with a wooden spoon until they are thoroughly combined.

Poteca

SWISS YEAST CAKE

A delicious sweet bread filled with a chewy walnut cream, Poteca (poh-tay-kah) may be served sliced and spread with butter.

TWO 1-POUND LOAVES

¾ oz. fresh yeast
4 oz. [½ cup] plus ½ teaspoon sugar
3 teaspoons lukewarm water
8 fl. oz. [1 cup] milk
4 oz. [½ cup] plus 2 teaspoons butter
1½ lb. [6 cups] flour
1 teaspoon salt
2 egg yolks, lightly beaten
FILLING
3 egg whites
4 oz. [½ cup] castor sugar
6 oz. [1 cup] walnuts, very finely chopped
grated rind of 1 small orange
grated rind of 1 lemon
TOPPING
2 to 3 tablespoons clear honey, warmed
12 walnut halves
6 glacé cherries, halved
2 angelica strips, cut into small pieces

Crumble the yeast into a small bowl and mash in the ½ teaspoon of sugar with a kitchen fork. Add the water and cream the

water and yeast together. Set the bowl aside in a warm, draught-free place for 15 to 20 minutes or until the yeast mixture is puffed up and frothy.

Pour the milk into a small saucepan. Place it over moderately high heat and scald the milk (bring to just under boiling point). Reduce the heat to low and add the 4 ounces [½ cup] of butter. When the butter has melted, remove the pan from the heat and allow the milk and butter mixture to cool to lukewarm.

Sift the flour, remaining sugar and salt into a warmed, large mixing bowl. Make a well in the centre of the flour mixture and pour in the yeast mixture, milk and butter mixture and the egg yolks.

Using your fingers or a spatula, gradually draw the flour into the liquid. Continue mixing until all the flour is incorporated and the dough comes away from the sides of the bowl.

Turn the dough out on to a lightly floured board or marble slab and knead it for 10 minutes, reflouring the surface if the dough becomes sticky. The dough should be elastic and smooth.

Rinse, thoroughly dry and lightly grease the large mixing bowl. Shape the dough into a ball and return it to the bowl. Cover the bowl with a clean damp cloth and set it in a warm, draught-free place. Leave it for 1 to 1½ hours or until the dough has risen and doubled.

Poteca is a very attractive sweet bread from Switzerland. Serve it sliced, on its own or with butter.

Meanwhile, using the 2 teaspoons of butter, grease two baking sheets.

In a medium-sized mixing bowl, beat the egg whites with a wire whisk or rotary beater until they form soft peaks. Using a metal spoon, carefully fold in the sugar, a little at a time. Beat the mixture until it is stiff and glossy. Fold in the walnuts and the orange and lemon rinds. Set aside.

Turn the risen dough out of the bowl on to a floured surface and knead it for about 5 minutes. Using a sharp knife, cut the dough into 2 pieces. Roll each piece of dough out to form a large, long rectangle. With a palette knife or spatula, spread half the filling on each piece of dough. With one of the long ends towards you, roll up each piece of dough Swiss [jelly] roll style. Carefully transfer the rolls to the prepared baking sheets, seam side down. Pull the ends of each loaf round to meet each other and make a circle. Wet the ends with a little water and press them together to seal, overlapping slightly.

Return the baking sheets to a warm place for about 30 to 45 minutes or until the dough has almost doubled in bulk.

Preheat the oven to hot 425°F (Gas Mark 7, 220°C).

Pots de Crème au Luxe is a creamy brandy and coffee-flavoured dessert.

Place the baking sheets in the oven and bake for 15 minutes.

Reduce the heat to moderate 350°F (Gas Mark 4, 180°C) and continue baking for a further 40 minutes. After removing the bread from the oven, tip the loaves off and rap the undersides with your knuckles. If the bread sounds hollow, like a drum, it is cooked. If it does not sound hollow, return the loaves, upside-down, to the oven and bake for 5 to 10 minutes.

Place the loaves on a wire rack to cool for 15 minutes. Using a pastry brush, brush with the honey. Decorate with the walnut halves, cherries and angelica.

Serve warm or cold.

Pots de Crème au Luxe
SMALL CUSTARD CREAMS

A richer version of the traditional small cups of custard, Pots de Crème au Luxe (poh d'krem oh looks) are flavoured with coffee and brandy.

6 SERVINGS

1 pint single cream [2½ cups light cream]
5 egg yolks
1 egg
3 tablespoons sugar
2 tablespoons coffee essence
2 tablespoons brandy

Preheat the oven to warm 325°F (Gas Mark 3, 170°C).

In a small saucepan, heat the cream over low heat. When the cream is hot but not boiling, remove the pan from the heat and set aside.

In a medium-sized mixing bowl, beat the egg yolks, egg, sugar, coffee essence and brandy together with a wooden spoon until they are just combined. Stirring constantly with the wooden spoon, gradually pour the cream on to the egg mixture, beating until they are well blended. Strain the mixture into another bowl.

Pour the mixture into 6 small ramekin dishes or custard cups. Place the filled dishes or cups in a baking tin and pour in enough boiling water to come halfway up the sides of the dishes or cups. Cover each dish or cup with aluminium foil.

Place the tin in the oven and bake for 25 to 30 minutes or until the custards are lightly set.

Remove the tin from the oven and leave to cool, then chill in the refrigerator before serving.

Pottage

Pottage is a thick, economical soup made from the cheaper cuts of meat and vegetables, although meat is not always used. The soup is cooked for a long time and barley, lentils and other pulses are often included to make it more substantial.

Potted Cheese, Meat, Fish, Game and Poultry

The tradition of potting good quality cheese, meat and fish derives from the early days of sailing when travellers used to take along such concentrated food to sustain them on their journey.

The meat and fish are first cooked, then usually minced [ground] or finely chopped and pressed into pots or terrines. Clarified butter is poured over the paste to preserve the contents.

Potted Cheese

This is a simply made cheese mixture for spreading on toast or savoury biscuits. It will keep for up to 10 days in the refrigerator. If you chill Potted Cheese in the refrigerator for longer than 4 hours leave it at room temperature for 1 hour before serving.

10-12 SERVINGS

1 lb. [4 cups] Cheshire or Cheddar cheese, grated
6 oz. [¾ cup] butter, softened
5 fl. oz. [⅝ cup] dry white wine
½ teaspoon grated nutmeg
⅛ teaspoon dry mustard
⅛ teaspoon cayenne pepper
6 oz. [¾ cup] clarified butter, melted

In a medium-sized mixing bowl, combine the cheese and softened butter. With a wooden spoon, beat the mixture until it is creamy.

Stir in the wine, nutmeg, mustard and cayenne and beat the mixture until it is smooth.

Spoon the cheese mixture into a 1½-pint [1-quart] terrine or mould and smooth the top with a table knife. Pour the clarified butter over the cheese mixture.

Cover the terrine or mould with aluminium foil and place it in the refrigerator to chill for at least 4 hours.

Remove the terrine or mould from the refrigerator. Remove and discard the foil and serve at once.

Potted Hare

This is a traditional English dish and, although recommended in the eighteenth century as part of a breakfast menu, it is now more usually served as a delicious and tasty first course, with hot buttered toast.

10 SERVINGS

2 lb. boned hare, cut into 1-inch pieces
4 fl. oz. [½ cup] red wine
1 tablespoon red wine vinegar
8 oz. unsalted pork fat, diced
1 pint [2½ cups] boiling water
1 teaspoon salt
½ teaspoon black pepper
½ teaspoon grated nutmeg
¼ teaspoon dried thyme
¼ teaspoon dried marjoram

Preheat the oven to cool 300°F (Gas Mark 2, 150°C).

Place the meat in a large mixing bowl and pour over the red wine, vinegar and enough water to just cover the meat. Set aside at room temperature for 2 hours. Drain the meat in a strainer and discard the marinade. Pat the meat dry with kitchen paper towels and set aside.

In a large frying-pan, cook the pork fat over moderate heat for 8 minutes, stirring frequently, or until it has rendered most of its fat. Add the meat to the frying-pan and cook it, stirring frequently, for 5 minutes or until it is evenly browned on all sides. Remove the pan from the heat and pour the meat and fat into an ovenproof casserole. Pour the boiling water into the casserole and stir in the salt, pepper, nutmeg, thyme and marjoram. Cover the casserole and place it in the oven.

Cook the meat for 2½ hours or until it is very tender when pierced with the point of a sharp knife.

Remove the casserole from the oven. Strain the contents of the casserole into a medium-sized mixing bowl. Place the meat on a board and, with a sharp knife, chop it very finely. Transfer the meat to a medium-sized terrine and set aside.

Place the mixing bowl in the refrigerator to chill for 20 minutes or until the fat has come to the top and is just starting to set. Remove the bowl from the refrigerator. Skim the fat from the surface and place it in a small saucepan.

Place the pan over low heat and melt the fat. Remove the pan from the heat and pour the fat into the terrine.

Cover the terrine with aluminium foil and chill it in the refrigerator for at least 2 hours before serving.

Potted Herrings

Potted Herrings make a delicious first course spread on thin, hot buttered toast, with a wedge of lemon squeezed over the fish. Alternatively, it can be used as an excellent sandwich filler. Potted Herrings may be kept for up to 3 days in the refrigerator.

8 SERVINGS

6 herrings, cleaned and roes reserved
½ teaspoon salt
½ teaspoon black pepper
1 tablespoon butter, softened
10 fl. oz. [1¼ cups] Court Bouillon
4 oz. [½ cup] clarified butter, melted

Preheat the oven to cool 300°F (Gas Mark 2, 150°C).

With a sharp knife, remove the heads and tails from the herrings. Rub the herrings all over with the salt and pepper.

Grease a large ovenproof dish with the tablespoon of butter. Arrange the herrings, top to tail, in the dish with the roes. Pour over the court bouillon.

Place the dish in the oven and bake the fish for 45 minutes or until the fish flakes very easily when tested with a fork.

Remove the dish from the oven. Drain the herrings and discard the cooking liquid. Remove and discard the backbones from the herrings. Put the herring flesh and roes in a strainer over a medium-sized mixing bowl. With the back of a wooden spoon, rub the fish through the strainer. Discard any pulp remaining in the strainer.

Spoon the mixture into 8 small pots.

Pour the clarified butter over the surface of the herrings. Cover the pots with aluminium foil and chill in the refrigerator until they are required.

A perfect first course — Potted Shrimps or Prawns with bread.

Potted Shrimps or Prawns

A traditional British speciality, Potted Shrimps or Prawns are very easy to prepare. White fish is often added to the shrimps or prawns and the mixture may be put into one big dish rather than small individual pots. Serve with thin slices of brown bread and garnish with watercress. Potted Shrimps or Prawns may be kept for up to 1 week in the refrigerator.

10 SERVINGS

5 oz. [⅝ cup] butter
¼ teaspoon ground mace
⅛ teaspoon cayenne pepper
½ teaspoon salt
½ teaspoon black pepper
1 lb. shrimps or prawns, cooked and shelled
3 oz. [⅜ cup] clarified butter, melted

In a large frying-pan, melt the butter over moderate heat. When the foam subsides, stir in the mace, cayenne, salt and pepper. Add the shrimps or prawns to the pan and coat them thoroughly with the seasoned butter. Remove the pan from the heat.

Spoon equal amounts of the mixture into 10 small pots, leaving a ¼-inch space at the top. Pour 1 tablespoon of the clarified butter into each pot. Cover the pots with aluminium foil and put them

in the refrigerator to chill for at least 2 hours.

Remove the pots from the refrigerator. Remove and discard the foil and serve at once.

Potted Tongue

An excellent way to use up leftover tongue, Potted Tongue is ideal for picnics or cold buffets where the food is prepared in advance. It may be kept for up to 1 week in the refrigerator. If Potted Tongue is chilled for longer than 2 hours leave it at room temperature for 1 hour before serving.

10 SERVINGS

8 oz. ox tongue, cooked and chopped
3 oz. [⅜ cup] unsalted butter, softened
½ teaspoon salt
¼ teaspoon black pepper
¼ teaspoon ground allspice
½ teaspoon grated lemon rind
2 fl. oz. [¼ cup] Marsala
3 oz. [⅜ cup] clarified butter, melted

Mince [grind] the tongue in a food mill or in an electric blender.

Transfer the tongue to a medium-sized mixing bowl and, with a wooden spoon, gradually beat in the softened butter. Stir in the salt, pepper, allspice and lemon rind. Stir in the Marsala and beat the mixture until the ingredients are thoroughly mixed.

Spoon the mixture into 10 small pots, leaving a ¼-inch space at the top. Pour 1 tablespoon of the clarified butter into each pot. Cover the pots with aluminium foil and put them in the refrigerator to chill for at least 2 hours.

Remove the pots from the refrigerator. Remove and discard the foil and serve at once.

Pouding d'Avocat

AVOCADO ICE-CREAM

A subtly flavoured ice-cream, Pouding d'Avocat (poo-ding dah-voh-kah) is made with sour cream and ripe avocados. Serve with a lemon sauce or just by itself. To make this dessert, you will need an ice-cream container equipped with paddles.

1 pint [2½ cups]

4 ripe avocados, halved and stoned
juice of 1 lemon
3 drops green food colouring
8 fl. oz. double cream [1 cup heavy cream]
8 fl. oz. [1 cup] sour cream
1 vanilla pod
3 egg yolks
2 oz. [¼ cup] sugar
3 fl. oz. [⅜ cup] water
3 egg whites, stiffly beaten

Using a teaspoon, scoop the flesh from the avocados and place it in a small mixing bowl. Pour the lemon juice into the bowl. Using a fork, mash the avocado flesh with the lemon juice and green food colouring until it forms a smooth paste. Set aside.

Place the cream and sour cream in a medium-sized saucepan. Set the pan over low heat and scald the cream (bring to just under boiling point). Remove the pan from the heat. Add the vanilla pod to the pan, cover it and set aside for 20 minutes.

Strain the cream into a small mixing bowl. Remove and discard the vanilla pod. Set the cream aside.

In a medium-sized mixing bowl, beat the egg yolks with a wire whisk or rotary beater until they are pale. Set aside.

In a small saucepan, dissolve the sugar in the water over low heat, stirring constantly. When the sugar has dissolved, increase the heat to moderate and boil the syrup until the temperature reaches 220°F on a sugar thermometer or until a little of the syrup dropped into cold water

Pouding d'Avocat is a really unusual and refreshing ice-cream made with avocados, sour cream and lemon.

forms a short thread when drawn out between your index finger and thumb. Remove the pan from the heat and let the syrup cool for 1 minute.

Pour the syrup on to the egg yolks in a steady stream, whisking constantly with a wire whisk or rotary beater. Continue whisking until the mixture is thick and fluffy. Using a metal spoon, gently but thoroughly fold in the avocado mixture. Stir in the cooled cream. With the metal spoon, fold in the egg whites.

Pour the mixture into the ice-cream container and freeze.

Pouding aux Fruits Sechés
DRIED FRUIT PUDDING

A filling and absolutely scrumptious steamed pudding, Pouding aux Fruits Seches (poo-ding oh frwee seh-shay) is made with a mixture of unusual dried fruit. All the fruit used may be obtained from most health food stores. Serve with Crème à la Vanille.

6 SERVINGS

3 oz. [⅜ cup] plus 3 teaspoons butter
5 oz. [1¼ cups] flour
½ teaspoon baking powder
½ teaspoon mixed spice or ground allspice
¼ teaspoon ground cinnamon

3 oz. [½ cup] soft brown sugar
2 eggs
4 tablespoons Apple Sauce
2 oz. [⅓ cup] dried apples, chopped
2 oz. [⅓ cup] dried bananas, chopped
2 oz. [⅓ cup] candied pineapple, chopped
2 oz. [⅓ cup] glacé cherries, halved
3 fl. oz. [⅜ cup] milk

Using 2 teaspoons of the butter, grease a 1½-pint [1-quart] pudding basin. Set aside.

Sift the flour, baking powder, mixed spice or allspice and cinnamon into a medium-sized mixing bowl. Set aside.

In a large mixing bowl, using a wooden spoon, cream 3 ounces [⅜ cup] of the butter until it is light and fluffy. Add the sugar and beat the mixture until it is smooth and creamy. Beat in the eggs, one at a time. Using a metal spoon, fold in half of the flour mixture. Stir in the apple sauce.

Add the apples, bananas, pineapple and cherries to the remaining flour mixture. Using a large metal spoon, fold the fruit and flour mixture into the batter. Stir in the milk.

Spoon the pudding batter into the prepared basin, smoothing the top with the back of the spoon. Cut out a circle of greaseproof or waxed paper 4-inches

Apples, bananas, pineapple, cherries and spices combine to make Pouding aux Fruits Sechés a super dessert.

wider than the rim of the basin. Grease the paper with the remaining teaspoon of butter. Cut out a circle of aluminium foil the same size as the paper circle.

Place the greaseproof or waxed paper circle and the foil circle together, the buttered side of the greaseproof or waxed paper away from the foil and, holding them firmly together, make a 1-inch pleat across the centre. Place the pleated paper and foil circle, foil uppermost, over the pudding basin. With a piece of string, securely tie the paper and foil circle around the rim of the basin.

Fill the lower half of a steamer three-quarters full of water and bring the water to the boil over moderate heat.

Place the basin in the top part of the steamer, cover with the lid and place it over the lower part of the steamer. Reduce the heat to moderately low and steam the pudding for 2½ hours, adding more boiling water if necessary.

Remove the steamer from the heat and remove the pudding from the steamer. Discard the paper and foil. Turn the pudding out on to a warmed serving dish and serve immediately.

Pouding de Viande
MEAT PUDDING

A useful recipe for using up leftover cooked meat, Pouding de Viande (poo-ding d'vee-ahnd) may be made with lamb, pork, chicken, or a mixture of these. It makes a filling dinner or lunch, served with a green vegetable.

4 SERVINGS

- 1 pint [2½ cups] béchamel sauce
- 4 egg yolks
- 2 tablespoons vegetable oil
- 1 large onion, finely chopped
- 2 lb. cooked lean meat, finely chopped
- ½ teaspoon salt
- ¼ teaspoon black pepper
- 1 oz. [2 tablespoons] plus 1 teaspoon butter
- 8 oz. button mushrooms, wiped clean and halved
- 10 slices day-old white bread, crusts removed and thinly buttered
- 4 oz. [1 cup] Gruyère cheese, grated

Pour the béchamel sauce into a medium-sized mixing bowl and, using a wooden spoon, beat in the egg yolks. Set aside.

In a large frying-pan, heat the oil over moderate heat. When the oil is hot, add the onion and fry, stirring occasionally, for 5 to 7 minutes or until it is soft and translucent but not brown. Add the meat, salt and pepper and fry, stirring occasionally, for 5 minutes. Remove the pan from the heat and set aside.

In a small saucepan, melt 1 ounce [2 tablespoons] of the butter over moderate heat. When the foam subsides, add the mushrooms and cook, stirring frequently, for 3 minutes. Remove the pan from the heat and mix the mushrooms into the béchamel mixture. Set aside.

Preheat the oven to moderate 350°F (Gas Mark 4, 180°C).

Grease a 3-pint [2-quart] ovenproof mould with the remaining teaspoon of butter. Line the sides and bottom of the mould with the bread, buttered sides facing inwards, overlapping each slice and reserving enough bread to make a lid.

Spoon a little of the meat and onion mixture into the bottom of the mould and cover with a little of the béchamel and mushroom mixture. Sprinkle over a little grated cheese. Continue making layers in the same way until all the ingredients have been used up. Cover with the remaining bread slices, buttered side down, trimming them to fit the shape of the mould. Cover the top of the mould with aluminium foil.

Place the mould in the centre of the oven and bake for 50 minutes to 1 hour or until the top is golden brown.

Remove the mould from the oven and remove and discard the foil. Run a sharp-edged knife around the edge of the mould. Hold a warmed serving dish, inverted, over the mould and reverse the two, giving the mould a sharp shake. The pudding should slide out easily. Serve immediately.

Pouilly Fuissé
A soft, fragrant white wine, Pouilly Fuissé is one of the best—and one of the most popular—of the white Burgundies. It is produced in a five-village area in the Maconnais region of Burgundy.

Pouilly Fumé
A delicate and aromatic white wine, Pouilly Fumé is generally considered to be the single best wine produced in the Loire area of France.

Pouilly Fumé is an excellent accompaniment to fish dishes.

Serve Pouding de Viande with a green vegetable for lunch or dinner.

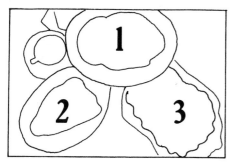

Three French chicken dishes fit for best dinner parties — 1 Poulet Brandade; 2 Poulet aux Cerises; 3 Poulet en Casserole à la Bonne Femme.

Poulet Brandade

CHICKEN WITH WINE AND BRANDY

A succulent yet easy-to-make dish, Poulet Brandade (poo-lay brahn-dad) may be served with Brussels Sprouts Creole and Duchess Potatoes for a really excellent meal. A well-chilled white Burgundy wine, such as Montrachet would be a good accompaniment.

4 SERVINGS

1 x 4 lb. chicken, cut into serving
   pieces
1 teaspoon salt
1 teaspoon black pepper
2 oz. [¼ cup] butter
2 shallots, finely chopped
2 garlic cloves, crushed
4 fl. oz. [½ cup] dry white wine
2 fl. oz. [¼ cup] brandy

Rub the chicken pieces all over with the salt and pepper and set aside.

In a deep, large frying-pan, melt the butter over moderate heat. When the foam subsides, add the shallots and garlic and cook, stirring occasionally, for 3 to 4 minutes or until the shallots are soft and translucent but not brown. Add the chicken pieces to the pan and cook, stirring and turning occasionally, for 8 to 10 minutes or until they are evenly browned.

Pour over the wine and brandy and bring the liquid to the boil, stirring occasionally. Reduce the heat to low, cover the pan and simmer the chicken for 20 to 25 minutes or until it is tender.

Using tongs, transfer the chicken pieces to a warmed serving dish. Keep warm while you finish the sauce.

Strain the pan liquid into a small saucepan and bring to the boil over high heat. Boil the sauce for 5 minutes or until it has reduced by about half.

Remove the pan from the heat and pour the sauce over the chicken. Serve at once.

Poulet en Casserole à la Bonne Femme

CASSEROLED CHICKEN WITH VEGETABLES

Poulet en Casserole à la Bonne Femme (poo-lay ehn kah-say-rohl ah lah bohn fahm) is a classic French dish of chicken cooked with bacon, potatoes, onions and herbs.

4 SERVINGS

1 x 4 lb. chicken
1 teaspoon salt
½ teaspoon black pepper
2 oz. [¼ cup] butter
1½ lb. small white onions, peeled
1½ lb. small new potatoes, scrubbed
6 lean bacon slices, rinds removed
   and diced
   bouquet garni, consisting of 4
   parsley sprigs, 1 thyme spray
   and 1 bay leaf tied together

Preheat the oven to moderate 350°F (Gas Mark 4, 180°C).

Rub the chicken, inside and out, with the salt and pepper. Set aside.

In a large flameproof casserole, melt the butter over moderate heat. When the foam subsides, add the chicken and cook, turning it frequently, for 8 to 10 minutes or until it is evenly browned.

Remove the chicken from the casserole and keep warm. Add the onions, potatoes and bacon to the casserole and cook for 10 minutes, shaking the casserole frequently.

Return the chicken to the casserole and add the bouquet garni. Cover the casserole and place it in the oven. Cook for 45 minutes to 1 hour or until the chicken is tender.

Remove the casserole from the oven and remove and discard the bouquet garni. Place the chicken on a warmed serving dish and surround it with the vegetables and bacon. Serve immediately.

Poulet aux Cerises

CHICKEN IN CHERRY SAUCE

A sweet and succulent sauce accompanies Poulet aux Cerises (poo-lay oh s'rees). A mixed salad, small roast potatoes and a well-chilled bottle of white Graves wine would round off the meal to perfection.

4 SERVINGS

1 x 4 lb. chicken
1 teaspoon salt
½ teaspoon black pepper
2 teaspoons fresh rosemary or 1
   teaspoon dried rosemary
2 oz. [¼ cup] butter
8 fl. oz. [1 cup] chicken stock

14 oz. canned stoned Morello
   cherries, drained and with 6 fl.
   oz. [¾ cup] of the can juice
   reserved
2 teaspoons lemon juice
2 teaspoons cornflour [cornstarch]
   dissolved in 2 tablespoons water

Preheat the oven to moderate 350°F (Gas Mark 4, 180°C).

Rub the chicken, inside and out, with the salt, pepper and rosemary. Set aside.

In a large flameproof casserole, melt the butter over moderate heat. When the foam subsides, add the chicken and cook, turning it frequently, for 8 to 10 minutes or until it is evenly browned. Pour over the stock and bring to the boil. Cover the casserole and place it in the centre of the oven. Cook for 45 minutes to 1 hour or until the chicken is tender.

Remove the casserole from the oven. Using two large forks, lift the chicken out of the casserole and transfer it to a warmed serving dish. Keep warm.

With a metal spoon, skim off any fat from the surface of the juices in the casserole. Pour the liquid through a fine wire strainer into a small saucepan.

Place the saucepan over moderate heat and add the reserved cherry juice and the lemon juice. Bring to the boil, stirring constantly.

Stir in the dissolved cornflour [cornstarch]. Reduce the heat to low. Simmer the sauce, stirring constantly, for 5 minutes or until it has thickened.

Add the drained cherries to the sauce and continue cooking for 2 minutes or until the cherries are heated through.

Remove the pan from the heat and pour half of the sauce over the chicken. Pour the remaining sauce into a warmed sauceboat and serve immediately, with the chicken.

Poulet aux Champignons

CHICKEN AND MUSHROOMS

A filling and tasty dish, Poulet aux Champignons (poo-lay oh sham-peen-yon) is also very decorative. Serve with pilaff for a scrumptious meal.

6 SERVINGS

3 tablespoons vegetable oil
1 medium-sized onion,
   finely chopped
1 garlic clove, crushed

Poulet aux Champignons, chicken cooked with wine, herbs and mushrooms, may be served with a mixed vegetable pilaff for a filling meal.

1 x 5 lb. chicken, cut into serving
    pieces
1 oz. [2 tablespoons] butter
1 lb. mushrooms, wiped clean and
    sliced
10 fl. oz. [1¼ cups] chicken stock
10 fl. oz. [1¼ cups] dry white wine
1 teaspoon chopped fresh thyme or
    ½ teaspoon dried thyme
½ teaspoon salt
¼ teaspoon white pepper
1 bay leaf
2 tablespoons cornflour [corn-
    starch] dissolved in 6 tablespoons
    water

In a large frying-pan, heat the oil over
moderate heat. When the oil is hot, add
the onion, garlic and chicken pieces to
the pan. Cook, turning the chicken pieces
frequently, for 8 to 10 minutes or until
they are evenly browned.

With a slotted spoon, remove the
chicken pieces, onion and garlic from
the pan and set them aside on a plate.
Pour off all the oil from the frying-pan.

Return the frying-pan to high heat and
add the 1 ounce [2 tablespoons] of butter.
When the foam subsides, add the mushrooms. Cook them, stirring constantly,

for 3 minutes. Remove the pan from the
heat and set aside.

In a large flameproof casserole, heat
the stock, wine, thyme, salt, pepper and
bay leaf over moderate heat. Stir in the
cornflour [cornstarch] mixture. Cook,
stirring constantly, until the mixture
begins to thicken. Return the chicken,
onion, garlic and mushrooms with the
cooking juices to the casserole. Stir well.
Reduce the heat to low, cover the casserole and simmer for 20 to 25 minutes
or until the chicken is tender.

Remove the casserole from the heat
and serve at once.

Poulet au Brocoli

POACHED CHICKEN WITH BROCCOLI

*A very succulent and easy-to-make dish,
Poulet au Brocoli (poo-lay oh braw-
c'ly) may be served with boiled new
potatoes and tomato salad. The cooking
liquid may be used as a base for soups and
casseroles.*

4 SERVINGS

1 x 4 lb. chicken
2½ pints [6¼ cups] water

2 teaspoons salt
2 oz. [¼ cup] butter
3 tablespoons flour
16 fl. oz. [2 cups] milk
½ teaspoon grated nutmeg
6 fl. oz. [¾ cup] Hollandaise Sauce
4 fl. oz. double cream [½ cup heavy
    cream], beaten until it is thick
    but not stiff
3 tablespoons sherry
1½ lb. broccoli, cooked and drained
3 oz. [¾ cup] Parmesan cheese,
    grated

Place the chicken in a large saucepan and
add the water and salt. Set the pan over
high heat and bring the water to the boil.
Reduce the heat to low and simmer the
chicken for 1 hour or until the chicken
is tender. Remove the pan from the heat
and allow the chicken to cool in the
cooking liquid.

In a medium-sized saucepan, melt the
butter over moderate heat. Remove the
pan from the heat and, with a wooden
spoon, stir in the flour to make a smooth
paste. Gradually add the milk, stirring
constantly. Return the pan to the heat
and cook, stirring constantly, for 2 to 3
minutes or until the sauce is thick and

smooth. Remove the pan from the heat and stir in the nutmeg. Set aside.

Stir the hollandaise sauce into the white sauce. Using a metal spoon, fold the cream and the sherry into the mixture. Set aside.

Preheat the oven to fairly hot 375°F (Gas Mark 5, 190°C).

When the chicken is cool enough to handle, take it out of the cooking liquid and place it on a chopping board. Discard the cooking liquid. Remove and discard the skin. Remove and slice the breast and leg meat.

Arrange the broccoli in a large oven-proof serving dish. Sprinkle over half of the Parmesan cheese. Arrange the chicken pieces on top of the cheese. Pour the sauce mixture over the chicken and sprinkle with the remaining cheese. Place the dish in the oven and bake for 30 minutes or until the top is deep golden brown.

Remove the dish from the oven and serve immediately.

Poulet aux Crevettes

CHICKEN WITH PRAWNS OR SHRIMPS AND WINE

An unusual combination of chicken and prawns or shrimps makes Poulet aux Crevettes (poo-lay oh kreh-vet) a delectable dish. Serve with boiled rice and a crisp green salad

4 SERVINGS

1 teaspoon salt
½ teaspoon black pepper
1 x 4 lb. chicken, cut into serving pieces
2 fl. oz. [¼ cup] olive oil
2 garlic cloves, crushed
1-inch piece fresh root ginger, peeled and finely chopped
3 shallots, coarsely chopped
10 fl. oz. [1¼ cups] white wine
2 teaspoons fresh marjoram or 1 teaspoon dried marjoram
10 oz. prawns or shrimps, shelled
1 teaspoon lemon juice
1 teaspoon cornflour [cornstarch] dissolved in 1 tablespoon water or white wine

Rub the salt and pepper into the chicken pieces and set them aside.

In a large flameproof casserole, heat the oil over moderate heat. When the oil is hot, add the chicken pieces and cook, turning frequently, for 8 to 10 minutes or until they are evenly browned. Using tongs, transfer the chicken to a plate and set aside.

Add the garlic, ginger and shallots to the casserole and cook, stirring frequently, for 3 to 4 minutes or until the shallots are soft and translucent but not brown. Return the chicken to the casserole.

Pour over the wine, add the marjoram and bring the liquid to the boil. Reduce the heat to low, cover the casserole and simmer for 45 minutes to 1 hour or until the chicken is tender.

Add the prawns or shrimps to the casserole, re-cover and cook for a further 5 minutes or until they have heated through. With the tongs, lift the chicken pieces out of the casserole and transfer them to a warmed serving dish. Using a slotted spoon, remove the prawns or shrimps from the cooking liquid and arrange them around the chicken.

Increase the heat to high and bring the liquid to the boil. Reduce the heat to very low, add the lemon juice and cook, stirring constantly with a wooden spoon, for 2 minutes.

Stir in the cornflour [cornstarch] mixture and cook, stirring constantly, for 3 minutes or until the sauce has thickened. Remove the casserole from the heat and pour the sauce over the chicken. Serve immediately.

For a really different meal, try this delectable Poulet aux Crevettes, a mixture of chicken, shrimps or prawns, marjoram, ginger and wine.

Tasty Poulet aux Girolles à la Crème, roast chicken served with a rich mushroom, bacon, garlic and wine sauce.

Poulet aux Girolles à la Crème

CHICKEN WITH MUSHROOM AND CREAM SAUCE

Delicious and sustaining, Poulet aux Girolles à la Crème (poo-lay oh jee-rawl ah lah krem) makes a magnificent centre-piece for a dinner party. Serve with Carottes au Neige and roast potatoes and, to drink, a well-chilled Pouilly Fuissé wine. The mushrooms used in this recipe are chanterelles but button mushrooms may be substituted.

6 SERVINGS

1 x 5 lb. chicken
1 teaspoon salt
1 teaspoon black pepper
1½ oz. [3 tablespoons] butter, melted
4 streaky bacon slices, diced
1 lb. chanterelle mushrooms, wiped clean and halved
2 garlic cloves, crushed
4 fl. oz. [½ cup] white wine
¼ teaspoon grated nutmeg
10 fl. oz. double cream [1¼ cups heavy cream]

1 tablespoon cornflour [cornstarch] mixed to a paste with 3 table-spoons water

Preheat the oven to hot 425°F (Gas Mark 7, 220°C).

Rub the chicken all over with the salt and pepper and place it in a roasting tin. Pour the melted butter over the chicken. Place the tin in the oven and roast the chicken for 15 minutes. Reduce the oven temperature to moderate 350°F (Gas Mark 4, 180°C) and continue roasting the chicken, basting it occasionally with the melted butter, for 1¼ to 1½ hours or until it is cooked and the juices run clear when one thigh is pierced with the point of a sharp knife.

Meanwhile, place the bacon in a medium-sized frying-pan. Set the pan over moderate heat and cook the bacon, stirring occasionally, for 5 minutes or until it is crisp and has rendered most of its fat. Add the mushrooms and garlic to the pan and cook, stirring occasionally, for 3 minutes. Add the wine to the pan and bring to the boil, stirring constantly. Remove the pan from the heat and stir in the nutmeg, cream and cornflour [cornstarch] mixture. Return the pan to low heat and simmer the sauce for 4 minutes or until it is thick and hot but not boiling. Remove the pan from the heat.

Remove the chicken from the oven and transfer it to a warmed serving dish.

Spoon the sauce around the chicken and serve at once.

Poulet Grillé à la Diable

GRILLED [BROILED] DEVILLED CHICKEN

Tasty grilled [broiled] chicken breasts, Poulet Grillé à la Diable (poo-lay gree-yay ah lah dee-ahbl'), is delicious served with boiled rice and stuffed vegetables.

4 SERVINGS

4 chicken breasts, skinned
1 oz. [2 tablespoons] butter, melted
½ teaspoon salt
4 tablespoons prepared French mustard
1 garlic clove, crushed
½ teaspoon cayenne pepper
½ teaspoon black pepper
4 fl. oz. [½ cup] olive oil
3 oz. [1 cup] dry white bread-crumbs

Preheat the grill [broiler] to moderate.

Pat the chicken breasts with kitchen paper towels. Using a pastry brush, brush them all over with the melted butter. Sprinkle over the salt.

Place the chicken breasts in the grill

[broiler] pan and grill [broil] for 5 to 6 minutes on each side, or until the chicken is evenly browned. Remove the chicken breasts from the grill [broiler] pan and keep warm.

In a small mixing bowl, combine the mustard, garlic, cayenne and black pepper. In a small saucepan, heat the oil over moderate heat. When the oil is hot remove the pan from the heat.

Add 1 tablespoon of the hot oil, a little at a time, to the mustard mixture, stirring constantly until the mixture is smooth. Using a pastry brush, brush the mixture over the chicken breasts.

Put the breadcrumbs on a plate and dip the chicken breasts into the crumbs, coating them thoroughly and shaking off any excess.

Return the chicken breasts to the grill [broiler] pan and pour over half of the remaining oil. Return the pan to the heat and grill [broil] for 8 to 10 minutes. Turn the chicken breasts over and pour over the remaining oil. Cook for a further 8 to 10 minutes or until the chicken is tender. Remove the pan from under the grill [broiler].

Transfer the chicken breasts to a warmed serving dish. Serve immediately.

Poulet à la Normande
CHICKEN WITH CALVADOS AND APPLE SAUCE

A combination of chicken, apples and Calvados, Poulet à la Normande (poo-lay ah lah nohr-mahnd) may be served with boiled rice and a tomato salad.

4 SERVINGS

1 x 4 lb. chicken
1 teaspoon salt
½ teaspoon black pepper
2 oz. [¼ cup] butter
1 large onion, coarsely chopped
1 lb. eating apples, peeled, cored and thickly sliced
6 fl. oz. [¾ cup] chicken stock
2 fl. oz. [¼ cup] Calvados
½ teaspoon dried sage
   finely grated rind of ½ lemon

Preheat the oven to moderate 350°F (Gas Mark 4, 180°C).

Rub the chicken, inside and out, with the salt and pepper and set aside.

In a large flameproof casserole, melt the butter over moderate heat. When the foam subsides, add the chicken and cook, turning it frequently, for 8 to 10 minutes or until it is evenly browned. Remove the chicken from the casserole and keep warm.

Add the onion to the casserole and cook, stirring occasionally, for 5 to 7 minutes or until it is soft and translucent but not brown. Add the apples and continue cooking, stirring frequently, for 2 minutes.

Pour in the stock and Calvados and add the sage and lemon rind. Bring the liquid to the boil over moderate heat, stirring constantly with a wooden spoon. Return the chicken to the casserole and baste it well with the liquid. Cover the casserole and place it in the oven. Cook for 45 minutes to 1 hour or until the chicken is tender.

Remove the casserole from the oven. Using two large forks, lift the chicken out of the casserole and transfer it to a warmed serving dish. With a slotted spoon, lift out the apple slices and arrange them around the chicken. Using a metal spoon, skim off any fat from the surface of the juices in the casserole. Pour half the juice over the chicken and apples and the other half into a warmed sauceboat. Serve immediately.

Poulet aux Pêches
CHICKEN WITH PEACHES AND ORANGE-FLAVOURED LIQUEUR

An extravagant dish perfect for that extra-special dinner party, Poulet aux Pêches (poo-lay oh pesh) is not difficult to make and looks and tastes spectacular. Serve with puréed potatoes and sautéed courgettes [zucchini]. Accompany this dish with a well-chilled white Burgundy wine.

4 SERVINGS

2 oz. [½ cup] seasoned flour, made with 2 oz. [½ cup] flour, 1 teaspoon salt and ½ teaspoon black pepper
4 chicken breasts, skinned and boned
4 oz. [½ cup] butter
4 fl. oz. [½ cup] white wine
2 medium-sized peaches, blanched, peeled, stoned and thinly sliced
2 fl. oz. [¼ cup] orange-flavoured liqueur
¼ teaspoon grated nutmeg
½ teaspoon salt
¼ teaspoon black pepper
4 fl. oz. double cream [½ cup heavy cream]
1 tablespoon cornflour [cornstarch] dissolved in 1 tablespoon water

Place the seasoned flour on a plate and roll the boned breasts in it, one by one, shaking off any excess. Set aside.

In a large frying-pan, melt 3 ounces [⅜ cup] of the butter over moderate heat. When the foam subsides, add the chicken breasts to the pan and brown them for 6 minutes on each side.

Pour in the wine and bring the liquid to the boil. Reduce the heat to low and simmer the chicken for 20 to 25 minutes or until the chicken is tender. With tongs, remove the chicken breasts from the pan. Keep warm while you prepare the sauce.

Add the remaining butter to the frying-pan and melt it over moderate heat. When the foam subsides, add the peach slices and cook, stirring occasionally, for 3 minutes. Add the orange-flavoured liqueur, nutmeg, salt and pepper to the pan and bring the mixture to the boil, stirring frequently.

Reduce the heat to low and stir in the cream, then the cornflour [cornstarch] mixture, stirring constantly. Return the chicken to the pan and cook the mixture, stirring occasionally, for 2 minutes or until it is hot but not boiling.

Remove the pan from the heat and transfer the mixture to a warmed serving dish. Serve at once.

Poulet Rôti aux Abricots
ROAST CHICKEN WITH APRICOTS

A delicious mixture of chicken stuffed with pork sausage meat and herbs and roasted with a wine and apricot sauce, Poulet Rôti aux Abricots (poo-lay roh-tee oh-zah-bree-koh) may be served with croquette potatoes and peas for a sumptuous meal. For a less expensive meal, substitute chicken stock for the wine.

6 SERVINGS

1½ oz. [3 tablespoons] butter
2 small shallots, very finely chopped
10 oz. pork sausage meat
4 tablespoons fresh white breadcrumbs
2 tablespoons double [heavy] cream
1 teaspoon salt
½ teaspoon black pepper
½ teaspoon dried thyme
1 teaspoon dried marjoram
1 tablespoon finely chopped toasted hazelnuts
2 lb. canned apricot halves, very finely chopped and with 5 fl. oz. [⅝ cup] of the can juice reserved
1 x 5 lb. chicken
1 tablespoon soft brown sugar
8 fl. oz. [1 cup] dry white wine
1 garlic clove, quartered

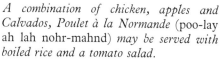

Superb Poulet Rôti aux Abricots — chicken stuffed with pork, herbs and hazelnuts and basted as it roasts with a wine, garlic and apricot sauce.

First make the stuffing. In a medium-sized saucepan, melt 1 ounce [2 tablespoons] of the butter over moderate heat. When the foam subsides, add the shallots and fry, stirring occasionally, for 3 to 4 minutes or until they are soft and translucent but not brown. Add the pork sausage meat and cook, stirring with a wooden spoon to break up the meat, for 6 to 8 minutes or until the meat has lost its pink colour. Beat in the breadcrumbs, cream, half the salt and pepper, the thyme, marjoram, hazelnuts and 2 tablespoons of the chopped apricots. Cook the stuffing, stirring constantly, for a further 3 minutes.

Remove the pan from the heat and set it aside.

Preheat the oven to hot 425°F (Gas Mark 7, 220°C).

Rub the chicken all over with the remaining salt and pepper. Spoon the stuffing into the cavity of the chicken and close the cavity with a trussing needle and thread, or skewers. Place the chicken in a medium-sized roasting tin and set it aside.

In a medium-sized saucepan, combine the remaining apricots, the reserved can juice, the brown sugar, wine, garlic and the remaining butter.

Set the pan over moderate heat and bring the mixture to the boil, stirring

constantly. Reduce the heat to moderately low and cook the mixture, stirring frequently, for 5 minutes or until the apricots are beginning to pulp.

Remove the pan from the heat and pour the mixture through a fine wire strainer held over a medium-sized mixing bowl. Using the back of a wooden spoon, rub the apricots through the strainer until only a dry pulp is left. Discard the pulp in the strainer. Set aside.

Place the roasting tin in the centre of the oven and roast the chicken for 15 minutes. Reduce the oven temperature to moderate 350°F (Gas Mark 4, 180°C). Spoon the apricot sauce over the chicken and roast the chicken for a further 1¼ to 1½ hours or until it is cooked and the juices run clear when one thigh is pierced with the point of a sharp knife. Baste the chicken frequently with the apricot sauce.

Remove the roasting tin from the oven. Using two large forks or spoons, lift the chicken out of the tin and transfer it to a carving board. Remove and discard the trussing thread or skewers and carve the chicken into serving pieces. Transfer the chicken pieces to a warmed serving dish and spoon over the stuffing.

Skim off and discard any fat on the surface of the apricot sauce. Pour the sauce over the chicken and serve.

One of the classic French ways to sauté chicken, Poulet Sauté à l'Archiduc is flavoured with Madeira and paprika. Serve with a mixed salad.

Poulet Sauté à l'Archiduc
SAUTEED CHICKEN IN MADEIRA-FLAVOURED CREAM SAUCE

To sauté chicken only tender young birds should be used. Most recipes for sautéed chicken have the same basic method of cooking the meat and it is the different sauces and garnishes which turn the chicken into the well-known classic dishes. Serve Poulet Sauté à l'Archiduc (poo-lay so-tay ah lahr-shee-dook) with a tomato and cucumber salad and a glass of chilled Pouilly Fuissé wine.

4 SERVINGS

1 teaspoon salt
1 teaspoon paprika
1 x 4 lb. chicken, cut into serving pieces
4 oz. [½ cup] butter
2 small onions, coarsely chopped
2 teaspoons lemon juice
4 fl. oz. [½ cup] white wine
6 fl. oz. single cream [¾ cup light cream]
2 tablespoons Madeira

1 tablespoon beurre manié
4 parsley sprigs

Sprinkle the salt and paprika over the chicken pieces and set aside.

In a large flameproof casserole, melt the butter over moderate heat. When the foam subsides, add the chicken pieces and cook, turning them frequently, for 8 to 10 minutes, or until they are evenly browned. Reduce the heat to low and add the onions. Sprinkle over the lemon juice.

Cover the casserole and cook for 20 to 25 minutes or until the chicken pieces are tender.

Using tongs, lift the chicken pieces out of the casserole and transfer them to a warmed serving dish. Keep warm while you finish the sauce.

With a metal spoon, skim off any fat from the surface of the juices in the casserole. Stir in the wine. Increase the heat to high and bring the liquid to the boil. Boil the liquid, stirring occasionally, for 10 minutes or until it has reduced by about half.

Remove the casserole from the heat and pour the liquid through a fine wire strainer into a small saucepan, rubbing the onions through with the back of a wooden spoon. Discard any pulp remaining in the strainer.

Add the cream, a little at a time,

stirring constantly. Place the pan over moderately low heat and cook the sauce, stirring constantly, for 3 minutes or until it is hot but not boiling. Stir in the Madeira. Add the beurre manié, a little at a time, stirring constantly until the sauce is thick and smooth.

Remove the pan from the heat and pour the sauce over the chicken. Garnish with the parsley sprigs and serve immediately.

Poulet Sauté au Basilic
SAUTEED CHICKEN WITH BASIL

A delicious dish, Poulet Sauté au Basilic (poo-lay so-tay oh bah-zil-eck) may be served with grilled [broiled] mushrooms and stuffed tomatoes. Accompany with a chilled white Muscadet wine.

2 SERVINGS

2 chicken breasts
½ teaspoon salt
½ teaspoon black pepper
2 oz. [¼ cup] butter

Poulet Sauté au Basilic is an easy to make and economical dish. Serve with savoury stuffed tomatoes and new potatoes for a simple meal.

4 fl. oz. [½ cup] dry white wine
4 fl. oz. [½ cup] chicken stock
2 teaspoons chopped fresh basil or
1 teaspoon dried basil
2 teaspoons beurre manié

Rub the chicken breasts all over with the salt and pepper.

In a medium-sized flameproof casserole, melt the butter over moderate heat. When the foam subsides, add the chicken breasts and cook, turning frequently, for 8 to 10 minutes or until they are evenly browned.

Reduce the heat to low, cover the casserole and cook for 20 to 25 minutes or until the chicken breasts are tender. Using tongs, transfer the chicken breasts to a warmed serving dish. Keep warm while you finish making the sauce.

Using a metal spoon, skim any fat from the juices in the casserole. Add the wine, stock and basil and bring the liquid to the boil over high heat. Boil for 10 minutes or until the liquid is reduced by about half.

Add the beurre manié, a little at a time, stirring constantly with a wooden spoon until the sauce is smooth and has thickened slightly.

Remove the casserole from the heat and pour the sauce over the chicken. Serve immediately.

Poulet Sauté à la Bordelaise

SAUTEED CHICKEN WITH POTATOES AND
ARTICHOKE HEARTS

A succulent and easy-to-make dish, Poulet Sauté à la Bordelaise (poo-lay so-tayah la bord-layz) may be served with a tomato and green pepper salad and lots of crusty bread for a really sustaining meal. A chilled Pouilly Fumé white wine would be excellent with this dish.

4 SERVINGS

1 x 4 lb. chicken, cut into serving pieces
1 teaspoon salt
½ teaspoon black pepper
4 oz. [½ cup] butter
2 medium-sized onions, finely chopped
1 garlic clove, crushed
4 fl. oz. [½ cup] white wine
4 fl. oz. [½ cup] chicken stock
1 tablespoon cornflour [cornstarch] dissolved in 3 tablespoons water
1 lb. potatoes, cooked and sliced
6 artichoke hearts, cooked and sliced

Rub the chicken pieces all over with the salt and pepper and set aside.

In a large flameproof casserole, melt the butter over moderate heat. When the foam subsides, add the chicken pieces and cook, turning them frequently, for 8 to 10 minutes or until they are evenly browned. Reduce the heat to low and add the onions and garlic.

Cover the casserole and cook for 20 to 25 minutes or until the chicken pieces are tender.

Using tongs, lift the chicken pieces out of the casserole and transfer them to a warmed serving dish. Keep warm while you finish the sauce.

Stir the wine and chicken stock into the casserole and bring to the boil over high heat. Boil the liquid, stirring occasionally, for 3 minutes or until it has reduced slightly.

Remove the casserole from the heat and pour the liquid through a fine wire strainer into a large saucepan, rubbing the onions and garlic through with the back of a wooden spoon. Discard any pulp remaining in the strainer.

Place the pan over high heat and bring the liquid to the boil. Reduce the heat to moderately low and add the cornflour [cornstarch] mixture and cook, stirring constantly, for 2 minutes or until the sauce has thickened. Add the potatoes and artichoke hearts and cook, stirring occasionally, for 3 minutes or until they are heated through.

Remove the pan from the heat and pour the sauce over the chicken pieces. Serve at once.

Poulet Sauté Chasseur

SAUTEED CHICKEN IN CHASSEUR SAUCE

An easily made but impressive dish, Poulet Sauté Chasseur (poo-lay so-tay shah-sur) may be served with a tossed green salad and sautéed new potatoes.

Poulet Sauté à la Provençale is a succulent dish flavoured with garlic, vegetables, wine and anchovies.

4 SERVINGS

1 teaspoon salt
½ teaspoon white pepper
1 x 4 lb. chicken, cut into serving pieces
2 oz. [¼ cup] butter
2 tablespoons vegetable oil

Poulet Sauté à la Provençale

SAUTEED CHICKEN WITH TOMATOES AND GARLIC

A colourful way of serving sautéed chicken, Poulet Sauté à la Provençale (poo-lay so-tay ah lah proh-van-sahl) makes an ideal main course for an informal dinner party. Serve with boiled rice or crusty bread and a green salad.

4 SERVINGS

1 teaspoon salt
1 teaspoon black pepper
1 garlic clove, crushed
1 x 4 lb. chicken, cut into serving pieces
2 fl. oz. [$\frac{1}{4}$ cup] olive oil
1 medium-sized onion, finely chopped
8 oz. mushrooms, wiped clean and halved
1 tablespoon flour
6 fl. oz. [$\frac{3}{4}$ cup] white wine
4 fl. oz. [$\frac{1}{2}$ cup] chicken stock
3 tomatoes, blanched, peeled, seeded and coarsely chopped
$\frac{1}{2}$ teaspoon dried oregano
6 black olives, stoned and halved
4 anchovy fillets, diced
2 anchovy fillets, halved

Rub the salt, pepper and garlic into the chicken pieces. Set aside.

In a large flameproof casserole, heat the oil over moderate heat. When the oil is hot, add the chicken pieces and cook, turning frequently, for 8 to 10 minutes or until they are evenly browned.

Preheat the oven to warm 325°F (Gas Mark 3, 170°C).

Reduce the heat to low and stir in the onion. Cover the casserole and cook for 20 to 25 minutes or until the chicken pieces are tender. Remove the casserole from the heat and, using tongs, lift out the chicken pieces and place them in an ovenproof serving dish. Cover the dish and place it in the oven to keep hot.

Increase the heat to moderate and add the mushrooms to the casserole. Fry, stirring constantly, for 3 minutes. Stir in the flour and cook for 30 seconds. Pour in the wine and stock, a little at a time, stirring constantly with a wooden spoon. Bring the sauce to the boil. Continue cooking, stirring frequently, for 10 minutes or until the sauce has thickened slightly.

Add the tomatoes, oregano, olives and diced anchovies. Bring to the boil, reduce the heat to low and simmer for 5 minutes.

Remove the chicken from the oven and pour over the sauce. Garnish with the halved anchovies and serve immediately.

4 oz. button mushrooms, wiped clean
10 fl. oz. [1$\frac{1}{4}$ cups] Chasseur Sauce, kept hot

Rub the salt and pepper over the chicken pieces and set aside.

In a large flameproof casserole, melt the butter with the oil over moderate heat. When the foam subsides, add the chicken pieces to the casserole and cook, turning them frequently, for 8 to 10 minutes or until they are evenly browned. Reduce the heat to low and add the mushrooms. Cover the casserole and cook for 20 to 25 minutes or until the chicken is tender.

Using tongs, lift the chicken pieces out of the casserole and transfer them to a warmed serving dish. With a slotted spoon, lift out the mushrooms and arrange them around the chicken.

Pour the chasseur sauce into a warmed sauceboat and serve with the chicken.

To carve poultry, use a sharp carving knife and a two-pronged fork with a thumb guard. Pull the leg away from the body and sever it through the joint.

If the bird is a large one, carve the meat from the breast in thin slices, slicing it parallel to the breastbone.

If the bird is small, the breast should be cut off in one piece with sharp kitchen scissors and then halved before serving.

Poultry

Poultry is the term used to describe all domestic birds which are reared for the table. This includes CHICKEN, DUCK, GOOSE, GUINEA FOWL, PIGEON and TURKEY. The classification of each species and how to cook them are described under the appropriate headings.

Poultry must be plucked, hung and drawn before cooking — these are now usually done by the butcher, before the poultry is sold.

If you wish to prepare poultry for cooking yourself, the bird first must be plucked — that is, its feathers removed as soon after killing as possible. The breast of the poultry is plucked first and the feathers are removed by pulling them sharply in the direction of the head. The down is removed by singeing.

The poultry is then hung for 2 to 3 days or, in the case of larger birds, for 5 to 7 days.

At the end of the hanging period, the poultry is drawn — its entrails are removed. The head, feet and sinews are generally removed at the same time. The heart, liver, gizzard and feet may be reserved for making stock.

It is important to remember that if frozen poultry is bought, it must be thoroughly thawed before cooking.

To carve poultry, use a large, sharp knife and a two-pronged fork. With the exception of very small birds, the legs are removed first. Pull the leg away from the body with the fork and sever through the thigh joint. Separate the drumstick from the thigh by cutting through the knee joint. To remove the wings, use the fork to hold down the pinion and cut through the shoulder joint. If the fowl is large the breast may be carved in thin slices, parallel to the breastbone. With a smaller bird, the breast is removed in one piece and then cut in half. If the bird has been stuffed, this is removed after carving and a small amount is served with the meat.

Pound Cake

The origin of this cake is confused, since Pound Cake has been adopted by both the United States and Great Britain as a rich, moist cake to serve on any occasion. The cake is so named because, originally, one pound quantities of butter, sugar, eggs and flour were used. This gave a very large cake, however, and today half the quantity is more common. Of all the many recipes for Pound Cake, no two seem to agree on the flavourings to be used — some use nuts, dried fruit or fruit juices, spices — either

mace or nutmeg — and others brandy. The proportion of fruit and nuts used is flexible and depends on personal preference. The cake will keep for up to 1 week.

ONE 2-POUND CAKE

8 oz. [1 cup] plus 2 teaspoons butter
8 oz. [1 cup] sugar
4 eggs
8 oz. [2 cups] flour
1 teaspoon salt
½ teaspoon mixed spice or ground allspice
8 oz. [1¼ cups] raisins
8 oz. [1⅓ cups] mixed glacé cherries, candied peel and chopped walnuts
2 fl. oz. [¼ cup] brandy
2 fl. oz. [¼ cup] orange juice

Preheat the oven to warm 325°F (Gas Mark 3, 170°C).

Using the 2 teaspoons of butter, grease a 2-pound loaf tin. Set aside.

In a large mixing bowl, cream the remaining butter with a wooden spoon until it is light and fluffy. Stir in the sugar and beat the mixture until it is smooth and creamy. Stir in the eggs, one at a time, beating well before each addition.

Sift the flour, salt and mixed spice or allspice into a medium-sized mixing bowl. Add the raisins and mixed glacé cherries, candied peel and walnuts to the flour and coat them well.

With a large metal spoon, fold the flour and fruit mixture into the creamed mixture, until the ingredients are thor-

oughly combined. Stir in the brandy and orange juice.

Spoon the cake batter into the prepared loaf tin and smooth the top with a table knife. Place the tin in the oven and bake for 2 to 2¼ hours or until a skewer inserted into the centre of the cake comes out clean.

Remove the tin from the oven and run a knife around the edge of the tin. Turn out the cake on to a wire rack to cool completely. Serve immediately or wrap it in aluminium foil and store until it is required.

A delightfully moist cake, Pound Cake is rich with fruit and brandy.

Pousse-Café

Pousse-Café (poos-kah-fay) is the name given to a drink consisting of a number of liqueurs, poured carefully into a tall liqueur glass so that they remain in layers.

The appearance of the drink is attractive, but the time and effort required to produce one perfect liqueur is not matched by the pleasure in drinking it. When pouring the liqueur, the heaviest liqueur must be used first and the lightest last to to prevent a blurring of the outlines. The liqueurs most often used are anisette, brown Curaçao, Cointreau, brandy, yellow Chartreuse, green Chartreuse, or crème de menthe, Parfait Amour, cherry brandy and Grand Marnier. The number of layers made may be three, five or, possibly, seven.

Pousse Café Gâteau

SPONGE CAKE WITH LIQUEUR-FLAVOURED ICING

Pousse Café (poos kah-fay) Gâteau is a rich and colourful dessert cake, flavoured with brandy and covered with a blend of different liqueur icings. The cake derives its name from the layered liqueur drink of the same name.

ONE 8-INCH CAKE

6 oz. [¾ cup] plus 2 teaspoons butter
8 oz. [1 cup] sugar
10 oz. [2½ cups] flour
2½ teaspoons baking powder
¼ teaspoon salt
3 eggs
4 fl. oz. [½ cup] brandy
2 tablespoons milk
3 fl. oz. single cream [⅜ cup light cream]

ICING

4 oz. [½ cup] unsalted butter
1 lb. icing sugar [4 cups confectioners' sugar]
2 teaspoons green Chartreuse
2 drops green food colouring
2 teaspoons orange-flavoured liqueur
3 drops orange food colouring
2 teaspoons brandy
2 drops yellow food colouring
2 teaspoons cherry brandy
3 drops red food colouring
2 teaspoons Parfait Amour
2 drops purple food colouring

Preheat the oven to moderate 350°F (Gas Mark 4, 180°C).

With the 2 teaspoons of butter, grease an 8-inch round cake tin and set aside.

In a large mixing bowl, cream the remaining butter with a wooden spoon until it is light and fluffy. Add the sugar and beat the mixture until it is smooth and creamy.

Sift the flour, baking powder and salt into a medium-sized mixing bowl and stir well to mix.

Beat the eggs into the creamed mixture, one at a time, adding a tablespoon of the flour mixture with each egg.

With a large metal spoon, fold in the remaining flour mixture. Stir in the brandy, milk and cream, stirring until all the ingredients are thoroughly combined.

Spoon the cake batter into the prepared cake tin, smoothing it down with the back of the spoon. Place the tin in the centre of the oven and bake the cake for 1¾ to 2 hours or until a skewer inserted into the centre of the cake comes out clean and dry.

Remove the tin from the oven and allow the cake to cool for 3 minutes.

Run a knife around the edge of the cake and turn the cake out on to a wire rack. Set aside to cool completely.

While the cake is cooling, make the icing. In a medium-sized mixing bowl, cream the butter with a wooden spoon until it is light and fluffy. Stir in the icing [confectioners'] sugar and beat the mixture until it is smooth and creamy. Divide the icing into 5 equal parts and place them in small mixing bowls.

Using a small wooden spoon, beat the Chartreuse and green food colouring into one bowl, beating until the icing is smooth and evenly coloured. Beat the orange-flavoured liqueur and orange food colouring into the second bowl, the brandy and yellow food colouring into the third, the cherry brandy and red food colouring into the fourth and the Parfait Amour and purple food colouring into the last bowl.

Using a large, sharp knife, cut the cake into 3 layers. Place 1 layer on a serving plate and spread it with 2 tablespoons of the green icing. Cover with another layer of cake and spread it with 2 tablespoons of the orange icing. Cover the icing with the remaining cake layer.

Spread each icing in sections over the top and sides of the cake, until all the icing has been used up and the cake is completely covered. Using a flat-bladed knife, gently swirl the colours into one another to make a decorative pattern. Place the cake on a serving plate and serve immediately.

A very unusual and decorative cake, Pousse Café Gâteau is made with five different liqueurs and food colours.

Poussin

A poussin (poo-sahn) is a very small chicken, aged between 6 and 8 weeks, and weighing between 12 ounces and 2 pounds. A poussin can be roasted, fried or grilled [broiled], and is generally served either whole or split in half.

To split a poussin, place it on a flat working surface and, using a sharp, pointed knife, split it through the breastbone. Using both hands, grasp each side of the poussin and bend back until the ribs crack. With a sharp knife, cut through the skin to separate the halves completely.

Poussin may be roasted whole, halved or split and opened out flat. Fried or grilled [broiled] poussin should be halved or split and opened out flat.

To roast poussin, preheat the oven to fairly hot 375°F (Gas Mark 5, 190°C). Melt 1 tablespoon of butter in a roasting tin and brush the poussin with more melted butter and sprinkle with a little salt and pepper. Place the tin in the oven and bake the poussin for 20 to 25 minutes, basting occasionally, or until the breast is tender when pierced with the point of a sharp knife.

To fry poussin, melt 1 ounce [2 tablespoons] of butter in a large frying-pan. When the foam subsides, add the poussin to the pan and fry it, turning occasionally,

for 18 minutes or until the breast is tender when pierced with the point of a sharp knife and the juices that run out are clear.

To grill [broil] poussin, preheat the grill [broiler] to high. Melt 1 ounce [2 tablespoons] of butter in the grill [broiler pan]. Place the poussin in the butter, skin side uppermost, and baste with the melted butter. Place the pan under the grill [broiler] and grill [broil] the poussin for 8 minutes, basting once. Turn the poussin over and baste with the butter. Grill [broil] the poussin for a further 8 minutes, basting once, or until the breast is tender when pierced with the point of a sharp knife.

Poussins au Gingembre
BABY CHICKENS WITH GINGER

This rather extravagant dish, Poussins au Gingembre (poo-sahn oh jahn-jamb-rer) is very simply cooked to make the most of the delightful sauce and the tender flesh of the chicken. Serve it with petits pois, braised celery and sautéed potatoes.

4 SERVINGS

4 poussins, cleaned and split
   through the breastbone
½ teaspoon salt

Poussins au Gingembre, baby chickens with ginger, lemon and wine sauce makes a super dinner party meal.

½ teaspoon black pepper
3 oz. [⅜ cup] butter, melted
SAUCE
1 oz. [2 tablespoons] butter
3-inch piece fresh root ginger,
   peeled and finely chopped
1 garlic clove, crushed
1 tablespoon tomato purée
1 tablespoon white wine vinegar
1 teaspoon soft brown sugar
½ teaspoon salt
½ teaspoon black pepper
10 fl. oz. [1¼ cups] dry white wine
8 fl. oz. [1 cup] chicken stock
2 tablespoons flour mixed to a
   paste with 3 tablespoons water
2 teaspoons lemon juice

First make the sauce. In a medium-sized saucepan, melt the butter over moderate heat. When the foam subsides, add the ginger and garlic and fry, stirring occasionally, for 3 minutes. Stir in the tomato purée, vinegar, sugar, salt, pepper, wine and stock and bring the mixture to the boil. Reduce the heat to low and simmer the sauce for 20 minutes. Remove the pan from the heat and strain the sauce into a small saucepan, pressing down with the back of a wooden spoon to extract the juices. Discard any pulp remaining in the strainer. Set aside.

Place the poussins on a working surface and, grasping each cut edge of breast with your hands, pull them apart until the ribs break. Rub each poussin with the salt and pepper.

Preheat the grill [broiler] to hot. Pour the melted butter into the grill [broiler] pan. Place the poussins, skin side up, in the grill [broiler] pan and baste them with the melted butter. Grill [broil] the poussins for 8 minutes, basting occasionally with the butter. Turn the poussins over, baste with the butter and grill [broil] them for a further 8 minutes or until the flesh on the breast is tender when pierced with the point of a sharp knife. (The poussins may have to be cooked in two batches.)

Meanwhile, stir the flour mixture and lemon juice into the sauce and bring

the sauce to the boil over moderate heat, stirring constantly. Reduce the heat to low and simmer the sauce for 3 minutes. Remove the pan from the heat and keep warm.

Remove the poussins from the grill [broiler] and place them on a large warmed serving dish. Pour the sauce into a warmed sauceboat and serve immediately, with the poussins.

Poussins Sautés au Citron

BABY CHICKENS COOKED WITH BUTTER AND LEMON

A useful recipe for a last-minute dinner party, Poussins Sautés au Citron (poo-sahn so-tay oh see-trawn) needs little preparation. Serve with a crisp green salad and new potatoes and, to drink, some well-chilled white wine

4 SERVINGS

4 poussins, cleaned and split through the breastbone
1 teaspoon salt
½ teaspoon black pepper
3 oz. [⅜ cup] butter
1 tablespoon vegetable oil

3 fl. oz. [⅜ cup] white wine
2 tablespoons lemon juice
10 fl. oz. single cream [1¼ cups light cream]
1 lemon, cut into wedges
2 teaspoons chopped fresh parsley

Rub the poussins all over with the salt and pepper and set them aside.

In a large frying-pan, melt the butter with the oil over moderate heat. When the foam subsides, add the poussin halves and fry them for 3 to 4 minutes on each side, or until they are evenly browned.

Reduce the heat to low, cover the pan and simmer for 15 to 20 minutes or until the poussins are tender.

Using tongs, remove the poussins from the pan and transfer them to a warmed serving dish. Set aside and keep warm.

Increase the heat to moderate and add the wine and lemon juice. Stir in the cream. Cook the sauce for 3 minutes, stirring constantly.

Remove the pan from the heat. Pour the sauce over the poussin halves and garnish with the lemon wedges and parsley. Serve immediately.

Poussins Sautés au Citron are perfect for a refreshing yet luxurious meal, served with parsleyed new potatoes and a mixed green salad.

Povoa Almond Cake

A delicious light cake made with eggs, Povoa Almond Cake is covered in a smooth icing made with sugar and egg white. Serve the cake in thin slices.

ONE 10-INCH CAKE

1 teaspoon vegetable oil
6 egg yolks
4 oz. [½ cup] castor sugar
6 oz. [1 cup] ground almonds
2 tablespoons milk
6 egg whites
ICING
1 lb. icing sugar [4 cups confectioners' sugar]
2 tablespoons hot water
1 egg white
¼ teaspoon almond essence
2 oz. [½ cup] slivered almonds

Preheat the oven to moderate 350°F (Gas Mark 4, 180°C). Line a 10- x 16-inch Swiss [jelly] roll tin with non-stick silicone or greaseproof paper. Grease the paper with the teaspoon of oil. Set aside.

Place the egg yolks and sugar in a medium-sized mixing bowl. Using a wire whisk or rotary beater, beat the mixture until it is thick and pale. Using a large metal spoon, fold in the ground almonds and milk. Set aside.

In a large mixing bowl, beat the egg whites with a wire whisk or rotary beater until they form stiff peaks. With the metal spoon, gently but thoroughly fold the egg whites into the egg yolk mixture. Pour the mixture into the prepared tin, smoothing it over with the back of the spoon.

Place the tin in the oven and bake for 15 to 20 minutes or until the cake is lightly browned and comes away from the sides of the tin.

Remove the tin from the oven and let the cake cool for 5 minutes. Carefully turn the cake out on to a flat surface covered with greaseproof or waxed paper, sprinkled with a little cornflour [cornstarch]. Remove and discard the paper lining from the cake and set the cake aside to cool completely.

To make the icing, place the icing [confectioners'] sugar, water and egg white in a medium-sized heatproof mixing bowl. Place the bowl over a saucepan half-filled with hot water and set the pan over low heat. Using a wooden spoon, beat the mixture until it is smooth and glossy and will coat the back of the spoon. Stir in the almond essence.

Remove the pan from the heat and remove the bowl from the pan. Set the icing aside to cool to room temperature.

When the cake is cold, using a sharp knife, cut the cake into 4 rectangles. Place one rectangle on a serving platter. Using a palette knife, spread one-sixth of the icing on to the cake and top with another rectangle. Make alternate layers with the remaining icing and the remaining pieces of cake. Spread the remaining icing evenly over the top and sides of the cake.

Sprinkle over the almonds and serve at once.

Prague Apricot Loaf

The Czechs are noted for their food, particularly for their beautiful — and fattening — cakes and breads. Sweet breads such as Prague Apricot Loaf are particularly popular and may be served with piping hot coffee.

ONE 16-INCH LOAF

½ oz. fresh yeast
5 tablespoons plus ½ teaspoon sugar
3 fl. oz. [⅜ cup] lukewarm milk
8 oz. [2 cups] flour
1 teaspoon salt
3 eggs, lightly beaten
2 oz. [¼ cup] plus 1 teaspoon butter, melted
FILLING
1 lb. [2⅜ cups] dried apricots, soaked overnight
3 tablespoons brandy
3 tablespoons sultanas or seedless raisins
2 oz. [½ cup] flaked almonds
½ teaspoon mixed spice or ground allspice

Crumble the yeast into a small bowl and mash in the ½ teaspoon of sugar with a fork. Add 1 tablespoon of the lukewarm milk and cream the yeast and milk together until they form a smooth paste. Set the bowl aside in a warm, draught-free place for 15 to 20 minutes or until the yeast has risen and is puffed up and frothy.

Sift the flour, salt and 4 tablespoons of sugar into a warmed, large mixing bowl. Make a well in the centre and pour in the yeast mixture, the remaining lukewarm milk, 2 eggs and the 2 ounces [¼ cup] of melted butter. Using your fingers or a spatula, gradually draw the flour mixture into the liquids. Continue mixing until all the flour is incorporated and the dough comes away from the sides of the bowl.

Turn the dough out on to a lightly floured board or marble slab and knead it for 5 minutes, reflouring the surface if the dough becomes sticky. The dough should be elastic and smooth.

Rinse, thoroughly dry and lightly grease the large mixing bowl. Shape the dough into a ball and return it to the bowl. Cover the bowl with a clean, damp cloth and set it in a warm, draught-free place. Leave it for 1 to 1½ hours or until the dough has risen and has almost doubled in bulk.

Meanwhile, make the filling. Drain the apricots and reserve 3 fluid ounces [⅜ cup] of the soaking liquid. Place the apricots in a small saucepan and pour over the reserved soaking liquid. Set the pan over high heat and bring the liquid to the boil. Reduce the heat to low and simmer the apricots for 20 to 30 minutes or until they are very tender. Remove the pan from the heat and purée the apricots in a food mill or blender.

Alternatively, rub the apricots through a fine wire strainer.

Transfer the apricot purée to a medium-sized mixing bowl and add the brandy, sultanas or seedless raisins, almonds and mixed spice or allspice. Beat with a fork until the ingredients are well blended. Set aside.

With the remaining teaspoon of butter, lightly grease a Swiss [jelly] roll tin or a large baking sheet. Set aside.

Turn the risen dough out of the bowl on to a floured surface and knead it for about 3 minutes. With a rolling pin, roll out the dough to a rectangle about 16-inches by 8-inches.

Spread the filling evenly over the rectangle, to within ¼-inch of the edges. Roll up the dough Swiss [jelly] roll fashion and transfer the loaf to the prepared tin or sheet. Cover the loaf with a clean, damp cloth and return it to the warm, draught-free place for 30 minutes or until the dough has almost doubled in bulk.

Preheat the oven to hot 425°F (Gas Mark 7, 220°C).

With a pastry brush, brush the top and sides of the loaf with the remaining beaten egg and sprinkle over the remaining sugar. Place the tin or sheet in the oven and bake the loaf for 10 minutes. Reduce the temperature to moderate 350°F (Gas Mark 4, 180°C) and continue baking the loaf for 30 minutes or until it is golden brown.

Remove the tin or sheet from the oven and allow the loaf to cool slightly before transferring it to a wire rack to cool completely before serving.

An unusual light cake which uses ground almonds instead of flour, Povoa Almond Cake has a smooth, white icing and tastes superb.

Prague Chicken

Prague Chicken is a delectable mixture of chicken breasts, marjoram and courgettes [zucchini] in a creamy cheese sauce.

4 SERVINGS

4 chicken breasts, skinned
1 teaspoon paprika
1 teaspoon salt
½ teaspoon black pepper
2 oz. [¼ cup] butter
2 teaspoons dried marjoram
1 lb. courgettes [zucchini], trimmed, washed and thinly sliced
1 teaspoon lemon juice
12 fl. oz. [1½ cups] béchamel sauce
10 fl. oz. single cream [1¼ cups light cream]
⅛ teaspoon cayenne pepper
1 bay leaf
2 oz. [½ cup] Emmenthal cheese, grated
2 oz. [½ cup] Parmesan cheese, grated

Rub the chicken breasts all over with the paprika and half the salt and pepper. Set aside.

In a large frying-pan, melt the butter over moderate heat. When the foam subsides, add the chicken breasts. Sprinkle over 1 teaspoon of the marjoram and fry the chicken breasts for 6

minutes on each side or until they are evenly browned.

Using tongs, remove the chicken breasts from the pan and place them, in one layer, in a large baking dish. Set aside and keep warm.

Add the sliced courgettes [zucchini] to the frying-pan and sprinkle over the lemon juice, the remaining salt, pepper and marjoram. Fry the courgettes [zucchini], stirring and turning frequently, for 6 to 8 minutes or until they are golden brown.

Remove the pan from the heat. With a slotted spoon, remove the courgettes [zucchini] from the pan and arrange them around and over the chicken. Set aside.

Preheat the oven to moderate 350°F (Gas Mark 4, 180°C).

In a medium-sized saucepan, beat the béchamel sauce and cream together with a wooden spoon. Stir in the cayenne, bay leaf, the Emmenthal cheese and half the Parmesan.

Set the pan over moderately low heat and cook the sauce, stirring constantly, for 6 minutes or until it is hot and smooth and the cheese has melted.

Remove the pan from the heat. Remove and discard the bay leaf and pour the sauce over the chicken and courgettes [zucchini] to cover them completely.

Prague Chicken is a nourishing dish of chicken breasts and courgettes [zucchini] sautéed with marjoram and baked with a creamy cheese sauce.

Sprinkle over the remaining Parmesan.

Place the dish in the centre of the oven and bake for 35 minutes or until the chicken is tender and the top is golden brown and bubbling.

Remove the dish from the oven and serve immediately.

Prairie Oyster

Prairie Oyster is most usually imbibed as a hangover cure, but it is also occasionally fed to invalids — perhaps on the theory that if it can remedy a hangover it can remedy anything! It is traditionally swallowed in one gulp.

1 SERVING

½ teaspoon Worcestershire sauce
⅛ teaspoon salt
½ teaspoon black pepper
1 teaspoon lemon juice
1 egg

Put all the ingredients except the egg into a cocktail glass and stir well. Break the egg into the mixture.

Serve at once.